Kinder Scout

Kinder Scout

The People's Mountain

Ed Douglas and John Beatty

Vertebrate Publishing, Sheffield
www.v-publishing.co.uk

Kinder northern edge above Nether Red Brook.

Snake woodlands and Seal Edge, viewed from Bamford Edge.

The Pagoda and Grindslow Knoll.

Moat Stone and the moon.

Kinder Scout

Ed Douglas and John Beatty

First published in 2018 by Vertebrate Publishing.

 Vertebrate Publishing
Crescent House, 228 Psalter Lane, Sheffield S11 8UT, United Kingdom.
www.v-publishing.co.uk

Copyright © Ed Douglas and John Beatty 2018.

Front cover: Freezing winter mist on Kinder Low summit (633 metres).
Back cover: Kinder Downfall fighting a westerly gale.
All photography by John Beatty.

Ed Douglas and John Beatty have asserted their rights under the Copyright, Designs and Patents Act 1988 to be identified as authors of this work.

This book is a work of non-fiction. The authors have stated to the publishers that, except in such minor respects not affecting the substantial accuracy of the work, the contents of the book are true.

A CIP catalogue record for this book is available from the British Library.

ISBN: 978-1-911342-50-2 (Paperback)

10 9 8 7 6 5 4 3 2 1

All rights reserved. No part of this work covered by the copyright herein may be reproduced or used in any form or by any means – graphic, electronic, or mechanised, including photocopying, recording, taping or information storage and retrieval systems – without the written permission of the publisher.

Every effort has been made to obtain the necessary permissions with reference to copyright material, both illustrative and quoted. We apologise for any omissions in this respect and will be pleased to make the appropriate acknowledgements in any future edition.

Design and production by Jane Beagley.

www.v-publishing.co.uk

Vertebrate Publishing is committed to printing on paper from sustainable sources.

Printed and bound in Europe by Latitude Press Ltd.

'Tall or short, near or far, some mountain watches over our native village like a tutelary deity. We spend our childhood in the shadow of our mountain and we carry it with us in memory when we grow up and leave the village. And however much our lives may change, the mountain will always be there, just as it has always been, to welcome us back to our home village.'
    Kyūya Fukada, *One Hundred Mountains of Japan*

'Once out of nature I shall never take
My bodily form from any natural thing,'
    W.B. Yeats, *Sailing to Byzantium*

Sand

It's early, but not that early. I've slept in a little, exhausted after yesterday's walk, more than twenty miles, and carrying camping gear too. There's a dull ache in my lower back, evidence, if it were needed, that after four decades in the mountains there's a price to pay, because that's nature: entropic, changeable, shifting. Things really do fall apart. For now, though, right here, I'm okay with that. The voice in my head seems stilled, that tyrant between my ears is weakened and distant. I feel a familiar odd pleasure in tiredness, the weary contentment after a great effort, sense the earth beneath my hip, cushioned by my sleeping mat, and, through the open door of the tent, watch streams of thin mist curling east over the moor, interspersed with patches of radiant blue. Yet the wind makes no sound. The air is wholly silent, making the scene ethereal, sprinkling it with a strange magic and so adding the moment to the precious store in the fraying basket of my memory.

Time passes. I pour water into a pan and get busy. The spell is broken. Soon I'm outside with a cup of coffee in my hands, boots half tied, contemplating my surroundings. I'm standing on a grassy gravel bank beside a shallow trickle of water, the thin nascent flow of the Kinder river. In front of me, on either side, are two small buttresses of gritstone barely a few metres high, the one on the right upright, like a sentry, that on the left sloping downhill and set in a steep bank of peat currently washed with sunshine. These are known as Kinder Gates, and before the route was changed, the Pennine Way, Britain's oldest long-distance footpath, passed between them. They are familiar landmarks, a kind of breastbone: close to, but not quite at the heart of Kinder Scout.

Its true heart lies not through these gates but off to the side, a little to my left, in the strange, indistinct centre of Kinder's broad, sprawling and awkward plateau, a vast hump of peat seamed and fissured with gullies – groughs is the northern word – which, in the wet conditions commonly experienced up here in the clouds, can be filled with water and ooze, sucking you down, and hard to navigate in heavy mist. It's a blank on the map, metaphorically these days, although even now in the age of satellites, as you stare at a dot of light on a GPS screen in the driving rain and try to reconcile its bright optimism with the murky reality in front of you, you can be left disoriented, turned around, confused and frozen. If you still want to get lost, come to Kinder Scout on a foul day.

And yet, deep in this confusion, you'll find something, not just the heart of this upland scrap of Derbyshire, but the heart of England also. Somewhere off to my left is one of England's more dramatic watersheds. Within a few squidgy yards, across the heather and moss, the water draining from beneath my feet will no longer trickle west, into the Kinder, and eventually into the Mersey Estuary, but funnel north-east towards Fair Brook or south-east towards Grinds Brook, flowing to the Trent and the North Sea. The mountain is at the cusp: of north and south, the tailbone of the Pennines. Equally it's at the heart of things, like a sombre spider on its web, with cities radiating out around it: Manchester, Sheffield, Derby and Stockport.

Opposite: The rock bluffs known as Kinder Gates, one of the few exposed gritstone features of the central plateau, are hidden in the central narrows of the River Kinder.

Written on its blank interior is our own story, a British story that extends far beyond the mountain's limit, paradoxically perhaps, given how empty the plateau appears to be. Kinder Scout holds a place in the popular imagination for the mass trespass held there in 1932, a near-mythological event in the fight for access to Britain's uplands, for many a critical moment, for others little more than a colourful distraction, even a stumbling block. But Kinder is undoubtedly the people's mountain, a focus for radicalism and liberty, rightly celebrated. It's the wild heart of Britain's first national park, that brave attempt to drag back the people's stake in its own natural heritage, another deliberate act of post-war social justice to set alongside the National Health Service.

But Kinder is even more than this. It tells a wider human story, about the very nature of our anxious, curious and acquisitive species. 'Literature is landscape on the desk,' the genial Chinese writer Lin Yutang suggested in *The Importance of Living*. 'Landscape is literature on the earth.' Many of the themes that compel us now, the collapse in biodiversity, our need for space, the balance between exploiting the Earth and conserving it, can be read first on the pages of Kinder Scout, downwind of the Industrial Revolution, half-poisoned, denuded and yet still-sacred ground, literally for some, a repository for all the messy contradictions that each of us brings, to add a sentence or two to the accumulated layers. My intention is to sift through these human stories, pick out some of the more significant landmarks in Kinder Scout's human history, and perhaps restore a few to public memory, like patching a drystone wall.

That's why I've walked up here, to try to understand, because Kinder is sometimes poorly understood, and even mocked or reviled. There have been many visitors over the years baffled by Kinder's appeal, even hostile to it. Partly also as a paean, a song of praise to somewhere that has been both backdrop and touchstone for most of my life, a place to mark the seismic changes of the passing years, somewhere to leave myself behind, but also somewhere to appreciate the quotidian, the day-to-day joys of an outdoor life. In doing so, I know that I must tread gently, because Kinder Scout means a great deal to a great many, and for each individual that meaning is different, sometimes subtly, sometimes in great measure.

In making this journey, I can't begin to do justice to all those different individual experiences, or even the range of experiences that people have enjoyed, endured, suffered or celebrated in this strange, expansive, opaque … what? How to define this landscape? Mountain? The term seems a little overblown for somewhere that barely scrapes over the 600-metre contour. Yet that hasn't prevented some of Kinder's admirers from drawing comparisons with other mountainous regions, in their enthusiasm over-promoting features as some kind of answer to the more dramatic appeal of more celebrated places. But Kinder Gates would barely serve a suburban bungalow let alone a grandiose house. The hill has marvellous rock climbs, although they're short; there's a bit of a summit, but it's not always easy to differentiate its location from the terrain surrounding it. There are parts of Aberdeenshire or the Berwyns where you can drive past similar hills and barely glance at them twice.

Then there is Kinder's curious topography, hardly mountain-like at all, if we take the child's view of a mountain being necessarily spiky and steep, a kind of Platonic Matterhorn, or in Samuel Johnson's dictionary, a 'vast protuberance of the earth'. Kinder is a tease: you climb steeply, from almost any angle, and then … nothing, just the sky above and a plateau ahead of you, and you're staggering on over a slimy plain where there should be some sort of climax. This clearly annoyed Alfred Wainwright, whose tastes in most things were meat and two veg: 'The terrain, everywhere difficult to traverse, rises very slightly to the insignificant summit of Kinder Scout, at 2,088ft. One wonders how this flat tableland came to earn its name as The Peak. Nothing less like a peak can be imagined.'

Given that he used local knowledge from Oldham rambler Len Chadwick, Wainwright must have known that Kinder earned its name as The Peak thanks to mislabelling on the part of the Ordnance Survey, an error pointed out by all sorts of writers thereafter. But he was correct to call Kinder a tableland. The mountain is what Americans would call a mesa, from the Spanish for table, or in parts of Venezuela and Guyana what the local Pemon people call a *tepui*. And here is the magic of it. Stand still at the centre of this tabletop, with the moor curving away uniformly around you, and you can experience something almost unique in Britain, something you can't on a conventional mountain: an abstract sense of space – a big, embracing nothingness.

Scratch out the modern roads, roll up the railway that emerges from the Cowburn Tunnel into Edale, and you can see the mountain for what it is and not be channelled into blinkers by how you arrived. Looked at from above, through the satellite's omniscient eye or on the contours of a map, Kinder has a harmony of shape, a graphic energy lacking in its neighbours: Bleaklow, Howden, Margery Hill. They seem amorphous and indistinct in comparison. Kinder appears to me like the outline of a terrier, head cocked, its crown Kinder's northern edges, its snout the steep rocks above Ashop Head sniffing towards Manchester, its slender neck, constantly narrowing thanks to the streams at either end, stretched between the steep cliffs of Kinder Downfall and the sharp angle of Fair Brook, ear cocked at Fairbrook Naze.

Patrick Monkhouse was one of several *Manchester Guardian* writers who appropriated the peak as their wild backyard. He quartered Kinder Scout's rambling bulk in his 1932 book *On Foot in the Peak*, published at the height of the post-war boom in outdoor activities and in the same year as the Kinder trespass: 'The Scout is perhaps four miles long, not as the crow flies but if you follow its major ins and outs. But it looks as long as eternity. That is the mark of greatness in mountains – not mere size, but the power to upset, to transcend, the normal measures of size. The highest point of Kinder Scout is barely above two thousand feet above sea level. But if you tell yourself that at the Ley Gate Head, it becomes either incredible or irrelevant. Two thousand feet is no great matter. It is less than the height of Whernside or Moel Hebog or Seat Sandal and many another summit, which falls far short of distinction, on which one looks unamazed. But here, face to face with the Scout, you feel the measuring-rod stretching and growing in your hands.'

Kinder has three distinct sides, like Everest, each with its own contrasting character and particular history: to the west, above the village of Hayfield, facing Manchester, and all that implies, the famous Downfall, where the Kinder plunges over tall crags in the crook of an angle in the edge, or on days when a strong westerly roars across the Cheshire plain, flying upwards in a drenching plume of spray visible for miles; to the north, colder, sterner, more sparsely inhabited, separated from the west by Ashop Head, a ruler-straight rampart of cliffs running east to where The Edge, as it is known, overlooking Ashop Clough, ducks sharply back south-west at Fairbrook Naze before turning east again, meandering a little past Seal Edge and into Blackden Brook. From Ashop Head eastwards Kinder has an apron of moors before the ground drops away: this is where most of the peak's grouse shooting now happens. East of Blackden the plateau slopes down and rather dissipates. 'This far eastern end of Kinder Scout,' Monkhouse wrote, 'is a calm, smooth greensward, compared to the north and west faces.' Kinder's southern flank, which, like the north, tapers to Kinder's east end above Hope Cross, rises above Edale and is wholly different again, a valley like a cupped hand, benign, half-secret, sheltering ancient farms on three sides, to the south by Mam Tor and Lose Hill, and in the lee of Brown Knoll and Edale Cross to the west, which, as the southern limit of Kinder's western end, closes the circle.

Where to see this sprawl to best advantage? Martin Doughty, one of the great recent champions of conservation in Britain, thought the ideal vantage point was his native New Mills, west of Kinder, facing the Downfall, the hill's defining landmark, tuned in perhaps to some of Kinder's ancient energy, when the geomancy of the Downfall, a cleft set deep between walls that seem to embrace you, to wrap around your back, was obvious to minds still open to such notions. My friend John Beatty, going to school on his motorbike, would crane his neck for this view of Kinder from the crest of Ravenoak Bridge in Cheadle Hulme, west again of New Mills, scanning the horizon for a brief glimpse of Kinder's ramparts of paradise. Until one day he glanced too long, clipped the back of a Jaguar and watched from the ground as a bus ran over his gauntlet, thrown down and off his fingers. Thus he escaped narrowly a more metaphysical visit to paradise to continue his lifetime's exploration of the mountain.

The way Kinder Scout opens so dramatically to the west contributes to the notion that it is somehow Manchester's mountain. Even so, there is a great passion for it on the other side of the Pennines. In 1900, Bert Ward, having at least attempted to advertise the formation of a new rambling club in Robert Blatchford's socialist *Clarion* newspaper, left Sheffield's Midland station with a group of fourteen men, women and children, the 'first workers' Sunday Rambling Club' in England. It was a beautiful autumn day, and where else would Bert Ward go than Kinder Scout, to walk what he termed the 'usual round'. But there was in 1900 little usual about it at all, for several reasons, not least that the railway through the Hope Valley was only completed in 1894, whereas lines stretching east from Manchester had been operating for decades. (Ward and his friends alighted at Edale station, where the platform sign now reads *Edale For Kinder*, as though the community there was offering its support.)

The other limitation was access, which had in Ward's day been a contentious issue for several decades. A bitter legal dispute aimed at restoring the public's right of way over William Clough and down Ashop Clough, a key section in Ward's circumambulation, had only concluded in 1897, after a campaign lasting two decades.

One of Ward's ramblers was Jack Jordan, who recalled this momentous day in the 1950s, remembering in particular the view from the top of Jacob's Ladder, the steep, twisting packhorse track that leads from Upper Booth to Edale Cross: 'From the top of it we looked across to Edale Rocks, Pym's Chair and Crowden Towers, and all of us knew that a new life was opening for us – and we hoped, for those to come after us.' It is quite something when a spectacular view contains the future. It was an act of imagination and faith on the parts of those who looked across Kinder's southern rim in 1900, since in those days Kinder's plateau was denied them, a prohibition enforced by gamekeepers patrolling the moor. Jordan, in his account, quoted, slightly inaccurately, Tennyson's *Locksley Hall*, written in the springtime of Victoria's reign. ('For I dipped into the future far as human eye could see, / And saw the glory of the world and the wonder that might be.') True, Jordan wrote, Kinder Scout 'was not the world, but it was a new world to us, traversed for the first time – even now, after fifty-seven years I still remember the thrill and the joy it gave me'. Tennyson wrote a sequel to *Locksley Hall*, more than forty years later, rueing the failed promise of the Industrial Revolution; the spirits of Kinder must have sympathised. In the years between, the population of Sheffield had tripled.

Bert Ward had deep Sheffield roots, inasmuch as anyone did in that mushrooming world of smoke and flame. His grandfather William had been born in the Derbyshire village of Ridgeway in 1814, when Sheffield's population was around 50,000. Ridgeway had long since harnessed its busy little streams to become a local centre for making scythes and sickles, but the scale was discrete, artisan; in August and September the smiths were back in the fields, using scythes they'd made to reap the harvest. What was happening in Sheffield was of a different order, and the booming city drew William in. He joined the ranks of Sheffield's enterprising 'little mesters', with works on Kelham Island on the River Don. Bert, like his father, was an Anglican Sunday school teacher, but, unlike his father, he was also part of the nascent labour movement and was, quite literally, thrown out of the church for his socialist activities.

For someone who spends a lot of time walking on the fringes of Sheffield, as I do, Bert Ward's presence is inescapable. He started his working life as an engineer fitter for a company making stays for corsets. He ended it as a civil servant with thirty-four years' service, turning down an honour on principle when he retired. Unusually, for a young fitter who'd left school at thirteen, he developed a passion for Spain, travelling there, learning the language and becoming involved in Spanish politics. But it's his rambling life that Ward is now known for, and when the Clarion Ramblers club was underway, he produced an annual handbook of upcoming walks that contained much else besides: lore, folk tales, quotations from favourite writers, like Emerson, Thoreau and Ruskin, history and, crucially, accurate information about boundaries and paths, grist to the mill of the access campaigns of the 1920s and 1930s of which Bert Ward was an integral part, as he was in the preservation of the landscape. The handbook managed to be local without being parochial, partly because Ward himself had strong roots and an internationalist outlook, thanks to his experience of Spain. His mantra, that a rambler made is a man improved, might seem hackneyed in the twenty-first century, but his kind of rambler was self-reliant, socially responsible, curious and determined.

Several times a week I pass his old house at Owler Bar, on the border of the Peak District National Park, an idea that must have seemed a distant dream when he was a boy, but which he lived to see realised. The moors around Owler Bar – Totley Moss, Blacka, Big Moor – were his daily bread, and are mine as well. They feature most often in his writings. Their high points are perhaps 200 metres lower than Kinder Scout, whose bulk dominates the horizon, a big dome muscling behind Lose Hill, but the interest is in the foreground, with the long, elegant sweeps of the Eastern Edges, culminating in Stanage.

In winter, though, Kinder is often shrouded in snow when the eastern moors are clear, and your eye is drawn and held fast to the dazzling horizon. Then you believe that it's not Glossop behind those hills, but the endless wastes of Hyperborea.

Another fine perspective is from Hollins Cross, where a track much older than recorded history crosses the ridgeline between Mam Tor and Lose Hill, between Edale and the Hope Valley. Stand facing north, and the southern mass of Kinder is spread before you, seamed with the watercourses that are slowly eroding it away, the deep, curving arc of Grindsbrook Clough straight ahead, Ollerbrook to the right of the fractured rocks of Ringing Roger, Crowden Clough, which Patrick Monkhouse thought 'sweetest of all the waters of Kinder', and beyond that, west again, the River Noe, whose name lends itself to one the earliest published references to Kinder, Michael Drayton's colossal tour of England's rivers, *Poly-Olbion*.

Drayton had been widely admired at the court of Elizabeth but was rudely expelled on the accession of James. His response was this epic portrait of a nation gathering a new sense of itself. Published in two volumes of thirty songs, the Noe appears in 'The Sixthe and Twentieth Song', published as part of the second batch in 1622. It also offers the name Nowstoll, or Noe Stool, for the hill that is its source – 'her great Sire' in Drayton's phrase. Drayton goes on to chastise, gently, Kinder – 'Faire Hill bee not so proud of thy so pleasant Scite' – as the Derwent quickly scoops up the Noe on its way to the Trent. There is a large rock perched on the rim of the plateau overlooking the Noe known as Noe Stool, but it doesn't seem remarkable enough to name a mountain of Kinder's scale.

That Drayton knew of Noe, tucked away in Edale, is testament to the sources he and his sometime co-author, the brilliant seventeenth-century scholar and jurist John Selden, could draw on, many of them heavily annotated and now in Oxford's Bodleian Library. The poem reveals what was well known of this corner of Derbyshire; there is a great deal, for example, on the quality and scale of sheep farming in the Derwent Valley, which in the Tudor period was booming. What Drayton certainly did not do was put on a waterproof ruff and gaiters and splash around the plateau.

Had he done so, his *Poly-Olbion* would have been a little more complete. No mention is made of the river that rises on Kinder's western fringe. The Eleventh Song in this epic survey covers Cheshire but the most remote tributary of the Mersey mentioned is the Goyt – 'downe from her Peakish spring' – that rises on Axe Edge Moor, a watershed to rival Kinder's. The Goyt meets the Sett, which rises under Edale Cross, at New Mills. The Sett meets the Kinder at Bowden Bridge above Hayfield, the Kinder's three-mile run now interrupted just upstream by the reservoir built in 1911 by the Stockport Corporation. Drayton's poem was illustrated with thirty maps, the work of engraver William Hole, based on the mapmaking of Christopher Saxton, who drew the first county maps of England. Saxton's atlas was widely admired when it was published in 1579, but while Hole's illustration for Cheshire and the fringes of Derbyshire shows the Goyt, only vague, suggestive wiggles fill the space where the Kinder and Sett might be.

Cartography and surveying advanced rapidly in the Elizabethan era, under royal patronage, redrawing minds too, anatomising the world in practically useful ways – especially to lawyers. But Michael Drayton's poem sprang from another Elizabethan compulsion, that of antiquarianism, most famously William Camden's hugely popular *Britannia,* a topographical and historical survey of immense scope and depth, which also captured the imagination of Elizabethan England. Drayton's work drew deep inspiration from Camden, the subtitle of *Poly-Olbion* being *A Chorographicall Description of Tracts, Rivers, Mountaines, Forests, and other Parts of this renowned Isle of Great Britaine, with intermixture of the most Remarquable Stories, Antiquities, Wonders, Rarityes, Pleasures, and Commodities of the same.* Chorography is writing about place, and rarely out of fashion since, but while Camden and Selden were serious scholars, Drayton was trying to entertain, capturing England's emerging sense of itself and its place in the world with creative wit. He casts the Peak as some kind of Greek rustic spirit, describing the district's 'wonders'. (Drayton has seven; Camden suggests nine.) The Enlightenment philosopher Thomas Hobbes, who toured the Peak District in 1626, recast these wonders in his Latin poem *De Mirabilibus Pecci.* The angler and Royalist Charles Cotton then reworked Hobbes back into English for his *Wonders of the Peake,* first published in 1681.

In the way of these things, there was a backlash: a 'Peak-lash'. Daniel Defoe, that elusive literary chancer, turned on Derbyshire's 'wonders', in his own 'chorographic' work, *A Tour Thro' the Whole Island of Great Britain.* It made sense to him, a man who knew how to write a headline, to shake things up, subvert the established view. The country west of the Derwent, of which Kinder is the summit, was, in his words, a 'houling wilderness'. He had a talent for such phrases, and liked this one so much he used it twice. 'I must say,' he wrote, after admiring the home of the Duke of Devonshire, where Hobbes had lived and worked as William Cavendish's tutor, 'if there is any wonder in Chatsworth, it is, that any man who had a genius suitable to so magnificent a design, who could lay out the plan for such a house, and had a fund to support the charge, would build it in such a place where the mountains insult the clouds, intercept the sun, and would threaten, were earthquakes frequent here, to bury the very towns, much more the house, in their ruins.' To Defoe, the High Peak, meaning Kinder Scout and Bleaklow, 'is the most desolate, wild, and abandoned country in all England'. Then, having dismissed the region as wastes, he adds a more intimate insult, one heard often since: 'The mountains of the Peak, of which I have been speaking, seem to be but the beginning of wonders to this part of the country, and but the beginning, or, if you will, as the lower rounds of a ladder.' Ouch. For Defoe, size mattered.

Given how much money he made, and that he was buried in a pauper's grave, it's safe to say Defoe had a taste for luxury. If he couldn't find a decent inn in the place he was visiting, he was generally prejudiced against it. He admires Doncaster largely for the quality of its hostelries and its manufacturing. Chatsworth is impressive and comfortable, but why would you bother with such wildernesses as the High Peak? Defoe liked to adopt a contrary line; it allowed him to pose. As a political journalist and spy, for both Whigs and Tories, he could happily defend more or less any position without much moral qualm. He never let the truth, or complexity, stand in the way of a good story. Disparaging a literary tradition, which is what he does in his denunciation of Hobbes and Cotton, and also Celia Fiennes, who made a similar journey in the 1690s, doing everything Defoe did but earlier and side-saddle, came naturally to him. Defoe's own style is robust and direct, and consequently antithetical to the poets he derides, just as they derided him, although Defoe had the sense to pilfer their material. In Drayton's poem the Peak's barren landscape is elegant: 'Like it in all this Isle, for sternnesse there is none, / Where Nature may be said to show you groves of stone.' Defoe's 'houling wilderness' gets straight to the point, like the man. Defoe likes stuff and material wealth, admires commerce, and hates pretension. Yet it's also true that he spends much more time and effort exciting his readers with tales of terrible places like Kinder Scout than he does with bourgeois accounts of market towns.

Larkin said: 'Man hands on misery to man.' The same is true for our view of landscapes. The quotations of famous writers are passed from book to book like viruses, infecting the present. Defoe's dismissal of the High Peak as both useless and charmless is often taken as an illustration of changing fashions in the appreciation of landscape, as though the word of one man could settle it. But it's fair to say there has always long been something divisive about the High Peak's true value as a landscape, irrespective of Romanticism or the alienating influence of the Industrial Revolution.

In the modern era, the division over Kinder Scout is most commonly the difference between those who pass through, often only once, and those who grow familiar with the moors over time. In Patrick Monkhouse's frame of reference, Kinder seems an old acquaintance, even a friend, a bit dog-eared, heavy going sometimes, far from perfect, but familiar. Another writer, John Hillaby, once a *Guardian* man himself, came this way only once at the end of the 1960s, walking the length of Britain to take the mood, and was dismayed by what he saw. 'Up there you blink. A silent and utterly sodden world. This, surely, is not the summit of the High Peak. Mounds of bare peat rise in all directions, like waves, or rather a field furrowed by a gigantic plough. On the top there are no signposts, no markers. Only the choice of channels between the chocolate-coloured peat.' Hillaby preferred to wear light boots, soft and comfortable, so he walked barefoot to preserve them while following a compass bearing. 'The peat extended for miles. It rose, gradually, in the direction of a mound of rocks. And it steamed, like manure. Manure is the analogy that comes most readily to mind. The top of Kinder Scout looks as if it's entirely covered in the droppings of dinosaurs.' Hillaby also felt oppressed by the surrounding cities creeping out towards him, impinging on his sense of space, somehow accentuating the barrenness he discovered there. 'There are people, I know, who speak highly of these south Pennine moors. They like the atmosphere of the wilderness. I am not among them. I found them extraordinarily depressing.'

Contemporary writers share Hillaby's gloom. William Atkins, an admired book editor from North London, described his journey across Britain's 'most forbidding and most mysterious terrain' in his book *The Moor*. When it comes to Kinder Scout, the same black dog trots in his footsteps. The naked hags suck him down, 'whose flat tops alone bore a cap of crowberry and heather, sometimes mere Mohicans of vegetation. It was as if these tables of peat had been excavated and dumped up here on the moor-top, fly-tipped.' He becomes disconnected from the landscape, adrift, until the main road rudely wakens him. 'The Snake Pass was a drugs route, a guns route; police pursuit drivers trained on it. "Think Bike" said the signs. Like most moorland passes, with their unbroken prospects and long straights, the accident rate is high, and the accidents are terrible.'

It's hard to read these things about somewhere I've known and loved intimately for almost forty years. The Snake Road has never been alien to me, never been a place of death. Crossing the summit on the way home from Manchester you are faced with a high, even sweep of moors into which the road sinks from view, the moorland seamed with black, like the roots of a tree, where the water has washed channels in the decaying bog. With no view of the road ahead, it feels like you are poised to go underground, that the moors will draw you in, swallow you up – take you to heart. And I like the intersection with the Pennine Way, the notion that I could just stop, get out of the car and start walking to the Borders.

Alfred Wainwright, in writing his *Pennine Way Companion*, made little secret of his dislike of Britain's oldest official long-distance footpath, which starts on Kinder, in those days up a badly scarred Grindsbrook Clough, these days skirting the mountain's base before climbing to Edale Cross and then along the plateau's western rim. He did his research a year or two before Hillaby and reached similar conclusions, describing the plateau as 'an open and uninviting landscape' and dismissing the River Kinder, judging the name 'an ambitious one for a sluggish trickle'. The surroundings are 'drab' and it's only on reaching the edge of the plateau that the walking becomes 'palatable', thanks only to 'extensive views to the west'. Whether Wainwright actually crossed Kinder in its entirety is open to question. On his first attempt in April 1966, as he wrote to his friend, the author Molly Lefebure, he turned back from the plateau in foul weather: 'a drizzle had set in, mist was falling, the path was a quagmire. I thought of Borrowdale, I thought ye gods what have I done, what am I doing in this godforsaken spot. Two hundred and fifty miles of this! I must be mad. Well I got up to the plateau, two miles, and into a wilderness of wet fog and snowdrifts and slimy peat hags, and my heart was in my boots. I turned back.' He still hadn't completed this section when he wrote to Len Chadwick about it more than a year later. So jaded did Wainwright become on his piecemeal walk up the Pennines, wondering why he had bothered, that he developed his own walk, not south to north but east to west, from the Cumbrian coast at St Bees to Robin Hood's Bay, a route that, in his own words, 'puts the Pennine Way to shame'. Despite his lukewarm impressions, the *Pennine Way Companion* sold briskly, like all his other books.

Wainwright's view of landscape seems wholly conventional to me. He adored Lakeland, had his formative experience there and left his perspective unchallenged thereafter, becoming a professional curmudgeon as the decades passed. (His choice of 'The Happy Wanderer' for the Radio 4 programme *Desert Island Discs* was presumably ironic.) The art critic and social reformer John Ruskin, dying at Coniston seven years almost to the day before Wainwright was born in Blackburn, also saw mountain scenery in definite terms: 'Mountains are to the rest of the body of the earth, what violent muscular action is to the body of man. The muscles and tendons of its anatomy are, in the mountain, brought out with force and convulsive energy, full of expression, passion, and strength; the plains and the lower hills are the repose and the effortless motion of the frame, when its muscles lie dormant and concealed beneath the lines of its beauty, yet ruling those lines in their every undulation. This, then, is the first grand principle of the truth of the earth. The spirit of the hills is action, that of the lowlands, repose … '

Ruskin was writing about the Alps, not the Lake District. He judged Britain's mountains 'too barren to be perfectly beautiful, and always too low to be perfectly sublime' but did allow that 'many deep sources of delight are gathered into the compass of their glens and vales'. The Victorian equivalent of, 'Yeah, not bad'. He was even less interested in the kind of high flat country that Kinder Scout epitomises. 'Inferior hills ordinarily interrupt, in some degree, the richness of the valleys at their feet; the grey downs of southern England and treeless *côteaux* of central France, and grey swells of Scottish moor, whatever peculiar charm they may possess in themselves, are at least destitute of those which belong to the woods and fields of the lowlands.' In other words, they provide an interesting contrast but that's about it. As for Defoe, for Ruskin: size mattered. But for different reasons, I think. Defoe, ever the journalist, wanted the remarkable – something novel, or useful. Ruskin had his towering, trembling aesthetic sense.

I sometimes wonder what Ruskin thought of Kinder Scout. He must have seen it, because he was a regular visitor to Derbyshire and valued its landscapes. His opposition in the 1860s to the railway through Chee Dale is well known, thanks to his remark that all the ruination would achieve would be that 'every fool in Buxton can be in Bakewell in half an hour and every fool at Bakewell in Buxton'. But he also opposed the railway between Totley and Chinley, the line that runs through Edale, judging it 'the invasion of virgin country', which, given his psychosexual reputation, is perhaps an unfortunate turn of phrase.

Totley was where, in the mid 1870s, Ruskin funded one of his idealistic social experiments, an attempt at communitarian living at what is now known as St George's Farm, but was known to Ruskin as Abbeydale. Living just round the corner, I often cycle past it. 'We will try to take some small piece of English ground, beautiful, peaceful and fruitful,' Ruskin announced. 'We will have no steam engines upon it and no railroads.' Except there was already a station at Totley, and his dream of a productive market garden and workshops full of happy artisans quickly foundered in the sort of finger-pointing and drift that too often plagues cooperative enterprises. Among the farm's more profitable activities was selling cups of tea to curious visitors. Ruskin knew he should be paying more attention to the commune's development, but was too busy working up some notes on St George's Church in Venice, whose stained-glass window is a better memorial to Ruskin than the failed experiment of St George's Farm. By the time the project was finally wound up, Ruskin had retreated to Brantwood, haunted by his failures, in a state of nervous collapse, unable to write and alienated from a newly industrialised world that had nature and beauty in full retreat. But Ruskin's idea did set people thinking. William Morris visited Abbeydale and the young Edward Carpenter also became involved, finding a new tenant for the farm.

Carpenter is a compelling figure, the sort of man who makes you wholly rethink the Victorian era, but not quite famous enough to escape the doom of being endlessly rediscovered. Born into a wealthy family, one of ten children, he was educated at Brighton College, living at home among six sisters, and then went up to Trinity Hall, Cambridge. An outstanding scholar, he took up Leslie Stephen's recently vacated fellowship at Trinity and consequently took holy orders. He was then offered the job of tutoring the future George V. But Carpenter was spectacularly ill-suited to serve the establishment. He is remembered now as a socialist with a strong dash of Indian mysticism, someone both Fabians and Marxists found annoying. But he was also a courageous advocate for gay rights, living if not quite openly, then with no shame for forty years with his partner George Merrill, born in the slums of Sheffield. Their relationship was the inspiration for Carpenter's friend E.M. Forster to write his novel *Maurice*.

Like Bert Ward, Carpenter was an admirer of Walt Whitman – though, unlike Ward, Carpenter reportedly slept with the poet, at least according to Allen Ginsberg – and under the influence of Whitman's collection *Leaves of Grass*, found a way to link his social conscience and his sexual preferences, a kind of 'manly comradeship' in his biographer Sheila Rowbotham's phrase. He quit the church and began an entirely new life more suited to his new ideals. 'I would and must somehow go and make my life with the mass of the people and the manual workers.' As Rowbotham described it, 'the north was a shock' for Edward Carpenter. He came first to Leeds as a lecturer for the University Extension programme, dreaming he would bring education to the masses, but discovering instead that audiences for his lectures were mostly middle class. If Leeds had been bad, then Sheffield was worse. The city was at that time, according to John Murray's *Hand-book for travellers in Yorkshire*, 'beyond all question the blackest, dirtiest, and least agreeable'. Carpenter was lecturing on astronomy, which he judged ironic since for three days the sky was barely visible through the smog and pollution. But he loved the open, wild country above the city, loved being outdoors tramping the footpaths, and resolved to live in the country, taking Thoreau as a more abiding influence than Marx. When Carpenter's father died and he inherited his share of the family fortune, he bought a large market garden at Millthorpe, a small village on the other side of the hill from Totley in north-east Derbyshire, and built a house.

Ruskin's social experiment at Totley had been for Carpenter 'the dim dawn or beginning of a new life for me'. He became absorbed in Sheffield's embryonic socialist community, but Carpenter was also prescient as an environmentalist, railing against the pollution – the filth, poisoned water and grim housing – ordinary people in Sheffield had to endure as the price of industrialisation. Younger socialist intellectuals, like George Bernard Shaw, mocked Carpenter; George Orwell was excoriating, judging Carpenter's type as an 'outer-suburban creeping Jesus'. (He was a great enthusiast for the wearing of sandals.) But his social liberalism, his ideas about sexuality and democracy, even his environmentalism, quietly endured to re-emerge at the end of the twentieth century. Some of those who participated in the trespasses of the 1930s, including on Kinder Scout, took direct inspiration from him. It says a great deal that Bert Ward helped organise an album signed by all the members of the Labour Cabinet when Carpenter turned eighty in 1924. Another well-known access campaigner, the philosopher C.E.M. Joad, called him the harbinger of modernity. 'What he wanted,' E.M. Forster wrote after Carpenter's death, 'was *News from Nowhere* and the place that is still nowhere, wildness, the rapture of unpolluted streams, sunrise and sunset over the moors, and in the midst of these the working people whom he loved passionately in touch with one another and with the natural glories around them.'

By contrast, when John Ruskin tried to marry his strong aesthetic judgement to his political ideals, the former overwhelmed the latter. He adored Alpine scenery, and consequently demanded that everyone else do so as well. His sense of self rested on his acute appreciation of art and nature, and the two were inextricably linked. Ruskin's judgement about mountain landscapes is one shared by many of my mountain-loving friends. There was something deeply architectural in his appreciation of its scenery, as though he were standing in a square in Venice admiring a palazzo. '[Mountains] seem to have been built for the human race,' he wrote in *Modern Painters*, 'as at once their schools and cathedrals; full of treasures of illuminated manuscript for the scholar, kindly in simple lessons to the worker, quiet in pale cloisters for the thinker, glorious in holiness for the worshipper.' They are, in Ruskin's estimation, the 'great cathedrals of the earth, with their gates of rock, pavements of cloud, choirs of stream and stone, altars of snow, and vaults of purple traversed by the continual stars'. Architects, and in Ruskin's mind, when it came to the natural world, that meant God, or some kind of divine progenitor, make reality. There's something virile about it, something unnegotiated, imposing a narrative. That's why a railway across a landscape Ruskin valued was a kind of personal insult; it violated his own ideas about what that space should be. That's why he raged against mountaineers treating the perfect peaks as 'greasy poles' for their narrow ambition. He reminds me of the more proprietorial kind of landowner, who resents being told his estate is more than his possession. As an aesthetic, it sounds authoritarian, even tyrannical, as though the working classes needed to be told what was and what was not beautiful because they had no chance of deciding for themselves.

Moorland seems to me a very different kind of space to mountains, less architectural and more abstract, more sculptural too. It is long curves and inflected lines, changing light and vast skies. (The name Heathcliff always struck me as a good piece of observation.) There is nothing to trap the eye, no place to reach, like the tops of hills. Moorland is less distinct, more equivocal than mountains and consequently, in a strange kind of way, more democratic, more accommodating. Barbara Hepworth, driving around West Yorkshire in the early 1920s with her father, newly appointed county surveyor, not only saw the hills as sculptures, she became absorbed into them, and they into her. 'I, the sculptor, *am* the landscape. I am the form and I am the hollow, the thrust and the contour.' The word 'moor', from the Anglo-Saxon 'mor', meaning bog or fen, was broadened, co-opted to translate the Latin word 'mons' and extended to cover heath. It was also largely synonymous with 'common', with all that implies. The Alps, ironically for Ruskin, were scenery for the age of steam; moorland seems more modern, more muted and less strenuous, less insistent.

Standing in front of Kinder Gates, I crouch down and scoop up a handful of pebbles, raking through them with my finger. They're white, of quartz, like small jewels, eroded out of the gritstone that caps the plateau of Kinder Scout. I've stood in the same spot in winter and seen similar stones locked in ice, as though in a cabinet, on display. It always pleases me when others notice the way Kinder's paths and channels are littered with these little bright shards. Mrs Humphry Ward's novel *The History of David Grieve* opens on Kinder Scout, where her hero grows up, and young David, out at night on the plateau, finds his way home by following these pebbles, 'gleaming white in the moonlight,' which, as she explains, 'wind and weather are forever teasing out of the grit, and which drift into open spaces'.

All mountains are entropic. They are quite literally falling to bits, washed away, blown to pieces, sucked down by gravity and always on the move. Stick around long enough and Kinder Scout will melt before your eyes. I'm squatting on top of a mountain dismantled by wind and rain, grains of sand washed away, and me with them, pretty soon. I've often thought that if we had time-lapse photography extending over tens of millions of years, if we could see, as geologists imagine, our planet shifting and wriggling, we'd have a radically different perspective on our overheating little spaceship, and also of its truculent crew.

Beneath my feet, under the gravel of the riverbed, successive layers of gritstone, shale, sandstone and more shale reach down for 600 metres to a final layer of limestone 3,000 metres thick. It's tempting to think of this sequence of layers like a cake, or an onion, but those are static comparisons and the formation of the rocks that make Kinder Scout was anything but static. Neither was the weathering and erosion that have produced its distinctive shape: the near-constant, restless wind driving rain across the plateau and, in the clear blue days of winter, the shattering frost.

The pebbles in my hand have already been on quite a journey, eroded out of a range of mountains that stretched from the Highlands to Scandinavia. Fragments like these, older than some of the stars in the sky, have been matched to parent rocks in Scotland. They were washed into a tributary of a vast river that drained those mountains, as the Ganges does the Himalaya, its delta located where the Pennines are now. When it was formed more than 300 million years ago, this vast, sprawling delta was at the equator, and has since drifted north by fifty degrees of latitude and is still going, pushed along on a tide of time, heading for the Arctic.

Sediment from this ancient range spewed out of the mouth of the river, losing momentum as it met the standing water of the sea. The heaviest fragments fell to the bottom of the ocean first. Lighter material washed out further to settle on the sea floor. It accumulated, thickened, the resting place for billions of sea creatures, squashed flat in this bottom 300-metre layer, called the Edale Shales. The delta grew, heavier material piled up, huge unstable banks of sand that would shift, squirting out a sluggish sandy broth that settled again, the process repeating itself over millennia, building up a fan of material over the shales that you can see in the landslip scars of Mam Tor: the Mam Tor Sandstones. These are 135 metres thick.

All the while, like the Ganges, our river kept shifting course as its channels choked with debris, thickening like a glutton. Slacker water, unable to support heavier material, left finer-grained deposits. You can see these, the Grindslow Shales, at the top of Grindsbrook, thin layers of biscuit-rock you can snap with your fingers. Then the swampy line of coast spread and expanded, and the delta was filled in with coarse-grained sand and pebbles, like the clutch I have in my hand; that too thickened, pressure built and with it heat, to create a cap of coarse-grained sandstone called Kinderscout Gritstone, the rocks now exposed on the plateau. Dour to some, for the rock climber it was alchemy, making stony gold from fragments.

Kinder's estuarine start in life is strangely appropriate. There's something littoral about the plateau, especially walking along the northern rim, as though you're pacing out time's shore. But it's not easy to visualise this constant, relentless movement of material – of braiding streams and sudden floods, and banks of shifting sand – when you're surrounded by rock. The spot where I'm standing, on top of the Kinderscout Gritstone, was buried in turn by a new delta. This one grew to a depth of 2,000 metres and was topped with the lush vegetation that became coal. Continents collided and the Pennines lifted a mile into the air. Time and wind and rain got to work. Standing here on the flat roof of Kinder, those layers are gone already, stripped away, as this one will be eventually.

Human history, human culture, is the same, an estuary thick with sediment, shifting course, settling here and then elsewhere, the steady accumulation of material, pressure, heat, amalgamation, change, and then erosion, exposing fragmentary clues to its origin, but without the movement, without the energy or noise that drove the pattern. Take Kinder Scout's name, a fossil itself, pored over by antiquarians and toponymists for clues as to its origin and pinned on to different cultures spread over centuries. The English professor Kenneth Cameron, who spent most of his career at the University of Nottingham and wrote the standard work on Derbyshire's place names, judged Kinder to be pre-Celtic. Other scholars have speculated that it's Brittonic, the Celtic language that fractured into Welsh, Cumbric and others. Some believe the name is derived from words connected to the mountain's topography; others that is a 'habitative' name, its meaning found in the hamlet of Kinder, most likely a named political entity long before the first written reference to Kinder – 'Chendre' – in *Domesday*. The name, still slippery and shifting, appears thereafter in a variety of spellings: Kender in 1275; Kendyr in 1285; Kunder in 1299; Kyndre in 1315.

The Downfall, the rocky precipice that defines Kinder's western aspect, is a captivating feature, especially for those of a more animist persuasion, and a boundary too, a watershed where east meets west, which adds weight to the idea that the name is a Celtic one for a boundary settlement. More recently, the linguist Jon Fyne, focusing on the dialects of north-west Derbyshire for his doctorate, made a potent argument for the Old English *cyne*, meaning fissure, or ravine. Given that the name Kinder has, historically, referred very much to the plateau's western end, this makes sense. The second part of the name, Scout, and in the late nineteenth century the mountain was usually called 'the Scout', comes most probably from the Old Norse *skúti*, meaning overhanging rock. This may upset those with a romantic leaning towards the Celts, but then history is often as much fashion as fact, especially when facts are thin on the ground. We usually project on to the past the concerns of today.

The same is true for individuals too. There are fragments here of my own past, a teenage boy looking for space to breathe and rocks to climb. Martin Kocsis, the author of the guidebook to Kinder Scout's rock climbs, felt the same: 'I remember the moment when I first realised what these moors meant to me. I was seventeen and was running across Featherbed Moss with some friends, yelling, screaming and laughing – the release was like nothing I'd ever known. I felt like something had changed irrevocably for the better.' Martin and I are just two among thousands of northern climbers who felt their universe expanding on the plateau of Kinder Scout. Doug Scott, the first Englishman to climb Everest, was another, the young explorer escaping the postwar gloom of Nottingham to cross Kinder Scout, discovering an imaginary Hindu Kush in Derbyshire.

Climbing was less romantic by the 1980s. The first time Andy Cave was up on these moors, he arrived at Edale station with a gang of mates from his mining village in South Yorkshire. The lads quickly set about making their mark. Having scrawled 'Royston Skins Rule OK' in large letters across the railway timetable, they headed to the pub for a few pints before taking the path up Kinder. Cave recalled two of them, twin brothers, dressed in matching Wrangler denim jackets and Dealer boots, buzzing rocks at the sheep to mitigate the boredom of going for a walk. 'The cloud dropped suddenly,' Cave wrote in his climbing memoir *Thin White Line*. 'I got out my map, but the twins called me a gay boy, so I put it away again and we trudged over the moor for hours disorientated, trying to find the northern edge by the Snake Pass Road. We peered down at a village at the end of the day, but it was Edale again; we had walked in a complete circle.'

Growing up in my own small world, where Kinder Scout was a sort of adventure kindergarten, there were such a rich variety of responses to Kinder's quiet appeal. Fell runners will tell you the same, stories from the mountain's famous races. So will those who track down the aircraft wrecks and other curiosities that pepper the mountain. There has been a cavalcade of artists drawing inspiration from its quiet lines: musicians, sculptors and painters, novelists and poets. There are the religious cranks and devoted ramblers, the half-interested picnickers and the dedicated conservationists. All comers. Kinder really is a mountain for the people. Over a lifetime looking in the mountain's face, my knowledge and appreciation of other human responses to this wild place has broadened and deepened and that has changed my own relationship with it. It's a place of constancy, a place to see the patterns of the universe. It's a place of change, and a place to see change: in ourselves and in the world around the mountain.

The mist-shrouded mire of Featherbed Moss.

Above: Crowden Brook gathers water from the Kinder plateau and carries it steeply down to the River Noe and eventually the Derwent, the Trent and the North Sea.
Opposite: The wind-sculpted rocks of the Pagoda, the Wool Packs and Pym Chair rear above the southern slopes of Kinder Scout, emphasising its plateau-like structure.

Sandy Heys. During the Carboniferous era 360 million years ago, coarse sands and gravel were laid down, forming the characteristic weathered boulders and tors that surround the plateau.

Noe Stool is a wind-eroded gritstone block perched high above the source of the River Noe between Edale Cross and the Wool Packs.

Residual woodlands of oak, birch and alder survive in the sheltered valleys that bisect the higher moorlands.

Frozen winter grasses and unearthly tors above Crowden Brook reflect the desolation that Daniel Defoe described as a 'houling wilderness' during his visit to the High Peak.

To gain the amphitheatre of Kinder Downfall at the head of Kinder ravine requires a treacherous scramble along exposed ledges.

Behind the icy curtain at Kinder Downfall.

Peter Nook is a relic plantation of mature larch and sycamore between Kinder Reservoir and the Downfall.

Frequently closed by winter snows, the exposed summit section of the Snake Pass that runs from Manchester to Sheffield reaches 512 metres above sea level, making it one of the highest major roads in Britain.

The rock-rimmed escarpment of Crowden Brook above Edale.

The natural textures and processes that form the landscape of Kinder Scout.
Top left: broken stems of common rushes swirl in a stream eddy; *top right:* lichens *Xanthoria* and *Rhizocarpon* form on exposed surface rocks; *bottom left:* quartz crystals form part of the coarse sediments that are a common constituent of millstone grit; *bottom right:* winter ice crystals halt water seeping through sand.

Above: On the north-eastern corner of the Kinder Scout massif is the colossal promontory of Fairbrook Naze overlooking the upper reaches of the Woodlands Valley.

Opposite: The summit of Lantern Pike (373 metres) above Hayfield is one of the finest viewpoints of the western flanks of Kinder Scout.

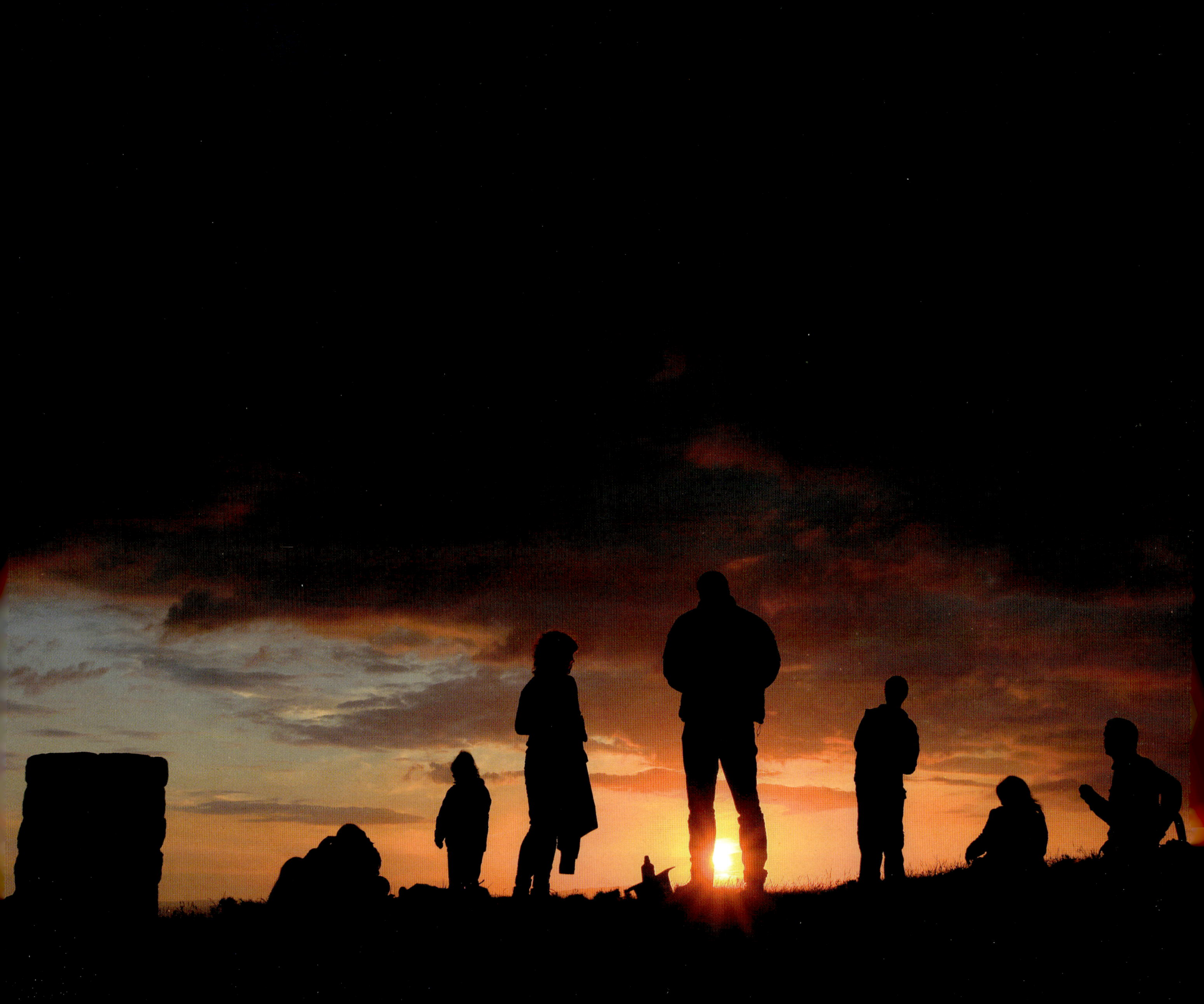

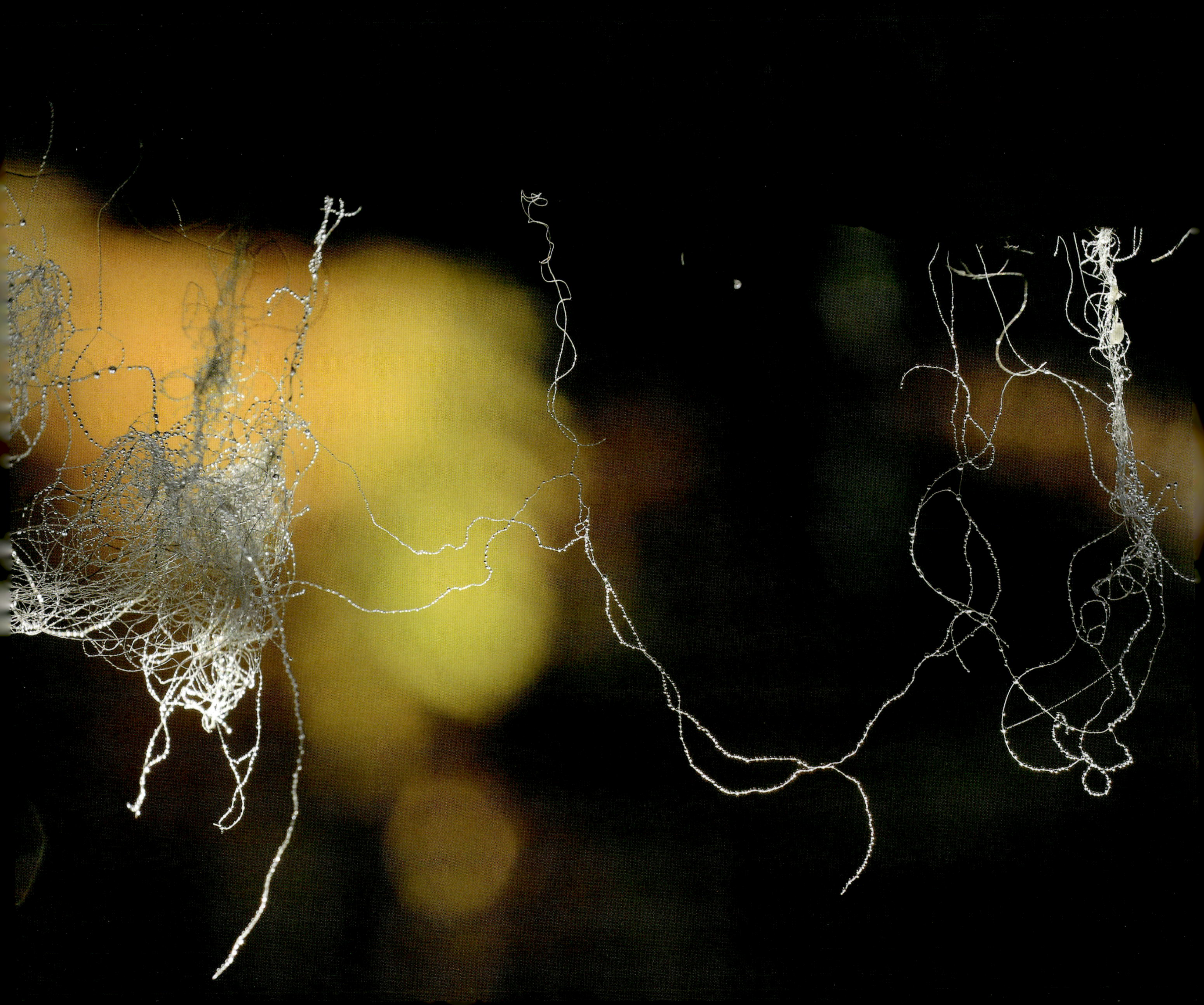

Sheep

Turning my back on Kinder Gates, I walk downstream towards the edge of the plateau, first on one side of the stream, then hopping across a couple of stepping stones to the other. After only a few minutes I enter another world. Instead of the closed, silent, blank interior of the plateau I am confronted with a sweep of space. The ground drops away below me in a jumble of blocks and crags; they incline towards the outstretched arms of the valley, waiting their turn to tumble down. I am at the top of Kinder Downfall. Away to the west are mill towns tucked into successive valleys – Chinley, New Mills, Stockport – at this time of day half concealed by morning haze. The far horizon is punctuated by Manchester's skyscraper, Beetham Tower, a quarter of the height of Kinder, piercing the clouds above it like a needle in a mattress. Like Kinder, it roars with noise in a brisk westerly.

Seattle looks up to the white bulk of Mount Rainier; Cape Town spreads beneath the slopes of Table Mountain; on a clear morning the volcano Mount Fuji is visible from the streets of Tokyo. And blessed Manchester – 'Cottonopolis' – has its Kinder Scout, watching over the city like a soot-smeared boggart. Stifle the laugh, and stand in Manchester's Ardwick, near the empty space where the Empire Theatre used to be, and you can look ruler straight down Hyde Road towards a distant purple smudge on the horizon. It may not seem like much, but from where I stand, on the top of Kinder Downfall sixteen miles away, things look a lot clearer.

Imagine a zip wire, strung between the Downfall and Beetham Tower. I zoom into Manchester and take the elevator to street level. Crossing Deansgate, tacking north-west, the People's museum on my right, I cross the Irwell, a river that ran with salmon 300 years ago but was a viscous flow of poison by the end of the nineteenth century. Now I am in Salford, walking along soulless Chapel Street, past the Crescent, one of the Irwell's meandering loops, its banks choked with plastic streaming from scrubby trees. At the university it's a sharp right into Peel Park. Named for Sir Robert Peel, who donated a thousand pounds, and opened in 1846, this was the first wholly free public park in the country; close by was England's first free public library as well. Cramming people for profit into filthy slums was not proving good for social cohesion. People needed space to breathe and think.

Queen Victoria saw the park in 1851, at the start of her first visit to Salford and Manchester, the first, in fact, by a British monarch for a century and a half. This was in the brittle aftermath of Chartism; to reassure her, Peel Park was packed with 80,000 schoolchildren singing the national anthem with loyal gusto. A painting of the visit, by the journeyman landscape artist George Hayes, shows the queen's coach arriving in a Peel Park surrounded by open spaces and long views. The *Manchester Guardian* called it 'one of the finest in the immediate neighbourhood of Manchester' – Salford's suburbs were still seen as an escape from the pollution of Manchester industry. When she came back four decades later near the end of her reign to open the Manchester Ship Canal, Victoria noted the city she was now seeing hadn't existed on her first visit.

Opposite: Filaments of teased fleece caught on the low branches of a larch tree in the Snake woodlands.

She praised Manchester's great warehouses, particularly the draper's warehouse on Portland Street built by the late Sir James Watts. When completed at the end of the 1850s it was by far the largest structure in Manchester, with three acres of floor space and 600 staff. Watts was lord mayor at the time and a friend of Prince Albert, whom he took shooting on his estate on Kinder Scout. Victoria admired the Albert Memorial too. Her husband had understood the power of Manchester's enterprise; the city's success was suffused with German influences. It must have all looked pleasantly bourgeois to the old queen, even if the city still had its radical edge.

Peel Park's views were no longer quite so expansive. At the start of the Great War, L.S. Lowry was a student at Salford Technical Institute overlooking Peel Park and returned to it as a subject again and again. He sketched the bandstand in 1925 and then did a version in oils in 1931, the crowds gathered around it, as one critic suggested, like iron filings around a magnet. In the distance mill chimneys belch smoke in a dirty sky, but the people seem rapt in their distraction. A more famous work, painted in 1944, shows the park full of his matchstick men, women and children, all anonymous, but this time disconnected, with no focus, seeking their own recreation. In the distance, a stream of people is entering the park through the Victoria Arch, an anachronism since the structure, in a Mughal style quoting the Brighton Pavilion, had been pulled down in 1937, shaken to bits by road traffic and a danger to the public. It might have been a metaphor.

Even so, just before the Great War and Lowry's arrival, this grimy scrap of green was the promise of heaven to the young Robert Roberts, raised just south of here in a long-demolished warren of slums, walled off in a fetid box formed by railways lines, Cross Lane and Oldfield Road, memorably sketched by Lowry. The air he breathed was poisoned by a nearby gasworks. You could buy a bucket of garden soil in Peel Park for a penny, and his mother tried a window box at home but the flowers wilted. 'You can rear a child, it seems, on coal gas,' she said, 'but it does for geraniums.' She was in good company. The gardeners at Peel Park regularly complained of the difficulty in getting anything to grow.

Roberts' parents ran a corner shop, an ill-considered investment financed with a legacy. Even the money they took across the counter 'had a sour, greasy smell'. His father drank, most usually leaving the running of the shop to his mother, whose fine intelligence and stamina survived the disappointment of a bad marriage long enough to raise seven children. Roberts became a writer and teacher, worked in Strangeways with illiterate prisoners, and preserved both his upbringing and his extraordinary mother in one of the great working-class memoirs, *A Ragged Schooling*.

Roberts and his family thought of themselves as living in a 'village', but that was a sour echo of Salford's more rural days earlier in Victoria's reign; their neighbourhood was, as Roberts reported, 'known to history as the world's first industrial slum', having been included in Friedrich Engels' 1845 work *The Condition of the Working Class in England*. (The book was first published in German; its English edition appeared in London forty-six years later. Bad news doesn't always travel fast.) Engels spent two years in the early 1840s working for his father's company Ermen & Engels at their factory in Victoria Mill at the end of Weaste Lane. In his free time, when he wasn't drinking at the Albert Club on Lawson Street, he paced the slums of Salford and Manchester with his Irish girlfriend Mary Burns, recording what he saw.

Even in Roberts' near-apocalyptic vision of urban poverty, the country still permeated city life, an ironical counterpoint to Marx's argument that the creation of industrial cities had rescued people from 'the idiocy of rural life'. The city was milking the country for people, as well as food. Children celebrated the coming of spring with a May queen. Cattle were walked into Salford town 'harried by dogs and bawling drovers' to what was then the largest cattle market in Britain. There were sheep too, down from the moors. 'It was not unheard of,' Roberts wrote, 'when a large flock of sheep was passing our street end, for a drover and his dogs seemingly to mishandle them, so that a score or so would suddenly "hive off" down a certain entry. There a backyard door swung conveniently open. Two fewer sheep ran out to rejoin the mainstream. For the next few days lamb sold cheap about the streets.' He remembered also the horror of watching an escaped heifer caught in a net and flung in the back of a cart, 'the terror in her great eyes', so that his own stung with tears.

The countryside was not then some distant place, with strange customs and obscure practices. Most of the people around Robert Roberts had family connections to rural life; they did not sentimentalise it but felt keenly the loss of nature from their lives. His mother worked for thirty years to escape the slum, half taunted, half-inspired with the memory of the first home she shared with her gregarious drunkard of a husband: 'A house in a lane by a river, and beyond, fields – almost the country!' She literally taught her son to make hay while the sun shined, sending him out to the waste grounds of Salford to cut grass with his scissors and then spreading it on the roof – '"tedding," my mother called it' – turning it next day before gathering the stalks into a miniature haycock which was set on the windowsill.

When, under the Liberal Party's welfare reforms, his mother got half a day's holiday, she took Robert to Peel Park. 'We sat on a high esplanade and looked far over the countless chimneys of northern Manchester to the horizon. On the skyline, green and aloof, the Pennines rose like the ramparts of paradise. "There!" she said, pointing. "Mountains!" I stared, lost for words.' The view now would feel more cramped to Roberts. A 1960s office block leans over the park, every shrub is thick with garbage and in the far distance those ramparts of paradise – not Kinder Scout but Scout Moor, north of Rochdale – are studded with wind turbines sixty metres high. On the other hand, he would find the air much cleaner and work to restore Peel Park is underway.

New horizons run throughout Roberts' book. As a boy he and his friends set off on a heroic journey to explore Cheshire, fashioning a tent from discarded sugar sacks so they could sleep out. (Joining the Scouts wasn't an option; they couldn't afford the uniform.) On the border, somewhere between Stretford and Sale, they reached their goal. 'Stout Cortez himself,' Roberts recalled, 'newly eyeing the Pacific could have registered no more joy.' Barely fifty metres inside Cheshire, two policemen – 'rozzers' – intercepted the explorers, pushing Roberts into a hedge. Having lost his gear, he fled back to Salford, where his mother promised him a new tent, once they'd emptied enough sacks, and advised he stay in Lancashire next time. Setting out on his exploration of the city's wilder corners, wearing the iron off their clogs, Roberts recalled how they 'went just as men climbed mountains, "because they were there": Boggart Hole Clough, Tootal Woods, Daisy Nook, the Pepper Hills and – Brindle Heath! A name for me a poem in itself.' Open spaces bred open minds: the natural amphitheatre of Boggart Hole Clough served as a meeting place for a cash-strapped Independent Labour Party in 1896, despite legal action to stop them.

Roberts kept his sense of adventure; early in the Second World War he moved to a smallholding called Wee Ting near Hebden Bridge belonging to his wife's German-born grandfather and stayed for almost two decades. He taught in Sweden, where he was cured of tuberculosis, before moving back to Manchester and the job at Strangeways. Yet the true exploration in *A Ragged Schooling* is political and social. The poverty of Salford's worst slums seems initially inescapable, a different universe from the cultural and intellectual progress being made elsewhere in Manchester. Yet even in the slums, change was gathering pace, ushered in by social reformers and pushed on by the war, so that the voiceless were suddenly articulate – and in no mood to be compliantly grateful. At the end of his story, Roberts tells how his parents and their friends, with enough savings for a short holiday in a posh hotel down south, were quizzed in turn by a woman who lived there year round on how each of them could afford it. How *industrious*, she simpered. Patronised, infuriated, Roberts' father told her: 'I got mine robbin' a bloody bank!' Sheep no longer, he had voted Liberal for the last time. 'It was enough,' he said, 'to turn you Bolshie.'

He didn't though, and in the end Robert Roberts' mother left his father, lived for a short time afterwards 'in a quiet, clean district near a park and a library', before dying, with 'a faint sardonic smile' on her lips. 'A final comment, perhaps,' Roberts wrote, 'on the world as she had known it.' The fate of women, his mother in particular, but all the women in his life, the pressures they faced, the resilience of some, the fragility of others, permeates *A Ragged Schooling*. Roberts was born in 1905 at the height of the women's suffrage movement, a year before the general election of 1906, when the arrival of cabinet ministers on the campaign trail drew militant suffragettes to picket their meetings. When Winston Churchill, deselected from Oldham and standing as a Liberal for Manchester North West, came to address a meeting at St John's Schoolroom on Deansgate, one of those militants was waiting for him, a tall, slim woman in her mid thirties, her pockets full of little flags with the words 'Votes for Women' painted in black enamel. After Churchill had been speaking for a while, the woman got to her feet and took out her white cotton pennant and called out: 'Will the Liberal government give the vote to women?' There was uproar, but Churchill appealed for order and invited her to the platform to speak. Despite being roughly handled not only by the crowd but by the chairman of the meeting too, she did so. The suffragette was Hannah Mitchell, who grew up within sight of Kinder Scout, knew the moors intimately and found in them, in the words of her grandson, 'a place of refuge from the anxieties of modern urban life'. She was still walking the moors in her seventies, after a lifetime of struggle and public service.

She was born Hannah Webster in 1871, at Alport Castles Farm, less than a quarter of a century after the publication of Emily Brontë's *Wuthering Heights*; her early life held some of that fiction's vision of the moors, a shifting blend of threat, freedom and the supernatural. ('I'm sure I should be myself,' Catherine Earnshaw pleads, as she lies dying, 'were I once among the heather on those hills.') There's a thread of that sentiment throughout Hannah's life, but Alport Castles Farm was no Thrushcross Grange. Hannah was shaped much more by the hard economic realities she experienced as a child and her burning sense of injustice at the place of women in society, captured in her memoir *The Hard Way Up*, unpublished in her lifetime but no less compelling than that of Robert Roberts. It is more *Hard Times* than Brontë, but underpinned by resilience and courage.

Her grandmother had kept the toll bar on the turnpike that ran through the Woodlands Valley, on the north side of Kinder Scout, the last of the great turnpikes to be built, sponsored through parliament by the local landowner, the sixth Duke of Devonshire, who built and operated a coaching inn called the Snake Inn halfway between Glossop and the now-submerged village of Ashopton. The pub became a well-known landmark, popular with sporting men escaping the day-to-day; prize fights and dog racing too. Above the door was the Devonshire's symbol, 'a serpent nowed, proper' – 'nowed' meaning knotted and 'proper' meaning as it appears in nature – and so the road, which twists through some high country, was known as the Snake. In 1871, with traffic limited by a slow economy, there was barely a living to be made at the toll bar, and so Hannah's parents put themselves into debt and took over the farm at Alport Castles, living thereafter with the constant anxiety of making the repayments. 'Life on those hill-farms at that time was very hard,' Hannah wrote, 'with no machinery and very little money.' If she had a fault, and there were those who found her overly stern, others who found her whimsical, it was understatement.

Hannah grew up in a world whose culture stretched back deep into the Middle Ages. Drayton had written in *Poly-Olbion* of the vast flocks of sheep in the Derwent Valley, on the other side of Alport Castles and flowing south to Chatsworth. There had been large flocks on the moors in the twelfth and thirteenth centuries, when the climate was warmer and drier and the High Peak was evolving from royal hunting grounds to stock farms. New houses were built, often illegally, on royal land. In those days there were still wolves in the Peak District, the memory of them preserved in place names, including Wolfstone in Woodlands: their days were numbered. Weekly markets were established in the thirteenth century to sell the wool and meat now growing on the moors. Huge tracts, including the Upper Derwent, were owned by the Premonstratensians – the White Canons – at Welbeck Abbey in Nottinghamshire. They were smelting lead too, that other great Peak District industry.

Upland farms have always been more vulnerable than those downstream, and the numbers of sheep – and people – rose and fell with the passing centuries. Even before the Black Death – the 'Great Pestilence' – wiped out a third of the human population, farming had contracted in the High Peak as livestock disease and failed harvests reduced income. After the plague, wages rose by half. Why farm marginal country if there was land or good wages available in easier places? The tide of man ebbed; the moors became wilder and less inhabited, then it turned once more and people slowly flowed back in. By the Tudor era sheep farming was booming again, demand for meat and wool surged, and new farms were built higher up the hillsides in wilder parts of the Peak. Rents increased by half for the five cattle booths in Edale: Upper, Nether, Barber, Grindsbrook and Ollerbrook. Alport's pasture, owned by the Duchy of Lancaster, was let to one John Savage. The moors had been a blank space to the Normans, their extent unrecorded. Now they were mapped, resources stretched and squabbled over, it became necessary to understand them. There was even an enquiry into overgrazing.

The Enlightenment offered new tools of understanding and new sorts of minds too. John Farey is one of those figures from the engine room of history, busily laying down the tracks on which progress can steam ahead. As mathematician, surveyor and geologist, he was a hugely prolific author of scientific papers but is remembered now for his series of fractions, immensely useful to musicologists, known as the Farey sequence. As a surveyor, publishing in the 1810s, he had much to say about the economic life of upland Derbyshire, drawing attention to the best breed, the 'Woodland or Moorland sheep', known in south-west Yorkshire as the Penistone: smallish, though big for a hill breed, white-faced, horned, long-legged but light in the forequarter and consequently well adapted to foraging over leggy heather moor. He detailed the names of Woodlands sheep breeders and drew attention to the shepherds' societies that met at Hayfield and Salter's Brook, on the north side of Bleaklow, to agree a marking system so that strays could be sorted. A sheep and wool fair was started in 1829, after Farey's time, at Ashopton, an event familiar to Hannah and her parents.

We get glimpses of this world from John Hutchinson, an enterprising Chapel-en-le-Frith author capitalising on the eighteenth century fashion for travelogues and grand tours. He might have lacked the literary skill of Celia Fiennes or Defoe, but Hutchinson was full of curiosity and not afraid to oversell his material. He published his *Tour Through the High Peak of Derbyshire* in 1809, a perspective underpinned by deep local knowledge. Along with the usual trips down caves and some hair-raising ghost stories, he offers us: 'the Romantic Scenery of the Woodlands, never before described.' The remoteness of the northern slopes of Kinder Scout is palpable, the numbers of sheep astonishing: 'the number of families in the Woodlands was easily ascertained to be forty-two, and the population two hundred, in a circuit of thirty miles. There is not any church or chapel, public house, shop, blacksmith, shoemaker, or mechanic, in the whole extent. The parish church being at Hope, a distance of eight or ten miles from some parts. The lower order of people are shepherds, and the farmers, as they are called, possess large flocks of sheep to the number of one thousand each.'

The hardness of life in Woodlands fascinates him; he describes eating oatcakes, because oats were the only crop that could cope with the short growing season. But even at the turn of the nineteenth century, before the railways and the turnpike, the world percolated in. At Over House, 'which is the farthest dwelling in the Woodlands,' he found two shepherds, one of whom, he wrote, 'I found rather intelligent. He had lately been, he said, to the West Indies on a frolic, with two of his countrymen, on board a merchant's ship. Unfortunately, his comrades on arriving at Liverpool, had been pressed into the king's service, and he alone had returned, to spend his days as a shepherd, upon the mountains, which he said he would never leave again.'

The mulish intelligence of High Peak sheep, a trope that continues into the twenty-first century, as anyone mugged by a woolly assailant for their sandwiches will attest, provides Hutchinson with one of his set-piece anecdotes. You can imagine him sitting in a Chapel public house to tell this story: 'Several years ago, a farm in this neighbourhood sold a quantity of sheep, to a person in Kent, which he forwarded according to a bargain. The drover having ascertained with the purchaser the number to be correct, returned with the sum for which they were sold. However, in the course of a few weeks, one of the same flock, well known by a particular mark, and his fine curling horns, was observed in the pastures of his old master, in the Woodlands.' The old owner checked with the new one: all sheep had been delivered.

'It seemed that he, the stranger in question, was dissatisfied with his new situation, and had determined to return. He therefore in all probability, crossed the Thames at London Bridge, or else swam over that river, and finding his way through the great metropolis, at length arrived in his native pastures, after a journey of above two hundred miles.' Two ewes set off with the ram, but never arrived. 'I have seen the horns, which are affixed to a carved piece of wood, resembling the head of a sheep, and hung up in the house of a very respectable gentleman of this country.'

After Farey and Hutchinson's time, there was a move towards the Derbyshire Gritstone breed – black-faced, hornless – also known as Dale o'Goyt, since the Goyt Valley is where they emerged in the late eighteenth century. Alan Virtue wrote a memoir of his life as a hill farmer in the mid-twentieth century at Rushop Hall, close but lower in altitude to Kinder Scout. He tried a few Derbyshire Gritstones on his land but found them too independent-minded. 'I bought off the Kinder Scout moors, through a dealer and turned them out, but the next day they were all missing. They all ended up back home on the old moors, and there they had to stay until the first official round up, when I promptly resold them, resolving not to try the experiment again. These moorland breeds will have the wild open spaces.' I can sympathise.

John Farey admired sheep but was not a fan of heather, which, in his judgement, was 'much too common'. He was pleased to note that: 'Within a few years past, nearly all the fine Limestone Hills between Asburne [sic] and Buxton were occupied by Heath, which is now happily becoming rather scarce there; and when the only remaining Commons, or unimproved Lands in the calcareous district, in Middleton, Yolgrave [sic] &c. shall have been inclosed, pared and burned, and limed &c. this noxious and useless Plant will, I hope, disappear altogether from this District.'

Farey offered lots of advice for getting rid of the noxious and useless heather from the Dark Peak as well as the White, but his advice was ignored. Fashions changed. Britain now has something like eighty per cent of the world's heather moorland and much money and effort is spent on seeing it thrive. It was the growing popularity of grouse shooting that meant Farey's advice was ignored and the heather preserved. The birds became better business than the sheep. By the time Hannah's parents took out their lease from the Duke of Devonshire on their farm, the economic prospects of sheep farmers were starting to fade.

In 1882 the first refrigerated ship carrying lamb and mutton left New Zealand. By the 1890s, eight million tonnes were being imported. Landowners saw more advantage in managing their moorland for grouse than sheep. The Manchester rambler Edwin Royce, who knew plenty of hill farmers from his tramps across the moors, wrote of the change: 'The old native will point to 50,000 sheep on the moorlands between Longdendale and Baslow sixty years ago but who could find 5,000 there today?' It was only with the outbreak of war in 1914 and the threat to food supplies that home-reared lamb recovered some of its advantage.

The life of hill farmers now is hard but historically it was brutally so. Alan Virtue farmed through the bitter winter months of early 1947, often cut off from the outside world, struggling against the outlandish amount of snow that fell. 'Sheep were buried without any hope of survival and many were found dead, frozen rigid in a normal standing position with their heads bowed.' When the snow finally began to melt, 'the savagery of the unprecedented conditions left us all in the district demoralised and frightened, that we should have to face anything like this again'.

Coal and fuel supplies were scarce, and for a while the Cowburn Tunnel into Edale was closed because of icicles. In Edale, the banks of a trench dug to the station reached up to the level of the telephone wires. Supplies were dumped on the platform and ferried to the farms by sled. At the request of the authorities, the Sheffield branch of the Council for the Preservation of Rural England organised sheep rescue parties of ramblers, climbers and members of the Youth Hostel Association, their first task to dig out 400 sheep stranded on Stanage. They discovered it was possible to jump off the top of the crag and land safely in the snowdrifts below.

Those were freakish conditions, but bad weather regularly claimed lives on the high moors. There was a pattern: someone walking between villages, often in late winter, was caught out by an unexpected snowstorm on the high country, became disoriented, then exhausted and ultimately frozen. Until you have experienced a white-out on featureless ground, the wind tearing at your clothes, your mind panicked, spinning in circles, it's hard to conceive how easily you can become lost. For example: in February 1692, Elizabeth Trout died crossing the moor on her way home from Tideswell market. Another: the curate at Bradfield wrote in the burial register on 25 August 1718: 'A coffin put in the earth with Bones of a Person found upon the high Moors, thought to be Richard Steade.' In 1724, the curate at Derwent buried a young couple, disappeared on the moors in a snowstorm decades before in January 1674. Their bodies had been discovered the following spring and 'they had lain in the moss twenty-eight years, and had been exposed every summer to the view of people who came out of curiosity for twenty years, which makes in the whole forty-eight years. They were laid in the moss twenty-eight years before I was born, and yet I buried them.' The preservation of flesh in the oxygenless peat being just one more way the moors seem to stretch time.

Children were especially vulnerable. There's a story framed on the wall of the Snake Pass Inn of two young boys who froze to death in January 1845 while trying to reach Glossop with their father, a 'travelling tumbler' called William Bullin. He survived, discovered more dead than alive a mile from the town by a search party. Even those most familiar with the moors, the shepherds who spent their lives on them, were at risk, like the legendary shepherd boy, Abraham Lowe, who lived with his widowed mother above the village of Derwent and died looking for their sheep below Back Tor in a winter storm, scratching, if the legend is true, the phrase 'Lost Lad' on a rock before he succumbed to exposure. (As a boy, I developed a complex fiction that Madwoman's Stones, at the eastern end of Kinder Scout from where the promontory of Lost Lad on Derwent Edge is clearly visible across the Woodlands Valley, was somehow connected, that the woman had been unhinged by the tragedy and, like Niobe, 'all tears', was turned to rock.)

Hannah Mitchell's father also succumbed to a winter storm, in 1902, many years after she had left home, caught in a snowstorm and led home by his sheepdog in a state of collapse, from which he died the following day. Hannah loved her father, judged him 'so kind a parent, so gentle in sickness, so indulgent in letting us off some of the hard work which even children had to do on these remote farms'. She thought him brave too, able to 'handle a savage horse or face an infuriated bull, and once I knew he had strangled a mad dog which attacked the sheep in the pen'.

He was not, however, able to 'shield us from my mother's virago-like temper'. A Yorkshire woman who arrived in the district as a maidservant, Hannah's mother was wholly unsuited to life as a farmer's wife in a remote Derbyshire valley. She had, Hannah recalled, a slim, girlish figure, shown off by the pretty frocks she liked to wear on Sundays. 'She could sing like a lark, and at times was perfectly charming. But her temper was so uncertain that we lived in constant fear of an outbreak which often lasted several days.'

Her mother always said she hated the dale from the first day she saw it, but Hannah was entirely at home roaming the moors. 'I loved the hills, loved to listen at night to "the rush of the mountain streams" or the "sound of a hidden brook", could respond to the beauty of a field of golden buttercups, hunt the hedgerows for wild violets, or climb the great tor for the primroses which grew in sheltered nooks known only to my father and me.' She was connected also to a way of seeing the High Peak that was far more rooted in time and place than the parade of educated travellers who came through the region, judging it sublime or terrible. Hannah was particularly devoted to her grandmother who lived with her only unmarried son in a small, sparsely furnished cottage at the end of the lane. 'She told me many stories of bygone days including the origin of the local Garland Day at Castleton, which she said was a survival of an ancient Druidical rite. She often spoke of the Druids and was the first person to tell me about the worship of mistletoe.'

Notions of Druidism, of an ancient British culture, were much in vogue in her grandmother's youth. Thomas Bateman had dug up what became known as the Druid's Stone on Kinder in the 1770s, discovering amulets beneath it. The theories and opinions that sprang from this antiquarianism were essentially myths, containing little or no reality of life in pre-Roman Britain. But that's rather to miss the point. Hannah's grandmother fulfilled a role familiar all over the world in remote communities, that of folk-healer and midwife, a woman judged by her neighbours to be in touch with the mysteries of life, who would sit talking with her long-dead husband and be amazed that Hannah couldn't see him. 'In earlier times,' Hannah wrote, 'she would have been burned as a witch.' She even had a spinning wheel in her bedroom.

Even in old age Hannah's grandmother would get up in the middle of the night to attend a confinement, a duty that was mostly unpaid. The old woman relied on an inherited bank of knowledge about the therapeutic effects of a range of herbs that she grew in the garden of her little cottage. 'Such a garden it was. All kinds of things grew here together in happy disorder: vegetables, flowers, and the herbs my grandmother used in her sick nursing, rue, wormwood, camomile, horehound, balm. For a long time I thought all herbs were bitter until I realised that mint, sage, marjoram and thyme were also herbs.' As an old woman, Hannah still dreamed of the daffodils that grew in profusion in her grandmother's garden. The cottage was torn down long before Hannah died, its stones used for walling, and I've looked in vain for any trace of the garden.

The closest school to the farm was in Derwent: a five-mile walk straight over Alport Castles with Kinder's northern rim at your back, and down past Birchinlee. Given the length of winter, and what might happen to a child caught out in a snowstorm, daily attendance was impractical and so Hannah's parents planned to send their six children to lodge there, starting with the two oldest boys. They brought books home and Hannah would bargain with them, doing their chores if they brought a book for her too. Hannah was desperate to go to school, but her mother wouldn't allow it, telling her she was needed at home. The seeds of her feminism were sown darning her brothers' socks.

In the meantime she took what learning she could find, practising her writing, picking up new words from visiting preachers like shells from a beach. She read anything she could find, cookery books, early Methodist magazines, lurid stories of murder and robbery, then, as now, immensely popular. She found more substantial works too, including a clean copy of Elizabeth Gaskell's *Cranford*. Through all this she had the support of her uncle, who lived with her grandmother and worked as a road mender and shepherd, later becoming a gamekeeper. Hannah told him that if her brothers got the vote when they grew up then she should do the same, law or no law. 'My uncle looked at me with a twinkle in his eye: "Aye lass, I believe you will."'

Even now Alport is a quiet dale, but in Hannah's youth visitors were extremely rare. One wet spring Sunday in 1879, as the children read in turn from the Bible round the kitchen table, Hannah's brother Will noticed a stranger coming up the lane, his tweed suit and knapsack soaked by the rain. While her mother organised hot food and dry clothes, the man showed the children his rucksack, since they were curious, never having seen such a thing before, how it left his hands free as he walked. In those days, walkers stuffed their pockets or carried a shoulder bag. Out of the sack came books, and Hannah was riveted. Did she read poetry, the man asked? She barely knew what it was but said yes anyway and was handed a copy of Wordsworth's poems, the rambler telling her that whichever of the children knew more of the poems when he returned would get to keep it for good. Hannah pored over the book, learned what she could, fancied herself like Lucy in the deceptively simple sequence of folk ballads Wordsworth wrote while living in Germany in the late 1790s: 'She dwelt among the untrodden ways / Beside the springs of Dove, / A maid whom there were none to praise / And very few to love.'

Hannah's mother couldn't tolerate her daughter's new-found passion and confiscated the book of poems, judging the time Hannah spent reading them 'wasted'. It disappeared from view, until, during the early 1940s, Hannah came to write her life story and she found the book again in the possession of her sister. Knowing that the visitor had scribbled something in the flyleaf, she turned the pages and discovered the identity of her benefactor: 'From Hans Renold, Manchester, April '79.' The name galvanised Hannah. She knew Renold; they had both been magistrates in Manchester. She knew him also as one of the city's leading industrialists, someone whose entrepreneurial ability was matched by his sense of social justice. Renold was the son of a baker and restaurant owner in the Swiss town of Aarau, at the foot of the Jura Mountains. From an early age it was clear he had a natural aptitude for mechanical engineering and as a boy he worked for a watchmaker. He studied at the polytechnic in Zurich, travelled to England as a young man, came to Manchester and found work at J. Felber & Co., machinery exporters. The year he met Hannah, he bought a chain-making business on Woden Street in Salford, just south of the slum Robert Roberts grew up in, borrowing the capital from his future father-in-law, the Unitarian businessman Charles James Herford. Within a year, Renold's fledgling business had developed a new kind of chain, one that worked perfectly on a new kind of transport – the bicycle. The lanes of Derbyshire were soon after full of cycling enthusiasts set free from the city thanks in part to Renold's inventions. He moved his premises to Brook Street in Manchester, continued both to be an innovative engineer and a model employer, and in 1943, when Hannah discovered her childhood link to him, was aged ninety and in the last weeks of his life. She wrote to him, and her letter was read to the old man, now blind, of how his gift of Wordsworth had inspired a little girl.

Renold's visit was not Hannah Mitchell's only literary encounter. A few years later, according to Hannah, two well-dressed women walked up the lane to Alport Castles Farm, and while her mother busied herself making tea for them, one of the women asked if her children were interested in reading; she was herself a writer and was hoping to include their dale in her next book. The writer was Mary Augusta Ward, fast becoming, under her married name Mrs Humphry Ward, one of the most famous and wealthy novelists in Britain. Within ten years she had earned, in today's terms, several millions, was hailed by Leo Tolstoy and admired by her friend Henry James. Her companion that day was her sister-in-law Gertrude Ward, then working as her secretary. The novel she was researching would become *The History of David Grieve* but the setting would not be the secret valley Hannah inhabited; it was changed to the western flank of Kinder Scout, helpfully, from a thematic point of view, overlooking the city of Manchester. Even so, the world Mrs Ward imagined, the ideas Mrs Ward espoused and the life of Hannah Mitchell wove together and then split apart with an uncanny intimacy.

Mrs Ward's background and upbringing could not have been more different from Hannah's. She was born in Australia, granddaughter of the famous headmaster of Rugby, Thomas Arnold. Her uncle was the poet Matthew Arnold. Her brother Willie was a journalist on the *Manchester Guardian* who was friends with the daughters of Elizabeth Gaskell and preparing new editions of her work at the time of his early death. Her sister Julia married Leonard Huxley,

son of the evolutionary biologist Thomas. Their two sons were Leonard and Aldous. Nothing made Mrs Ward more proud than her own pedigree. Her father, Tom Arnold, was an academic driven from his post in Tasmania when he converted to Catholicism, later reverting to Anglicanism, and then going back to Catholicism. His religious toing and froing infuriated his wife, not least because he kept squandering good jobs. But agonies of religious conscience were grist to Mrs Ward's creative mill and a major theme of her novels.

She made a series of visits to the High Peak in the 1880s gathering material and taking in the scene, although the inspiration for the novel came later. After completing the opening chapters, originally set in the Derwent Valley, close to Hannah's home, she revisited the area. (There is a tantalising reference in the diaries of Gertrude, who accompanied the author, to an avalanche from the edge above Derwent village.) Then the two women took a dogcart to Glossop and continued to Hayfield, staying in Upper House Farm, before it became James Watts' shooting lodge, where Gertrude's brother Willie joined her. Next day they climbed up the Downfall and took in the view. This fresh perspective made her move the opening of the novel to Kinder Scout, within sight of Manchester. This was much neater for her plot. Her hero, David Grieve, survives a rural childhood of poverty and hard work shared with his wild and ultimately untameable sister Louie. They are orphans, taken in by their uncle Reuben and aunt – called Hannah – who farm on the flanks of Kinder Scout, have narrow religious views and are often cruelly strict. Just as Hannah Mitchell sought escape in books, so does David, 'whose joys lay in free moorland wanderings with the sheep, in endless reading', and is roundly mocked by his sister for it.

He hides from his aunt and uncle in a derelict smithy, symbolic of a fading pattern of life, 'a spectator for ever of that younger, busier England'. (She had read Louis Jennings's recently published *Rambles Among the Hills*, the best evocation of Kinder Scout's landscape available, and visited the old smithy he mentions.) Metal work had been part of the local Hayfield economy since at least the thirteenth century. Trees were felled for charcoal to smelt iron, the slag heaps now underwater in Kinder reservoir, the metal worked in small smithies attached to farms. There are hints of this industry in local names: Cutler's Green, Ashes Farm.

Looking up from above Hayfield, Mrs Ward captures some of the landscape's abstract appeal, but she can't resist bringing things to some kind of climax: 'A magnificent curving front of moor, the steep sides of it crowned with black edges and cliffs of grit, the outline of the south-western end sweeping finely up on the right to a purple peak, the king of all the moorland around.' If the summit of Kinder is a king, then he's more likely one of those democratically inclined Scandinavian kings who rides a bicycle and is, anyway, a woman. Turning the other way, looking out from the smithy, David could see his future: 'From the old threshold the eye commanded a wilderness of moors, rising wave-like one after another, from the green swell just below whereon stood Reuben Grieve's farm, to the far-distant Alderley Edge. In the hollows in between, dim tall chimneys veiled in mist and smoke showed the places of the cotton towns – of Hayfield, New Mills, Staleybridge, Stockport; while in the far northwest, any gazer to whom the country-side spoke familiarly might, in any ordinary clearness of weather, look for and find the eternal smoke-cloud of Manchester.'

Otherwise, Mrs Ward massages Kinder Scout like clay to fit her narrative. She has David and Louie visiting Edale – this is before the railway tunnel pierced Kinder like a skewer through meat, so that all the juices ran out – to have their fortunes read by gypsies. Their uncle, who is essentially a good man put upon by a harridan, becomes anxious that they will be caught out by nightfall returning home. 'If they conno see their way when they get to the top o't'Downfall,' he says, (Mrs Ward's attempt at the local dialect leans towards the Pythonesque), 'they'll stay there till it gets morning, if they've ony sort o'gumption.' To miss the familiar packhorse route from Edale to Hayfield and end up at the top of the Downfall, the siblings would need to be hopelessly drunk.

If the geography is wonky, Mrs Ward does succeed in catching the interaction of people and landscape on the cusp of change between a more rooted traditional culture and something more ersatz, whipped up to sell train tickets and guidebooks, drawing on diffuse Romantic sentiments about wild land. She focuses on the Mermaid's Pool, an unremarkable rush pond marked on the modern Ordnance Survey map below Sandy Heys and the Downfall. There's some evidence this had once been a feature in the Downfall, a kind of grotto formed by an arch and ceiling over the stream, which better fits the legend of a mermaid bathing on Easter's eve, and the lucky man who catches a glimpse of her living forever. When the arch collapsed, the myth shifted with it, because it was a good story that needed to survive.

Louie asks her uncle about the pool and they discuss its various names, which include, improbably, 'Hamadryad', since a hamadryad is a Greek tree spirit and a lack of trees is a feature of Kinder's landscape. 'Aye, soom faddlin kind of a name they gie it – I know – those Manchester chaps, as cooms trespassin ower t'Scout wheer they aren't wanted. T'ain't ov ony account what they an their books coe it.' Mrs Ward makes a point of telling us that whereas Reuben is generally a humble man, when it comes to ramblers he doesn't hesitate to show his superiority and turn them away. He also offers Louie another name, the Witch's Pool, and recalls that in his grandfather's time a witch was drowned in it. He names her as Jenny Crum, tells how a local eccentric, Lias Dawson, an older friend of David's and a 'queer dreamer', was tormented by her and suffered losses on his farm, a common trope in stories about witches across northern England and Scotland. David, droving sheep into Yorkshire with his uncle, begins quizzing shepherds and farmers about witches, and hears stories of 'mysterious hares coursed at night by angry farmers enraged by the "bedivilment" of their stock, shot at with silver slugs, and identified next morning with some dreaded hag or other lying groaning and wounded in her bed – of calves' hearts burnt a' midnight with awful ceremonies, while the baffled witch outside flung herself in rage and agony against the close-barred doors and windows.'

Mrs Ward sensationalised the fragments she picked up during her visits north from her home in Oxford, but she was drawing on cultural strands stretching back to the Elizabethan era, like the North Berwick witch trials on which Shakespeare drew for *Macbeth*, and on the paranoia of James I about women, especially old women, who could control the elements and conjure disease, a paranoia underpinned by fear of Catholic plots. No wonder Hannah Mitchell thought her grandmother would have been burned.

Mrs Ward's curiosity about Kinder Scout was limited; the role of the moors was simply to sprinkle the flavours of Wordsworth over her creation. Her real interest was in Manchester where conflicting ideas and futures were jostling for space, the perfect cockpit in which to throw David Grieve. When he gets there, he quickly sheds his dialect, which is a relief since her rendition of it is painful. Mrs Ward also made sure, for the benefit of southern readers, to distance David from his northern nonconformist upbringing by giving him an exotic backstory, a fickle and doomed French mother and a father who has prospered somewhat in London. Although she allows him a brief and fervent religious phase, he abruptly turns his back on Methodism, gets drunk and flees to the city, where, with 'the constant presentiment of a wide career', he begins a long and chastening journey towards prosperity, social responsibility and the established church. Nonconformity, an essential motif in the fabric of communities in the shadow of Kinder Scout, is narrow and stupid, as illustrated by David's limited uncle and aunt. First, Mrs Ward sends him – rather improbably – to Haworth to buy sheep with his uncle, where he meets someone who had known the Brontë sisters – the novel opens in the 1860s – and encourages him to read *Shirley*, which in turn provokes an existential crisis. 'The old free life on the moors with the long hours for reading seemed to him now a mere dull drifting – not living at all.'

The contrast with Hannah Mitchell is stark. Just as hungry for learning, she doesn't share David Grieve's view of Manchester as 'the golden city on the horizon to which the pilgrims of wealth go up'. She was no less aware of the 'tug of the great current which had been sweeping all the while past the quiet mountains and the sheep walks'. But she would have been content enough 'with more leisure and plenty of books' to have 'lived happily in this quiet place'. (What she lacked, more than anything, was a room of her own.) And while she became a socialist and suffragette, the joyful, communitarian aspect of her Methodist upbringing stays with her for life, particularly the 'Love Feast', held each summer in her father's barn on the first Sunday in July, an early Christian tradition, known in Greek as *agape*, that was revived by Protestant sects like the Moravians, who in turn influenced the Methodist Charles Wesley.

As a child, Hannah looked forward to the Love Feast like almost nothing else. The farm buildings were whitewashed inside, the barn swept and the floor spread with bracken and rushes. Rough planks set on large blocks served as seats and a trestle table as a platform. Her mother, as fearsome in her temper as Aunt Hannah in David Grieve, 'baked bread, pies and cakes, roasted a great piece of beef, and boiled a ham'. The congregation arrived on foot, since coaches couldn't get up the narrow track. Many of them would have walked anyway, coming from as far afield as Bradwell. Resentment at the closure by grouse shooting interests of the ancient footpath up William Clough and down Ashop Clough was connected to the need of local people to reach places of worship in the Woodlands Valley, including the Love Feast. Limiting freedom of movement across the moors had a religious angle. Many years later, after she had supported the campaign to overturn this illegal closure, Hannah wrote a short pamphlet on the Love Feast, and in researching its history discovered how the festival grew out of the 1662 Act of Uniformity, which excluded nonconformist Protestants from public office and suppressed nonconformist worship.

'At this remote spot,' Hannah wrote, 'men and women assembled to worship God in their own way, and, one hopes, were never discovered by their enemies. Tradition has it that John Wesley himself had preached in the barn, so it seemed a natural supposition that the founders of the Wesleyan Society should choose this spot, already consecrated by those early worshippers, for their annual festival, and to it we all return, making our yearly visit like pilgrims returning to a shrine.'

Although little read outside academia now, and largely forgotten, *The History of David Grieve* is an absorbing-enough novel, even though, when it was published in 1892, it was already old-fashioned, both in its structure, similar to the biographical fiction of Dickens, and in its moral and philosophical complacencies. Hannah Mitchell doesn't offer any judgement, but you feel that if the novel had meant anything to her, she would have mentioned it. She and several friends did club together to buy a copy of Thomas Hardy's *Jude the Obscure* when it was published soon after *David Grieve*, a far more harrowing exploration of England's rapid social change and the thwarted intellectual ambitions of the working classes – more modernist than Romantic. Its hero, Jude Fawley, has ambitions of going to Oxford, learns Latin and Greek, but is ultimately crushed by circumstance, class and convention. He is the antithesis of David Grieve: 'I was perhaps, after all, a paltry victim to the spirit of mental and social restlessness, that makes so many unhappy in these days.'

There were good reasons Hannah might prefer *Jude the Obscure* to *David Grieve*. Towards the end of the latter, David Grieve tells his wife: 'Socialism, as a system, seems to me, at any rate, to strike down and weaken the most precious thing in the world, that on which the whole of civilised life and progress rests – the spring of will and conscience in the individual.' Hannah Mitchell might have argued that her springs of will and conscience were overflowing and found their best expression in the Independent Labour Party. But I suspect it went deeper than that. In *David Grieve*, the women are ciphers, with the exception of David's wild sister Louie, who as a child impersonates the witch Jenny Crum, ignores social convention by sleeping around and is made to pay for it. David's wife Lucy, her name a genuflection to Wordsworth, dies at Rydal, having been so devoid of ideas that the more elevated circles David attains consider her unworthy of him.

The meeting between Mrs Humphry Ward and Hannah Mitchell is a compelling moment. The grand Victorian novelist, on the hunt for stories and ideas, meets a working-class girl desperate for learning, trapped and bewildered by poverty but determined to break society's limitations on her gender. And yet Mrs Ward chose to write a novel about a naturally brilliant young man, a hero from the Thomas Carlyle mould, whose progress is trailed or hampered by women who largely stand and watch. It's not surprising they would find themselves on opposite sides of the coming struggle over universal suffrage. Mrs Ward became the chair of the Women's National Anti-Suffrage League, which argued that men and women were for reasons of nature different in their abilities, and that much of the world – the military, heavy industry – was beyond women. By then, her literary reputation was waning. Much of her wealth was dissipated meeting tax demands and the gambling debts of her son, a Conservative Member of Parliament who was dropped by the party for his outspoken opposition to women having the vote. When she died in 1920, the family home was sold. Virginia Woolf wrote: 'Mrs Ward is dead; poor Mrs Humphry Ward; and it appears that she was merely a woman of straw after all – shovelled into the ground and already forgotten.'

Had Hannah Mitchell stayed where she was, in Alport Dale, an emblem of rural continuity, she would have been just the sort of person William Wordsworth wrote poems about, like Lucy. But when she ran away, first to Glossop, then to Bolton, she became one of the nameless urban poor, a nuisance to be kept out of the countryside. She had become the sort of tourist the ageing Wordsworth, dressed like a shepherd and misplacing his false teeth, claimed would destroy his Lake District if the railway arrived. ('Is then no nook of English ground secure / From rash assault?') Harriet Martineau, the feminist sociologist and a friend of Mrs Ward's family, lived near Wordsworth. After William's death she continued visiting Mary, as *The Prelude* was published, and wrote a sketch of her when she too died. 'It was a rather serious matter to hear the Poet's denunciations of the railway,' she recalled, but Mary had been 'kindly, cheery' and it was so unlike her when she said 'that a green field with buttercups would answer all the purposes of Lancashire operatives, and they did not know what to do with themselves when they came among the mountains.' But Hannah Mitchell knew.

Although they lived in the same boarding house in Bolton, Hannah came to know her husband Gibbon Mitchell at a public meeting about the campaign to reopen the path on Kinder Scout's western flank, that linking Hayfield to the Woodlands Valley. Given her affection for the Love Feast her family had hosted, it was an issue close to her heart, a spiritual matter as well as one of customary freedoms. The Hayfield, Kinder Scout, and District Ancient Footpaths and Bridle-paths Association was one of many local footpath lobby groups that sprung up in the 1870s, and with a public collection of £1,000 hired the radical lawyer Richard Pankhurst as counsel. Pankhurst, whose wife was the suffragette Emmeline Pankhurst, had been, with Emmeline, a founder member of the Independent Labour Party with their friends Keir Hardie and George Bernard Shaw. Known as the 'Red Doctor', he campaigned on a wide range of issues: independence for India, land nationalisation – at the time a popular idea among Liberals as well as socialists – and women's suffrage. He had also written the legislation for the Married Women's Property Act of 1882.

Gibbon Mitchell, like Hannah a keen walker, was already calling himself a socialist, and found in Hannah a natural ally. They both joined the Independent Labour Party, and that's where Hannah stayed throughout her political life, suspicious of the new Labour Party's 'rigid constitution' that was, she believed, an infringement on personal liberty. There was always something rebellious about her. She was turned down at first as a town councillor, for being a feminist and 'not amenable to discipline'.

The gap between the rhetoric of committed young socialist men and the reality of domestic life disillusioned Hannah to some extent: 'They expected that the girl who had shared their weekend cycling or rambling, summer games or winter dances, would change all her ways with her marriage ring and begin where their mothers left off.' She faced, as Colm Toíbín wrote of Henry James's sister Alice, 'the dilemma of a woman in an age of reform pulled between the rules of her upbringing and the need to change those rules'. Men, Hannah believed, had in their natures something of the self-willed, dependent child in them. 'They expect to be regarded in public as pillars of strength and cosseted in private like delicate children.' That was no less true inside the Independent Labour Party, which proved reluctant to campaign for votes for women, prompting Emmeline Pankhurst and others to form the Women's Social and Political Union in 1903. It was entirely natural for Hannah to join them.

Hannah saw her work as a suffragette as her most important contribution; she called it the 'great experience'. But there was disillusionment here too. After an intensive period of campaigning, including a night in Strangeways after which her husband, much to Hannah's fury, bailed her out, the public speaking, the constant threat of being jostled and abused, caused her to suffer a nervous breakdown. She was left bitter at the realisation that despite working closely with them, none of the Pankhursts bothered to see her or even enquire about her. Following the lead of her friend Charlotte Despard, she left the Pankhursts for the Women's Freedom League. (Edward Carpenter, an active, if sporadic campaigner, sent his friend Despard a pound for the new organisation. There was in Sheffield more of a synergy between ramblers and suffragettes.)

'The year which followed my breakdown was hard to bear,' Hannah wrote. 'I suffered from fits of depression when I was often tempted to end my life. At such times I sought the open air, and often walked miles until I felt normal again.' To the end of her life, the moors gave her sanctuary, somewhere to escape to, and there are fragmentary images of her reaching some kind of accommodation with all she had been through later in her life. Writing her memoirs, she discovered forebears on her mother's side had been Chartists, radical roots for her own campaigning. A newspaper reporter at the Love Feast in July 1950 catches sight of her, now aged seventy-eight, light streaming through the barn window on to the straw-covered floor just as it had done when she was a child.

The snow-blasted great ravine of the River Kinder as it flows west from the Downfall.

Looking west from Kinder escarpment on a cold November afternoon. Mist swirls around the outlying flanks of South Head, Chinley Churn and Charles Head, hiding the vast conurbation of Manchester beyond.

The Snake woodlands descending towards Sheffield from the Snake Pass are riven with deep valleys including Blackden Brook (pictured), Ashop Clough, and the Alport Valley, the childhood home of Hannah Mitchell.

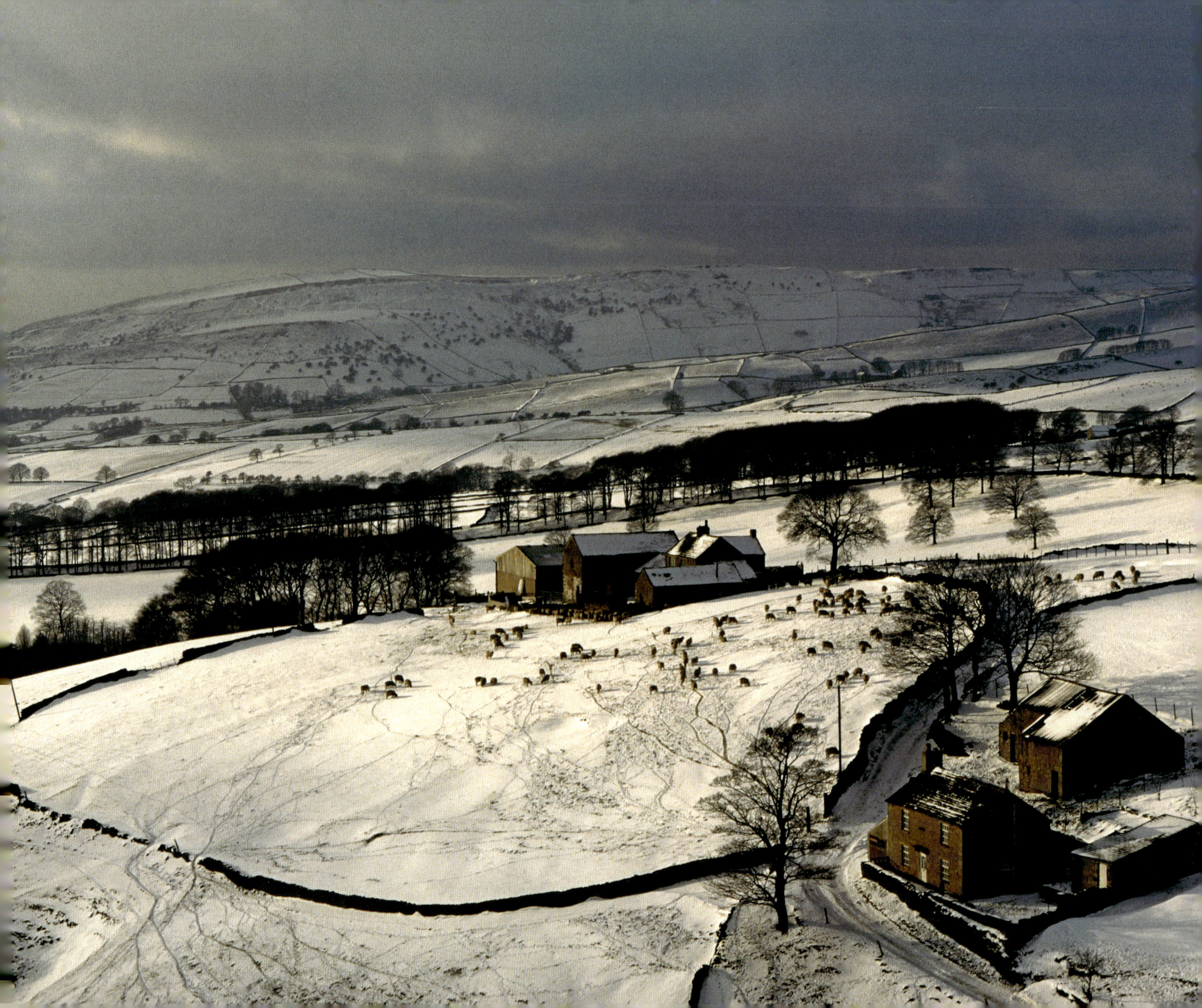

Opposite: Bettfield Farm near Rushup Edge and the distant Cracken Edge of Chinley Churn.
Above: Overlooking Shireoaks in Roych Clough a natural spring line once supported high hill farmsteads.

The Derbyshire Gritstone black-faced sheep originated in the nearby Goyt Valley in the 1770s. As one of the oldest hill breeds in Britain it is robust and hardy with a dense fleece to withstand the rigours of winter in the Peak.

The mysterious Mermaid's Pool high above Peter Nook in the Kinder ravine.

In January 2010 severe weather struck the high moors of Kinder Scout inundating the mountain and surrounding hills for two weeks. Many roads in the Peak were blocked with snow and rail services were cancelled.

Simon Kinnear on the deep and steep ascent under Crowden Tower.

Late winter afternoon on the Pagoda.

Moorland grasses at Crowden Head (632 metres), illuminated at sunset.

Top left: the remote slopes of Nether Red Brook; *top right:* the Pagoda; *bottom left:* frozen pools in the River Kinder; *bottom right:* Coldwell Clough.

The summit of Kinder Low (633 metres) in winter raiment.

Above Hayfield, Middle Moor looks into Coldwell and Tunstead cloughs with Mount Famine, South Head and Kinderlow End beyond.

Top left: imagining Hannah Mitchell in Snake woodlands; *top right*: celebrants at the Love Feast, Alport Barn, Alport Valley; *bottom left*: the loving cup shared during the annual Love Feast; *bottom right*: Alport Barn.

Common cottongrass *(Eriophorum angustifolium)*.

Alport Barn, site of the annual Love Feast.

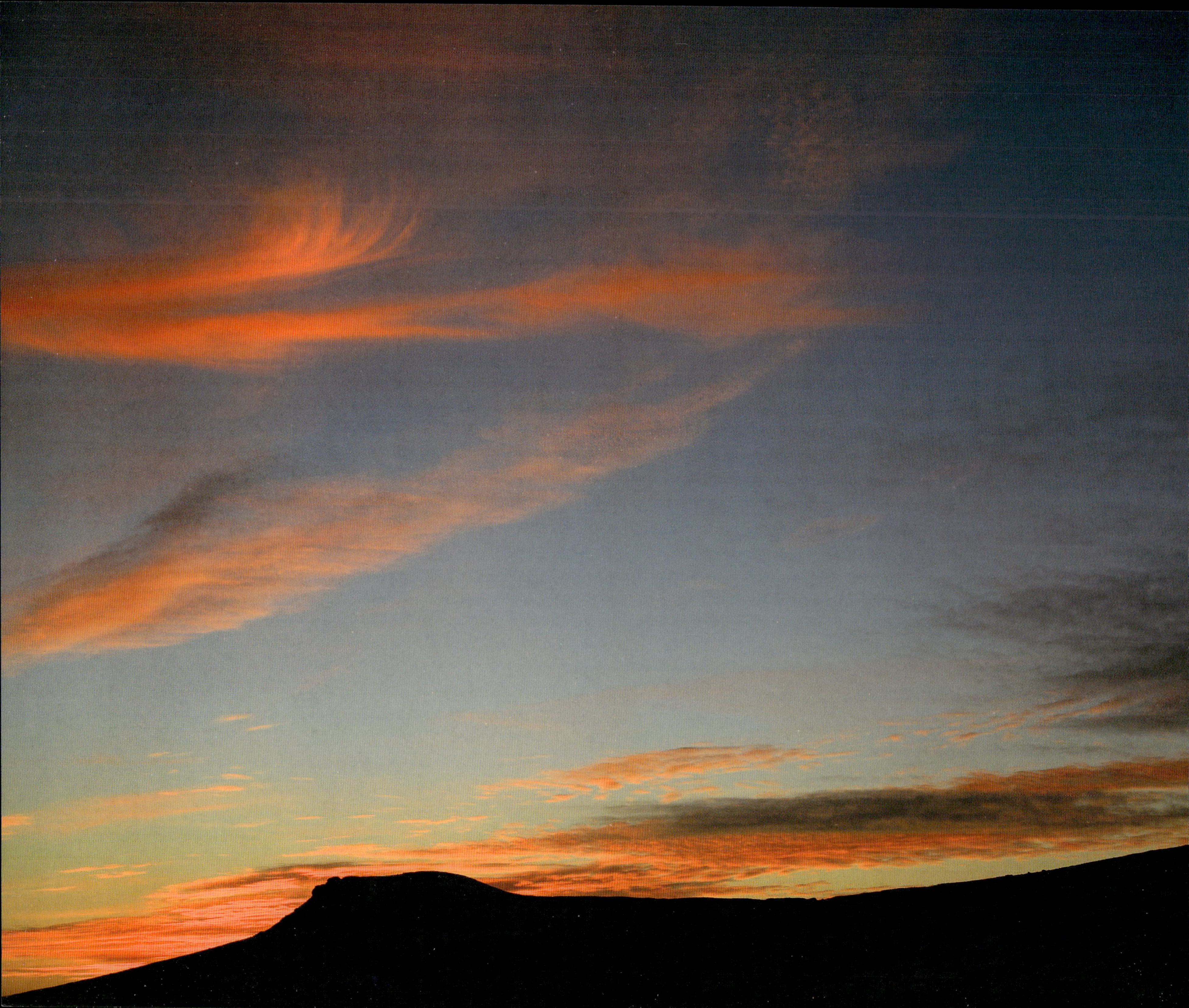

Flight

Leaving the Downfall, walking west past Sandy Heys, Manchester is glittering on the horizon. I watch an aircraft banking over the moors to the north. The circuit of the plateau has often felt to me like a long, slow circle in the sky, as though you're in a holding pattern, tilting slightly as you watch the clouds go past, enjoying the distant views. The aircraft levels off, then settles into its final approach to the airport south-west of Stockport, its runway pointing ruler-straight towards where I now stand, face to the wind.

At the western tip of the plateau, snouting towards Manchester, I start my own descent, taking the steep path off the rim, dropping about sixty metres before climbing back up a little to reach the cairn of crumbling rocks at the summit of Mill Hill. Settling down for a break, I take out a thermos and my map and examine the ground to the east of where I'm sitting. I've marked a small black dot a couple of hundred metres away, today's objective, and lift and lower my head between map and hillside. The trail to Chunal Moor seems to head in the right direction. I drain my coffee and then trot down the slope, stopping every so often to scan the ground to my right. A fork appears, zeroing in on a patch of bare peat a few dozen metres ahead of me. I'm conscious of a fluttering in my stomach.

The first wreckage I see is an engine sitting upright on the peat, or what is left of an engine: a cylindrical block of anodised metal with circular holes and a rusty spindle emerging from the centre of its flat end. It has two similarly rusty cogs at its base. This forlorn, weathered relic is part of an aircraft, a B-24 Liberator bomber. It was, temporarily, part of a delivery squadron, had taken off at half past ten on the morning of 11 October 1944 from an air base at Burtonwood, near Liverpool, heading for RAF Hardwick to join its American squadron, at the time flying supplies for Allied troops advancing across Europe. A quarter of an hour later, flying through heavy turbulence and an overcast sky, the pilot spotted a hill just below him through a gap in the clouds and, far too late, hauled back on the stick. The aircraft ploughed into the moor, which slopes uphill at a comparatively gentle angle, and gouged its way through the peat before finally coming to rest. There was no explosion. Liberators ordinarily had a crew of eleven but for a delivery run there were just two men on board and both survived with minor injuries. Had they met Kinder Scout at Ashop Head, they might not have been so lucky.

The official enquiry into the accident amounts to a few sheets of paper and some bad photographs: for a wholly avoidable accident to an expensive aircraft it seems rather thin. The rank of the pilot, Creighton Houpt, is given as both first and second lieutenant. There are several spelling errors and some obvious conclusions not drawn. For example, Houpt told the enquiry he'd been flying at 2,800 feet, but the aircraft crashed into the moor below the summit of Mill Hill at little more than 1,600 feet. Investigators concluded that the aircraft's altimeter was working correctly. So who was right? At least one account suggests the flight engineer Jerome Najvar

Opposite: High evening cirrus clouds above Swine's Back and Edale Rocks.

thought the pilot was at the wrong altitude. Houpt had plenty of experience flying B-24s but crews on delivery flights were under intense pressure. The enquiry didn't pursue it. There was, as they used to say, a war on. Aircraft were being lost on a regular basis and at least this time no one died. Kinder Scout is peppered with wartime wrecks where the crew did not survive. And in August 1944, a few weeks earlier, another B-24 due for delivery crashed into a school in the Lancashire village of Freckleton, killing sixty-one people, including thirty-eight children. In that context, Houpt's oversight was little more than a mishap. Authorisation was given to remove anything dangerous or valuable and burn the rest, although at least one machine gun had already disappeared. (It was hidden, lost and recovered years later rusted away.)

It's not hard to imagine Najvar's growing sense that something was badly wrong, the last few panicked seconds, the sudden burst of adrenaline, the rush towards the ground and then the scream of tearing metal as the aircraft scraped across the gritstone just beneath the surface of heather. To reach Hardwick, in west Suffolk, there must have been enough fuel on board for the aircraft to burn. But it didn't and the two men crawled out of the wreckage. Houpt was more seriously injured, with a fractured jaw, but they were both able to walk down Hollingworth Clough – a 'mountain creek' in Houpt's testimony, a glint of the Rockies in Derbyshire – to the road linking Little Hayfield and Glossop. A lorry stopped to give them a lift, taking the injured flight crew, Houpt told the enquiry, to 'a public house' where he called Burtonwood for help.

After so many years it's impossible to know, but it seems likely the two Americans were dropped at the Grouse Inn below Chunal Moor, the closest pub to where they were picked up, and one with connections to the birth of aviation. The moor was the site of the University of Manchester's Kite Flying Upper Atmosphere Station, established by Arthur Schuster, a brilliant physicist and able teacher and administrator, who had transformed the university's department with a large new laboratory and set the stage for his successor Ernest Rutherford, among the greatest physicists in history. From a Jewish family who converted to Christianity, Schuster was born in Frankfurt, but his father moved to Manchester to oversee the family textile business and Arthur followed him, becoming a British citizen in 1875. The kite flying research was crucial work in understanding how the atmosphere worked and how that information might be applied to the embryonic aviation industry. Schuster continued to take an interest after he retired, when the centre became the responsibility of Joseph Petavel, who had been a lecturer in mechanics under Schuster but in 1908 became a professor of engineering and director of the Whitworth Laboratories. A significant part of Petavel's career was concerned with the theory of gas engines and aeronautics, defining subjects of the twentieth century.

Aviation is a powerful part of Manchester's story, and Kinder's too. In 1910, Alliott Verdon Roe and his brother Humphrey, born in Eccles, established A.V. Roe & Co. – later Avro – at their first aircraft factory on Great Ancoats Street. By the Second World War 75,000 men and women were working in aircraft and component factories in Trafford Park alone, Ford building Merlin engines for Spitfires and Lancasters, Avro, by then owned by Hawker Siddeley, turning out Lancaster and Halifax heavy bombers at their factories in Woodford near Stockport and Chadderton near Oldham. Plenty of their workers explored Kinder Scout. The access campaigner Benny

Rothman worked for Avro in the mid 1930s and then at Metropolitan-Vickers, which made Lancasters under licence. John Beatty's father worked for Avro at Woodford from 1938, at the start of a career in aviation lasting forty-one years. He recalled test pilots bringing their Lancaster bombers up Ashop Clough and descending quickly over William Clough and Hayfield to the strip at Woodford during the blackout. John's mother drove a tractor towing the aircraft to and from their hangers. Every so often, out walking or cycling, I'll hear the guttural roar of the four Merlin engines of the Battle of Britain Memorial Flight's Lancaster, going to or from Derwent reservoir, where the Dambuster pilots trained for their mission.

Chunal Moor rises to a hilltop called Harry Hut. I'm not sure anyone now knows who Harry was, but there are some stones suggesting there was once a shelter there. It's an oddly cheery name for such a raw place, and one with such an ancient human connection. Signs of human activity, hunting parties on the move 8,000 years ago, have been excavated here, not quite the Palaeolithic culture of Derbyshire's Creswell Crags, but old enough. When I conjure an image of those young Edwardian scientists, lodging at The Grouse, out on the moor, braced against the wind, flying their kites and recording their findings, and then, less than forty years later, Lieutenant Houpt crashing his huge machine nearby, I can't help thinking of Bowie: look at those cavemen go.

In the spring of 1908 a young man arrived at The Grouse for the first time to begin his own researches. Ludwig Wittgenstein, then nineteen years old, was born in the same week as Adolf Hitler, and was in fact at the same school as Hitler in Linz for a year. Born the last of eight children into one of the wealthiest families of Habsburg Vienna, Wittgenstein had been struck as a boy of eight or nine by a simple question with a complicated answer: why should you tell the truth when it's to your advantage to tell a lie? He came to Manchester because, in the way of a genius, he could see how the new obsession with aviation, often derided in the press as a world peopled by cranks and eccentrics, was the future, and as an able mathematician and mechanical engineer he could profit from that, something that would please his father, even though his youthful interest in philosophy had taken over his intellectual life. And so the handsome young Wittgenstein, immaculately dressed, drawn from one of the most cultured families in Europe, could be found lodging at a remote Derbyshire pub to fly kites from the skirts of Kinder Scout. Food arrived via the Hayfield Road once a week on a pony and trap. The story goes that bottles of beer were stored in the pub's only tin bath.

The presence of German speakers like Schuster and Wittgenstein in Manchester was unremarkable. For much of the nineteenth century, Manchester's commercial boom had attracted industrialists and merchants from many parts of Europe but particularly the aspirational middle classes of the German states. They called what was happening in the city *Das Manchestertum*, or *Das Manchesterliberalismus*. In 1861, a third of all the city's foreign residents were German. Elizabeth Gaskell has her northern mill owner in *North and South* state proudly: 'We are Teutonic up here in Darkshire ... We stand up for self-government, and oppose centralisation.' Gaskell's house on Plymouth Grove was, in the middle of the nineteenth century, a nexus for Germans and German-Jews, who often converted to Unitarianism, becoming members of her husband William's Cross Street Chapel. Her daughters, as we have seen, kept open house for *Manchester Guardian* journalists like Willie Arnold. The influx of liberally minded Germans reminded the north of England of its Anglo-Saxon liberties.

The *Manchester Guardian* journalist James Agate, born in the Lancashire town of Pendleton, was between the wars one of the leading theatre critics in London for *The Sunday Times*: 'In my time Manchester was a city of liberal culture, awareness and gaiety, which it owed almost entirely to the large infusion of German-Jewish brains and taste.' (Writing this in the late 1920s, he also decried the arrival in the city of the 'cheap and flashy Yid'. More of whom later.) Neville Cardus, the *Manchester Guardian*'s brilliant music critic and cricket writer, born in the Manchester district of Rusholme, thought it 'nothing to Manchester's discredit that she owes much of her renown in music to the habits and devotion [of the] pre-[Great] War colony'. He meant in particular Sir Charles Hallé, born Karl Halle in the German region of Westphalia, who founded the city's famous orchestra and the Royal Manchester College of Music. Cardus had been introduced to the wealthy German-Jewish families of Victoria Park by his friend the violinist Adolph Brodsky and recalled hearing German spoken from carriages leaving Hallé concerts. The writer W.G. Sebald thought the German and Jewish influence was stronger in Manchester than in any other European city.

By the time Wittgenstein arrived, there were around 1,300 Germans in Manchester, low compared to London but significant in their impact. Around a tenth of Manchester's merchants were of German descent. They transformed the cultural life of the city and as they settled down and married into the existing middle classes, particularly from nonconformist, Unitarian circles, a new and highly distinctive regional culture was created, one that permeated politics and influenced education in the city. It was also a culture that loved establishing clubs – *verein* in German – not least the Schiller Anstalt, famous for its musical evenings. Friedrich Engels might have been unusual in having a relationship with a working-class Irish woman, but he was typical in drinking at the Albert Club, serving on its committee in the 1860s. (Engels was also typical in needing to escape an increasingly authoritarian political climate at home in Germany, having returned to Manchester in 1849.)

Such clubs catered almost as much for physical well-being, particularly in the outdoors, as they did for cultural or intellectual enrichment, and these outdoor clubs had an immense and lasting impact. The principal of Owens College, later the first vice-chancellor of the Victoria University of Manchester, was Alfred Hopkinson, one of five brothers who were all enthusiastic mountaineers. Several members of the family married into Manchester's German community. Arthur Schuster and his brother Felix were also mountaineers, taking it up as students in Geneva in the 1860s. Their cousin Claud, born in Manchester, would become president of the Alpine Club in 1938. Hopkinson was also an early president of the Rucksack Club, founded in 1902 as Lancashire's answer to the Yorkshire Ramblers' Club. C.E. Montague, de facto editor of the *Manchester Guardian* in the last years of the nineteenth century, when C.P. Scott was at Westminster as a Liberal MP, was also a keen walker and climber, frequently on Kinder Scout, despite the threat of gamekeepers. His friend Oliver Elton, a literary academic who taught at Owens College, wrote a memoir of Montague, capturing this atmosphere of robust self-improvement through association. 'There were groups that bicycled, walked, talked, dined, smoked, laughed, and disputed together.'

Wittgenstein was not so clubbable. 'I make my own oxygen,' he once said, and Kinder Scout proved a good place to breathe. He wrote to his sister Hermine on 17 May 1908, complaining about the food and the incessant rain but exulting in his isolation and loving the work: 'I have to provide the observatory with kites – which formerly were always ordered from outside – and to ascertain through trial and error their best design; the materials for this are ordered for me by request from the observatory. To begin with, of course, I had to help with the observations, in order to get to know the demands, which would be made of such a kite. The day before yesterday, however, I was told that I can now begin making independent experiments … Yesterday I began to build my first kite and hope to finish it by the middle of next week.'

The isolation of life at The Grouse made Wittgenstein long for company. 'Because I am so cut off I naturally have an *extraordinarily strong* desire for a friend and when the students arrive on Saturday I always think it will be one of them.' As it happens, he did develop a friendship, with a student four years older than he was, William Eccles. By the autumn Wittgenstein was back in Manchester, for the next couple of years working on his design for a jet engine, patenting a design for a propeller, going to concerts at the Hallé and studying mathematics. This led him to Bertrand Russell and back to philosophy. It was likely for the best: one contemporary thought Wittgenstein's 'nervous temperament made him the last person to tackle such research'. Wittgenstein's most accessible biographer, Ray Monk, described the philosopher's life as 'an ongoing battle with his own nature'.

In the autumn of 1909, another student arrived at the university's engineering department to study aeronautics for whom the same thing could be said. His name was Siegfried Wedgwood Herford and while there's no evidence he and Wittgenstein met, it seems likely. Herford's contemporaries regarded him as the greatest climber of his or any generation before the Great War. There's a photograph of him standing alongside George Mallory outside a mountain hut in North Wales. Herford looks rather stuffy and old-fashioned with his pipe, next to the soulful Mallory, but there's little doubt that had Herford survived the war, he would also have been on Everest in 1924. More than that, his immense practical intelligence meant he would have made a great contribution elsewhere. The *Manchester Guardian* called him 'a man of beautiful character and great gifts'. You could not find a better example of that chivalrous, doomed Edwardian generation than Siegfried Herford and yet at some profound level he remains an enigma, a puzzle, the secrets of his life elusive. There are traces of him though on Kinder Scout.

Siegfried Herford was born into one of Manchester's most prominent Unitarian families, and one with strong German connections. His mother was Marie Betge, daughter of the chief postmaster of Bremen, who arrived in Manchester as a teacher. Siegfried's name emphasised his German half; he would grow up bilingual. His father was Charles Harold Herford, an English literature professor and nephew of the Unitarian minister William Henry Herford. Charles's sister had married Hans Renold, the bicycle chain manufacturer and Hannah Mitchell's benefactor. Charles Herford would become a noted Ben Jonson scholar, but at the time of Siegfried's birth was teaching at Aberystwyth.

His early years were spent exploring the hills above the town with his sister May, later a Classics lecturer and Siegfried's close ally. Both were precociously creative, presenting visitors with specially composed verses. She called him by his nickname, 'Seaweed', and they shared a fantasy world, imagining themselves kings of two closely allied states on Mars. 'We consulted together on affairs of state,' she recalled, 'we swore oaths of loyalty to one another and the very mountains of our respective lands was honour bound not to exceed one another in height.' This shared imaginary world, fed by the space and physical freedom of hills not unlike those in the High Peak, allowed the brother and sister to be whomever they chose to be. You sense that Siegfried was never so open again.

In 1901, Charles Herford became the Victoria University of Manchester's first professor of English, and the family returned to its roots. It was a very different kind of Edwardian world to that of Robert Roberts in Salford. They lived in a large new house in Didsbury, built to Charles's own specification, with rooms for a cook and a maid. The new electric tram system was starting service, whisking the family into town. There was a large garden too, and Siegfried, who already had a tendency to run wild, would climb up the apple tree like a gorilla and throw fruit at people. Returning to Manchester also put the family back in the heart of their Unitarian community, one that was influential in the city. Socially progressive, it was dedicated to public service, put the application of reason at its heart, wasn't doctrinaire but was obsessed with education. Academic performance was a given. If it sounds controlled, Siegfried certainly found it so.

The obvious place to send him to school was Lady Barn House on Mauldeth Road, founded by Siegfried's great uncle William Henry Herford. He had tutored the son of Byron's daughter Ada Lovelace at Hofwil, a progressive school in Bern based on the radical theories of Frederick Froebel. What he saw there changed William Herford's life. He opened his own school and translated Froebel's work *The Education of Man* into English: 'Education consists in leading man, as a thinking, intelligent being, growing into self-consciousness, to a pure and unsullied, conscious and free representation of the inner law of Divine Unity.' Education for William Herford was not about exams or the demands of industry or the professions; it was about the child, the whole child. This approach appealed hugely to Manchester's German immigrants and those of German extraction; half of the pupils in the school's first ten years had German names.

Paradoxically, given that Lady Barn's ethos was all about the child's inner volition being expressed, and that it believed in outdoor play, Siegfried did not prosper. It would be futile to speculate what the problem was, but the boy was volcanically energetic with a fierce and very specific intelligence for mathematics. He was obsessed with numbers. Wandering around the hills above Aberystwyth, the Romantic appeal of distant hills had to be accompanied with precise measurements of heights and distances; these were contrasted with other mountains, like Everest. And if Siegfried's specific demands weren't met, he would lose interest and withdraw, a habit which, combined with his powerful physical presence, could be alarming for his parents and sister. Lady Barn wanted to turn out rounded, well-adjusted, cultured boys and girls who would benefit society. Siegfried may well have benefitted society, but he wasn't rounded: he was intense, volatile and restless.

Charles Herford wasn't the first successful parent too focused on his career to be able to respond to a child not fitting in, but Siegfried's unhappiness was especially awkward, because he was rejecting Charles and Marie's Unitarian world, a world they believed in and one that defined them. To their credit, they tried something different, and sent him to a preparatory school called Boxgrove House on the Surrey Downs, removing him from progressive Froebel and handing him over to the ethos expounded by Mrs Humphry Ward's grandfather, Thomas Arnold: cold baths, corporal punishment, cricket and a hectic schedule. Arnold's vision was not child centred; it was about meeting challenges and becoming leaders. Siegfried liked the sound of that, and he excelled, especially in maths.

After Boxgrove, Siegfried returned home to Didsbury and started at the prestigious Manchester Grammar School. Yet the same difficulties in his behaviour resurfaced. He did well at school, but at home he oscillated between long, moody silences and outbursts of temper. So his parents went one better than Boxgrove, and sent him to Hermann Lietz's school at Schloss Bieberstein, a Baroque castle eight miles east of Fulda in Hesse, right in the heart of Germany. Lietz was about as far removed philosphically from Froebel as it was possible to get. He wasn't interested in culturally rounded, socially responsible burghers. Lietz was educating Plato's guardians of the Republic: men, and only men, who could lead society through the upheavals industrialisation had unleashed.

Lietz came from a fascinating sequence of educators that started with Cecil Reddie, a friend and guest of Edward Carpenter at Millthorpe, where the two discussed Reddie's plans for a new kind of progressive school. This he founded in 1889 at Abbotsholme in Derbyshire, near to Dovedale. Reddie had been a bit too progressive for Clifton College in Bristol, where he and Carpenter first met, insisting Clifton should introduce sex education. Reddie's own homosexuality was necessarily secret, but his greater difficulty was an abrasive personality: he was constantly falling out with backers and staff. Reddie's curriculum focused on science and modern languages, and so he often hired foreign teachers. Hermann Lietz was one of them. When Lietz went back to Germany, he started his own schools modelled on Abbotsholme but with a strong pan-Germanic flavour. Lietz in turn influenced Kurt Hahn, who founded Gordonstoun and the Outward Bound movement. The British outdoor movement is inextricably meshed with German educational philosophy.

Siegfried Herford prospered in Germany under Lietz, but even better was the school expedition to Iceland, the sort of venture public schools now offer routinely, but which in 1909 was almost unknown. His parents were opposed but Siegfried wasn't going to be stopped. The wildness, the strangeness of the landscape, the occasional moments of danger seemed like challenges Siegfried was designed to meet. He was in his element. He had always been a physically strong, attractive child. One of his mother's friends called him a 'Sun God', spending so much time outside that school friends assumed he'd spent the holidays on the Riviera rather than cycling with his father.

Cycling was something Charles Herford and his strong but silent offspring could share. They toured North Wales together in the spring of 1907. Charles wrote: 'At Betws we bought some biscuits and chocolate, and a MG [*Manchester Guardian*], and started up the road for Pen-y-Gwryd: I had some difficulty in persuading S to stop at the Swallow Falls. What was a waterfall, when Snowdon was coming?' A passion for the new activity of bicycling was almost inevitable, given that Siegfried's devoted aunt Mary was married to Hans Renold. It's also likely that the link, and Siegfried's visits to the factory on Brook Street, inspired his interest in engineering, if not aeronautical engineering, which is what he elected to study at the University of Manchester from the autumn of 1909 under the direction of Joseph Petavel.

Home from Iceland and studying in Manchester, Herford's proximity, his passion for mountains and his growing interest in climbing meant two things: first, that he would quickly find himself mixed up with the Rucksack Club, and second, that he would climb on Kinder Scout. Other crags drew him first. He climbed for example on Laddow Rocks on the north side of Longdendale with J. Anton Stoop, a native of the Swiss town of St Gallen, on the edge of the Appenzell Alps. Stoop was a mountaineer deprived of his mountains working at a shipping office. The *Manchester Guardian* ran an article about some of the climbs being done at Laddow and the Rucksack Club discovered Stoop one day halfway up the cliff with the article in his hand. Siegfried climbed also with the genial Stanley Jeffcoat from Buxton, whose favoured crag was Castle Naze, near Chapel-en-le-Frith, and with whom Siegfried would climb his most famous British route in 1914 on Scafell, the *Central Buttress*. He climbed also with Sandiford – no first name has been traced – and it was to Sandiford that John Laycock wrote asking for details of rock climbs on Kinder Scout, as he was preparing a guidebook to the increasing numbers of routes on gritstone. Sandiford said he had been there most with Herford, and arranged a meeting at the Downfall.

All three sides of Kinder Scout are fringed with outcrops and all offer good routes of differing character. The Downfall has scale and looms above your head, massive and rambling. The tors and crags on the southern rim catch the sun and are full of rough, bulging buttresses, sculptural and tactile. The crags of the northern rim are more sombre, dark even, but with elegant lines of geometric simplicity, like *Jester Cracks* and *Legacy*. Modern climbers seem more reluctant than their forebears to hike up to the side of Kinder for only fifteen or twenty metres of climbing. And the gritstone at Kinder's summit, being older than and formed differently to the millstone grit of Stanage, feels more abrasive on the hands, being essentially grittier gritstone. But it's worth every bit of the struggle. Climbing on Kinder has a depth and scale that belies the brevity of the climbs. These are adventures that have more in common with the mountain crags of Wales but with that sense of space and air so characteristic of the High Peak.

It might be surprising to those with no knowledge of climbing that a man from Sheffield was first to climb on Kinder, given the difficulties of access. Surely it would be Manchester men, stalwarts of the Alpine Club like the Hopkinsons, or Arthur Schuster? Yet in the late nineteenth century such rock climbing as existed was considered training for the Alps, a way to experience the mountains at home while waiting to get back to the real thing. The sport of rock climbing for its own sake was embryonic and few of those drawn from the ranks of the Alpine Club would consider gritstone cliffs – brutish and short, if not always nasty – as worth their powder. It was left to a working-class man from Sheffield to explore Kinder Scout, one who is known well to climbers but who dropped from view in less arcane circles. His name was J.W. Puttrell, 'Jim' Puttrell, born in 1868, son of a builder who lost everything in the Great Sheffield Flood of 1864 but who eventually prospered.

Jim Puttrell was judged to have weak ankles as a young boy and wore leg irons for a while, but when he discovered the Peak District on his doorstop, he overcame any lingering disability. He made a crossing of Kinder's plateau on New Year's Day of 1884 or perhaps 1885, when Hannah Mitchell was still living in Alport. Few gamekeepers were outside in the depths of winter so his passage was untroubled, but he faced the endless sequence of peaks and troughs of peat alone, separated from friends who followed a lower route. He walked forty miles that day. His early climbs were, necessarily, done alone, on the crags of Wharncliffe on the east bank of the Don, more coarse sandstone than grit. The public were, at the pleasure of the Earl of Wharncliffe, free to visit on Mondays, Thursdays and Saturdays. With no rope or anyone to hold one, his early explorations were of necessity dangerous. But Puttrell stuck with it. Climbing and the Peak were too rich with experience for him not to try.

Puttrell started work for the cutlery firm Mappin & Webb in 1883, and after years exploring on his own, persuaded a young silversmith called William Watson, just fifteen, to join him on his adventures. In 1890, the year before Siegfried Herford was born, he and William camped under a boulder high up in Grindsbrook Clough and next morning did the first rock climbs on Kinder, on Nether Tor and Upper Tor. One of them, *Primitive Route*, is still graded as Severe, good going for Victorians. Then the gamekeepers spotted them and the two young men were bundled off the crag.

Puttrell was still doing new routes on Kinder when Herford appeared on the scene, having in the meantime made the first explorations of many of the crags of the Dark Peak. By then he was at the centre of a small social circle of climbers, cavers and walkers who had formed themselves into a club called, in a philological nod to Kinder's supposed Celtic origins, the Kyndwr. Its inspiration was Ernest Albert Baker, a librarian with a first in English and a master's in Classics who moved to Derby from his native Bath in 1893. Baker had arrived as a fly fisherman but after meeting Puttrell and his friends put aside the rod to write the seminal early work on climbing and walking in the Peak District. In doing so he left readers with the impression that he, Ernest Baker, had been the inspiration and leader of the adventures he described, rather than his companions, whose names often didn't feature at all. Baker would later run the University of London's School of Librarianship and write a ten-volume *History of the English Novel*. Puttrell, the cutlery worker who quit school at fifteen, later part of the family painting and decorating business, died before he completed his autobiography, which was lost. His friends remembered a generous and likeable man, sturdy, famously punctual, but one perhaps who did not know his own worth.

It was John Laycock's aim to update the information available in books like Baker's and that required fieldwork. His encounter with Siegfried at the Downfall, most probably in February 1910, was much more than a sharing of information. Herford left a powerful impression on Laycock, 'a tall, strongly built young man with fair hair, blue eyes and regular features. Herford's manner was then, as always, pleasing and unassuming.' Herford climbed so much that he was inevitably promiscuous in his partnerships, but there was a special bond between him, Laycock and Jeffcoat, not least on Kinder Scout where they climbed some of the best early routes there: *Variety Crack*, the elegant, expansive *Mermaid's Ridge*, the *Twin Chimneys* and *Downfall North Corner*.

His finest new route on Kinder Scout was on the wind-eroded buttress called the Pagoda, on the plateau's southern rim. It's known as *Herford's Route* and is now graded Hard Very Severe, cutting edge in 1910 and one of the hardest climbs done before the Great War. Yet it is even more revealing of Herford's own personality, a series of awkward moves interspersed with niches of safety from which to contemplate the next one. The climb matches intensity and doubt with periods of calm. Climbing it a hundred years after Herford's death, I never felt closer to this beautiful, enigmatic, brilliant man. I used every modern contrivance available to me, but could still read in the rock that admixture of focused effort and impetuosity that marked him out.

Laycock's research into the climbers of Kinder Scout and other gritstone crags were written up, but the manuscript, finished in 1911, remained unpublished for another two years. The Rucksack Club had promised it would appear under the club's name and at its expense, but changed its mind as the implications of Laycock's work became clearer. Kinder was forbidden ground, and while some climbers explored it surreptitiously, the Rucksack Club was sufficiently well connected to apply successfully for permits from the owners. A guidebook might be seen as an incitement to trespass, and the committee, under the influence of the solicitor Charles Pickstone, withdrew its support. Laycock, a lawyer himself and later a distinguished one, was enraged, accused the committee of moral cowardice, and resigned from the club that he had joined as a founder member. *Some Gritstone Climbs* was finally published in 1913 by the printing department of an insurance company with financial support from four friends. It was dedicated to Siegfried Herford.

A lengthy, sneering review in the *Yorkshire Ramblers' Club Journal* reflected the snobbery and ignorance of the mountaineering establishment, judging that Laycock's groundbreaking book was 'liable to be dismissed by a percentage of mountaineers as a Baby Book on Toy Climbs'. Shorter climbs are dismissed as 'fancy gymnastics' that with a soft landing would 'lose most of their terror'. The review illustrated the failure of Victorian climbers to appreciate how short technical climbs might eventually move standards forward in the mountains. The review warned: 'It is to be hoped they would never be attempted at any considerable altitude.'

The lack of imagination of what climbing might become was typical: Herford was ahead of the game. Within a few months of Laycock's book, he had led the first ascent of *Central Buttress* on Scafell, an electrifying moment in the history of British rock climbing but also an extension of the approach he had taken on Kinder Scout and other shorter cliffs. His most famous achievement also overshadowed his third season in the Alps in the summer of 1914, when he climbed the south-west ridge, the *Rote Zähne*, of the Gspaltenhorn, in Switzerland's Bernese Oberland. It was one of the most significant first ascents in the Alps by a British party before the war, and a beautiful one too. He climbed with the guides Josef Knubel and Hans Brantschen, his British partner being the poet and educationalist Geoffrey Winthrop Young, a man who was wildly romantic about mountains and young men, Herford being no exception. The climb was long and complicated with difficult sections of rock climbing, requiring the group to abseil and then pull down the ropes, committing them to the climb, like bolting the emergency exit in a theatre that could catch fire at any moment. This dazzling achievement, completed on 14 July, two weeks before war was declared, is like an exclamation mark at the end of the golden years of Edwardian adventure. Nothing would be the same again.

The gathering clouds of war had mingled with the smog of Robert Roberts's slum in Salford. Games of cowboys and Indians gave way to street battles between British and Germans, often featuring a foreign spy to add a dash of paranoia. 'Rising anti-German feeling started to show itself openly. One poor mongrel in our area, part dachshund, suffered wretched cruelties at the hands of boys "paying out the German sausage dog". Well before August 1914 women bruited it among us that Mrs Pratz, wife of the local German pork butcher, had given a customer a shilling in change with the remark "You'll soon have the Kaiser's head on that!" Mother, hearing this, called it rubbish.'

In 1935, Roberts married a woman called Ruth Dean, who was born Ruth Dehner. Her grandfather came to Britain from his small hometown in Baden-Württemberg in the 1880s to escape the rising tide of German militarism, much as Arthur Schuster had done. He opened a butcher's shop in Hebden Bridge, raised six children, one of whom, Albert, Ruth's father, started his own butcher's in Sheffield. Ruth was born there in 1911. After war broke out, when Albert was away on business, a gang came up the street shouting they would 'get' the young German lad Albert had recently hired. Ruth's mother was suffering the onset of multiple sclerosis, but her Sheffielder shop assistant, Lilly Kirk, broad and tough, told the boy to hide upstairs in the attic. Then she stood, arms folded, in front of the cellar door. As the thugs arrived: 'Any bugger that tries to go down into t'cellar will 'ave ter deal wi' me furst! And he'll get a reet thumpin'!' Even so, Albert changed the family name and enlisted as a stretcher-bearer so he could serve and still meet his personal commitment to pacifism.

When the war started, anti-German sentiment was more muted in Manchester than elsewhere in the north, but Arthur Schuster, a naturalised British citizen who had made the university's physics department one of the best in the world, found himself under suspicion. He was accused of spying and was forced to remove radio equipment from his house. His brother, Sir Felix Schuster, issued a statement declaring the family's loyalty. In May 1915, prompted by the sinking of the *Lusitania*, there were anti-German riots in Manchester. German-owned shops and homes were attacked. The secure and admired position Germans held in Manchester's public life was gone. Schuster was by then president of the British Association for the Advancement of Science. Before the organisation's meeting, held that year in Manchester, he faced calls for his resignation or for the meeting to be suspended. The meeting went ahead, and Schuster spoke of the 'common aims of science and humanity', of 'intellectual freedom, which is more than material prosperity'. On the same day he learned his son had been wounded at Gallipoli.

By the summer of 1914, Siegfried Herford had finished the aviation research that would earn him a master's, but the government was investing in ships, not aircraft. The outbreak of war was a personal crisis for Siegfried's mother Marie. Her husband and children were English but she was German. She told her son: 'It is your country and you must fight for it.' Siegfried applied for a commission, as one of Plato's guardians should, and, while he waited for the War Office to react, spent time in France acting as despatch runner for Geoffrey Winthrop Young, who was working as a correspondent for the *Daily News*, reunited in a way neither could have anticipated on the Gspaltenhorn. He also worked as an ambulance driver for the Red Cross, writing two reports of dangerous honesty for the *Manchester Guardian* about his work on the front line: 'The Germans have behaved much better than is made out, and the British officer has certainly great admiration for the German soldier.'

Although published anonymously, it's possible that despatches like this, coupled with his German name, his German education and German mother, made the War Office hesitate in offering him a commission. His biographer, Keith Treacher, found no evidence that he was officially turned down, as his friends John Laycock and C.E. Montague believed, but reached the reasonable conclusion that the War Office was 'conveying their intentions by saying absolutely nothing'. So in an act of self-destructive petulance, he enlisted in February 1915 as an ordinary private in the infantry and was sent for basic training. He enjoyed his last leave with his family in November at a farmhouse near Machynlleth, and then May watched as her brother's train pulled out of Dovey Junction. She never saw him again.

Mrs Humphry Ward used a novelist's artistic freedom to describe Kinder Scout's plateau in *The History of David Grieve*, finding an analogy with the Romantic fascination for ice and glaciers. But her words eerily prefigured the Great War, still a quarter of a century in the future: 'The top of the Peak is, so to speak, a vast black glacier, whereof the crevasses are great fissures, ebony-black in colour, sometimes ten feet deep, and with ten feet more of black water at the bottom. For miles on either side the ground is seamed and torn with these crevasses, now shallower, now deeper, succeeding each other at intervals of a yard or two and it is they which make the crossing of the Peak in the dark or in mist a matter of danger sometimes even for the native.'

As ramblers explored the plateau, illicitly or otherwise, they photographed it too, using the cheaper more portable cameras then becoming available. A photograph by Sheffield rambler Frank Packhard is particularly haunting. A group of seven men in flat caps and puttees standing in a grough three metres deep, surrounded by walls of black ooze, one figure resting his elbow on his knee as he stands on a bank of peat, as though poised for action. Their faces look out from those 'great fissures' echoing images that are more familiar, of men in trenches waiting to go over the top, smeared in mud.

By January 1916, Siegfried was at Festubert, on the front line in Flanders. Robert Graves, who Siegfried knew from Geoffrey Winthrop Young's Easter climbing parties at Pen-y-Pass, left a grim description of the battlefield, not long before Siegfried arrived, in *Good-bye to All That*. The British Army map described the ground the British held as: 'Marsh, sometimes dry in summer.' Much like bogs on Kinder. The defences Graves's battalion dug sank into the mire. Troops sheltered in dugouts filled with water. The Germans were close enough to hear their talk. Siegfried would have known what they were saying.

At the end of the month he was sent with five other men to one of the front's 'island trenches', dug into the mud in front of the main trench, and told to hold it for four days. Any notions of the glory of war Siegfried might once have entertained had long since perished; on his last leave he had told his family how much he loathed the sordidness of it all. On 28 January he wrote to his sister May: 'Today is quite a fair day, for a change. We have nothing to do except sit tight in our little island and keep a watchful eye on the periscope at which a German is taking some sporting shots.' Three hours later a German rifle grenade exploded in the trench, tearing Siegfried Herford in two.

Herford's friends all wrote to his parents to express their sense of loss. C.E. Montague, a man who had famously dyed his grey hair black so he could go to the front at the age of forty-seven, was one of many to acknowledge Herford's brilliance:

'All English rock climbers who knew him would say that he was the best of them all.' Arthur Thomson, a big-hearted man who had suffered polio as a boy and whose climbing career was consequently a triumph of character over disability, caught something of how so many felt about Herford: 'He was so very different from other people one encounters in everyday life – I don't refer to climbers now – who have little or none of his generosity.' For the rest of his life, the memory of Herford would bring a smile to Thomson's face.

His father, perhaps from guilt, believed that joining up was the only path open to Siegfried to prove his loyalty, but he could have served in other ways: remaining with the Red Cross, training as a pilot or applying to the Royal Aircraft Establishment. At the time of his death, Herford was trying to transfer to the Friends' Ambulance Unit. His death and the manner of it seem unusually pointless in a deluge of deaths, a brilliant engineer who came top of his year at Manchester butchered in a muddy hole. Even at the end of the slaughter, anti-German hysteria remained, a phenomenon C.E. Montague called, in his startling war memoir *Disenchantment*, 'that shabby epidemic of spite'.

Siegfried Herford's interior world, the enigmatic centre of his soul, wholly disappeared: no letters or diaries pierce the veil. There are only hints. John Laycock told Herford's grieving parents: 'For many years he has been my dearest friend, and a great deal more.' The latter phrase is enigmatic; his biographer considered it as evidence Siegfried might have been gay. Laycock was certainly devastated by Siegfried's death, as he was by Stanley Jeffcoat's. Two of that tight little circle were now gone, and he quit Europe – and climbing – for life as a barrister in Singapore. Later he founded a liberal political party that provided Singapore's first prime minister, Lee Kuan Yew.

He also married, and adopted a daughter; they grew orchids together in the garden he created. There is a photograph of Laycock taken in the fifties, bull-necked and puffy faced, not long before his death in 1960, and it's hard not to draw comparisons with the photograph taken of him at Castle Naze almost fifty years earlier. He sits on the right of Jeffcoat, who puffs on his pipe, smart in a three-piece suit and tie, a dog at their feet, and on Arthur Thomson's left, also smoking. On Thomson's left is Herford, in a heavy polo-neck sweater, his legs wrapped in puttees. He's still a teenager.

Herford was close as well to Geoffrey Winthrop Young, a substantial and influential figure in the history of mountaineering, whose own record was impressive but who also mentored some of the brightest talents, including George Mallory and Siegfried. In the years before the war, Young became a more dominant influence on him than Laycock. But the bisexual Young had barely concealed secrets. He was twice sacked, from both Eton where he was teaching and the Schools Inspectorate, for his sexual proclivities. He was clearly attracted to Herford, and Herford seemed happy enough to go along with Young to boxing booths in the slums of London, to watch young, working-class men beat each other. 'There is no risk,' Maynard Keynes wrote to Lytton Strachey of being gay, 'so long as no one has anything to do with the lower classes, or people off the street.' There could be no blackmail if both lovers had something to lose. Young had no such qualms. He liked risk, and paid the price. There is a paradoxical distance between Young's affected, sentimental poetry and his trips to Berlin's gay underworld, but all of him is there to see. With Herford it's a blank. And there is nothing to show that he shared either Young's bed or his sexual preferences.

Laycock's phrase 'and a great deal more' captures, for me, something about Herford that many others tried to convey. Their meeting at Kinder Downfall stayed with him, that first image burned in his memory. Not that it matters, but my guess is it wasn't about sex; it was about a sense of freedom – freedom to be yourself, to try out new roles, to escape the pressures created in your own mind, or in the minds of others, to be joyful, carefree. Kinder wasn't just an escape, it was a crucible. Laycock knew he would never find that world again, that it had died with Jeffcoat and Herford; it was useless to look for it. That's why he went halfway round the world to play golf and grow orchids and never climb again. Herford, who epitomised the promise of youth, had helped him make sense of the world, and now he was gone.

Herford has several memorials: his war grave just outside Beuvry in Pas-de-Calais; the weighty metal tablet erected in 1924 on the summit of Great Gable listing all those in the Fell & Rock Climbing Club, almost a third of the membership, who lost their lives in the war. Siegfried's name appears above that of his friend Stanley Jeffcoat. He also has his own personal memorial, a stained-glass window by the Arts and Crafts artist Caroline Townshend, presented to Platt Chapel by his great friend C.E. Montague. It is based on a photograph of Herford on the Third Pinnacle of Sgùrr nan Gillean on Skye, perched on the toes of his nailed boots, his hemp rope tied around his lower chest. Townshend removed Herford's wool cap to reveal his head more clearly, but she lost the beautifully poised tension in Herford's body and legs that speaks to his natural ability on rock. He looks almost saintly, saints being Townshend's more usual subject matter. There are clouds beneath his feet and birds above his head. The sun is rising. A critic at the time noted that 'the whole effect is of transfiguration'.

When Platt Chapel closed in 1970, money was raised to move the window to the Outward Bound centre at Eskdale, a neat link to the Lietz school where Siegfried finished his education. His sister May, by then in her eighties, was at the rededication.

Herford's fellow aviation student Ludwig Wittgenstein spent the war in the Austro-Hungarian Army, serving with astonishing courage and writing *Tractatus*. In late 1918, David Pinsent, among the greatest minds of his generation and Wittgenstein's lover at Cambridge, was killed in a plane crash at Farnborough, where he had been working as a test pilot. Wittgenstein was lucky to survive the depression the news inflicted. 'I might say:' he wrote a few years later, still hunting down the truth of things, 'if the place I want to reach could only be climbed up to by a ladder, I would give up trying to get there. For the place to which I really have to go is one that I must actually be at already.'

Siegfried Herford's truth is in his rock climbs, the invisible lines he drew on wind-seamed crags, ladders leading nowhere but back to Herford himself. They capture something of his talent and character. In that sense, you can still find Siegfried Herford on Kinder Scout, the place where he first found himself and his place in the world. You can run your hands over the rock that he was first to touch, trace your fingers over his moment in time. And in a way know it, and him, as your own.

Opposite left: the summit of Mill Hill lies to the north of Ashop Head. It is a step away from the rigours of the higher plateau of Kinder Scout and leads you north to the Snake road and Bleaklow, or west to Chunal Moor and the now-abandoned Grouse Inn. *Opposite right:* carcass of red grouse predated by the now rare and persecuted peregrine falcon.

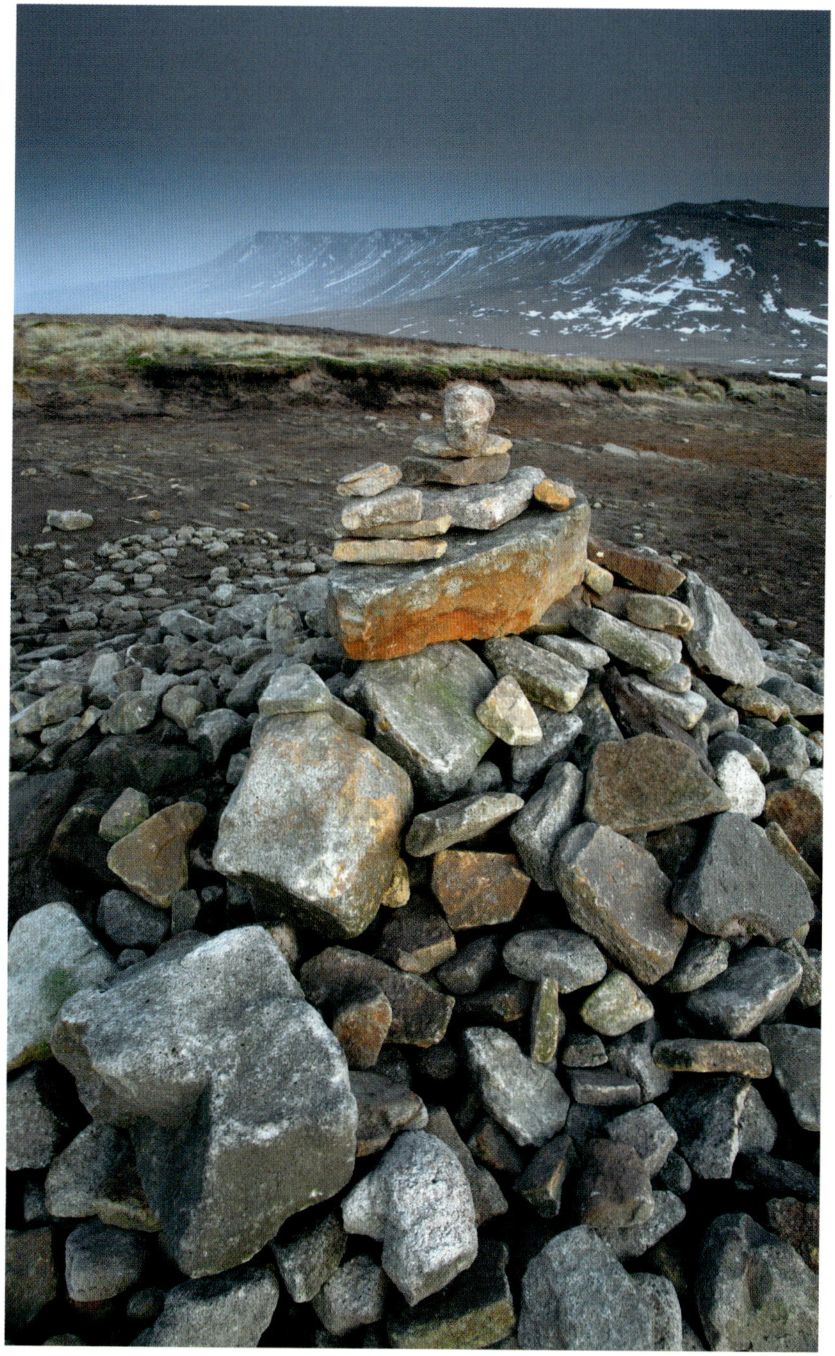

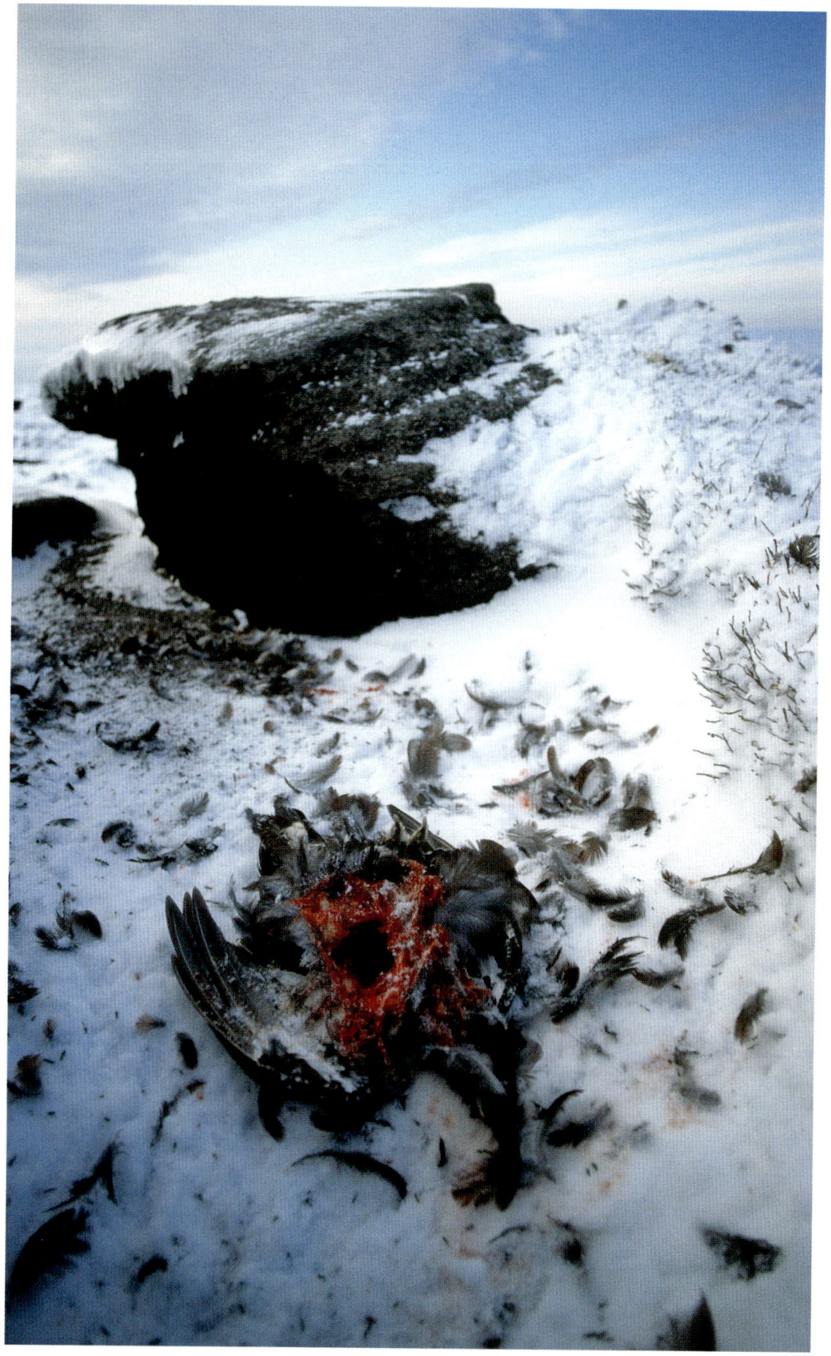

Remains of aircraft wrecks on Kinder Scout. The main period of aerial activity over Kinder was during World War Two when many flights were made across the Pennines. Limited navigational aids and low cloud were often the principal causes of aircraft accidents over the moors.

Common cottongrass *(Eriophorum angustifolium)* is found in poorly drained acid soil conditions, such as areas of degraded peat bog. This grass flowers between late June and August and is a familiar species growing here on Featherbed Moss, and round many waterlogged pools on Kinder.

82 Kinder Scout

After heavy snowfall on Kinder plateau, the peat hags often become inundated with deep drifts, giving plenty of fun for the exuberance of youth.

Frozen peat mire on Grindslow Knoll above Edale.

Limonite, a hydrous iron-oxide deposit on the streambed of Ashop Clough.

Kinder Low in mid-afternoon winter mist. The plateau at Kinder Low's summit resembles subarctic tundra. Recent restorative planting schemes have transformed the eroded landscape.

Top left: rooks nesting in the sycamores above Edale Church graveyard; *top right:* spider web in hogweed at Barber Booth, Edale; *bottom left:* sheep carcass in Whitemoor Clough, Chapel Gate; *bottom right:* icicles in Cluther Rocks.

Jaggers Clough. The old name *jagger*, recorded as early as the 1300s, was given to someone in charge of packhorses who most likely carried iron ore across the Peak.

This is the landscape of millstone grit that attracted pioneer rock climbers, artists and sculptors at the turn of the nineteenth century. Kinder Low (633 metres).

Scattered across the moors between Crowden Tower and the Pagoda, the Wool Packs are a mass of gritstone rocks that have been weathered by wind and ice to form unusual mushroom-like shapes.

Above: The harebell *(Campanula rotundifolia)* is a delicate bell-shaped plant of hillside and heath and is common on the drier grassy flanks of Kinder Scout.
Opposite: The Mermaid's Ridge was first climbed by Siegfried Herford in 1910. This steep buttress guards the entrance to Kinder ravine and is a fine example of the rough and exposed climbs that form the ramparts of Kinder Scout.

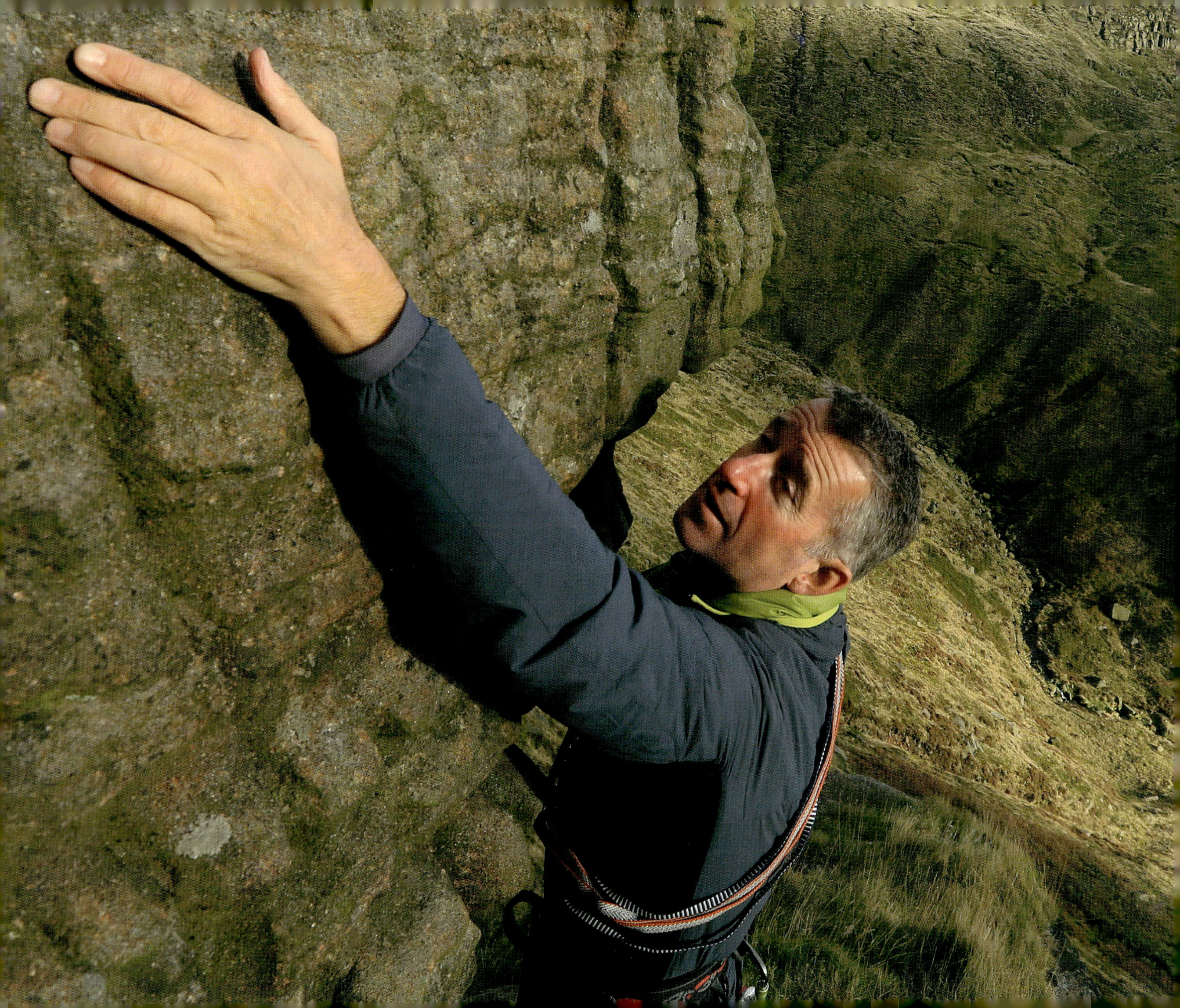

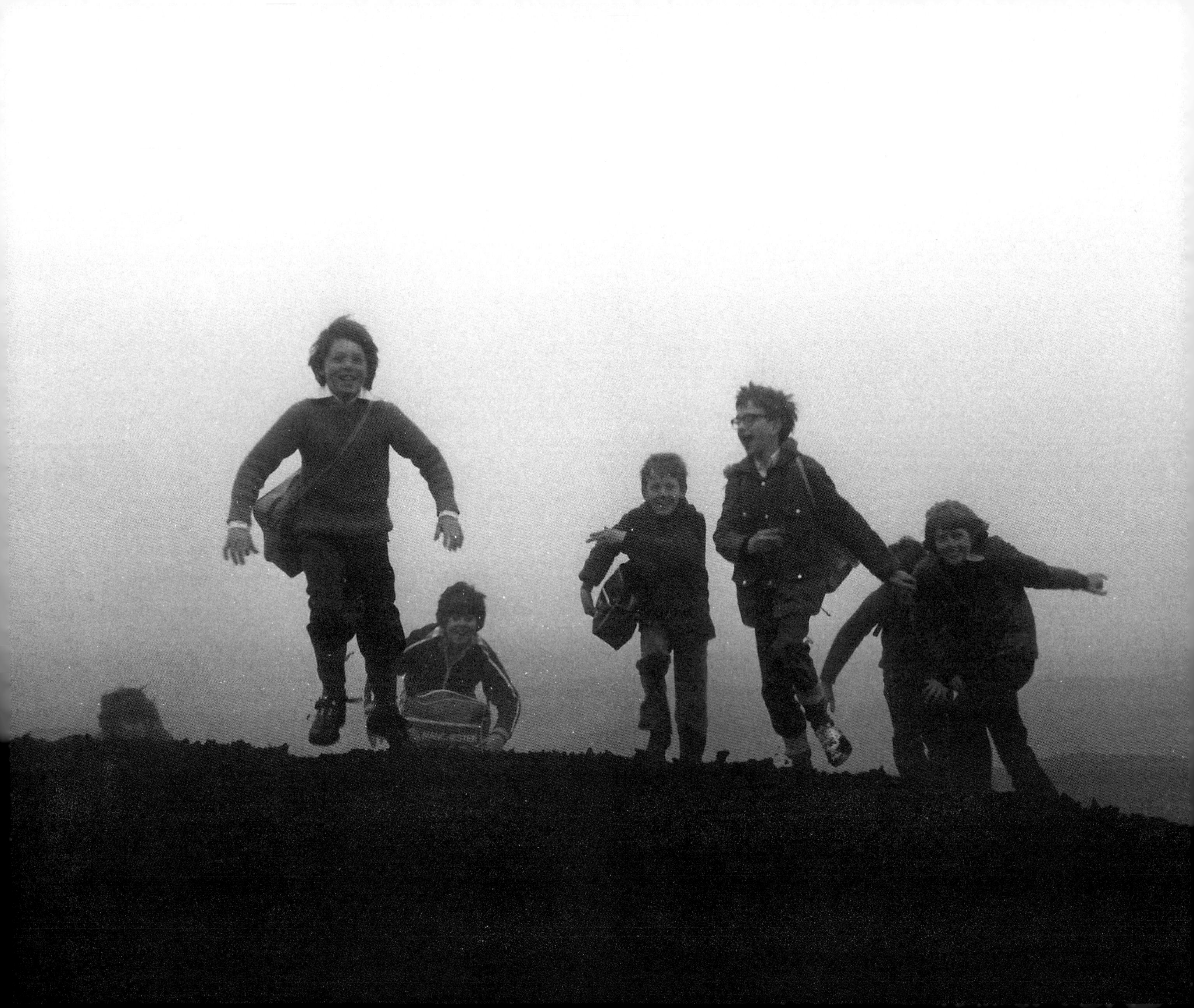

Grouse

Leaving the anodised bones of Lieutenant Houpt's wrecked aircraft, I retrace my steps uphill, cross the summit of Mill Hill and then drop down to Ashop Head. This is the most dramatic threshold on Kinder Scout, a pivot between the wild Pennine country of Yorkshire to the north, and the mill towns of Derbyshire tucked away in lower, more sheltered valleys to the south. Below Ashop Head, on the southern side, is William Clough, its steep banks covered in tussocks of white grass and heather, the neighbouring path dropping down to the track that leads to Hayfield. In the medieval era, there was forest in the bottom of this steep valley, but the trees went for charcoal to feed the village's small-scale iron smelters. Their slag heaps are now drowned in the reservoir, along with the confluence of William Clough and the River Kinder. The denuded hillside east of William Clough is now better known as the location for an encounter between a massed group of ramblers and a smaller number of gamekeepers almost ninety years ago, an event whose meaning is still fiercely debated, even discounted, a sacred achievement or an overblown sideshow: the Kinder Mass Trespass.

In April 1932, a young man arrived at the offices of the *Manchester Evening Chronicle* on Withy Grove to give an interview about a demonstration planned for a few days later on Kinder Scout. Benny Rothman was short, barely five feet tall, but genial and persuasive. A gymnast at school, now a keen cyclist and walker, he was obviously fit and energetic. He was also a communist and a Jew, having grown up in the then predominantly Jewish district of Cheetham Hill.

Manchester's German-Jewish population had been part of the social fabric of Manchester for much of the nineteenth century, but Benny Rothman was not from German stock. His parents were Romanian. Faded family photographs show relatives in north-eastern Romanian towns like Braila, where Benny's father Isaac was born in 1869, and the beautiful Carpathian town of Piatra Neamt. What you can't see is the increasing prejudice Benny's parents faced. Christian Romanians, especially in the north-eastern province of Moldavia, blamed Jews for their economic woes, and as the century wore on, a sequence of draconian laws were passed until it was almost impossible to get a job without full citizenship and almost impossible for a Jew to become a full citizen. Those who could afford it emigrated. Tens of thousands of Romanian Jews left around the turn of the century and Isaac was one of them.

He went first to New York and worked as a steward at sea before settling in Manchester in 1908, marrying another Romanian émigré, Freda Solomons, known as Fanny, whose father had gone to Canada, returned to Romania then settled in Manchester. They rented a house on Granton Street in Hightown and had five children: Phyllis, Leah, Bernard, Rosa and Gersh. Money was scarce: their wedding photograph was paid for in instalments. But Isaac did what he could. He rented a stall at the markets in Glossop and Shaw, or a 'gaff', as the novelist Howard Jacobson remembered it from his days with his dad on a similar circuit of northern markets just after the Second World War: 'They had to start

Opposite: A school day out in 1975. In the twentieth century Kinder plateau above Red Brook was a desolate place of eroding peat, but held its place in the imagination of Manchester workers eager to experience 'the freedom of the hills'.

from nothing, and selling nylon stockings or pillowcases on a market stall was as good as any. A hundred years before, they'd have been pedlars selling reels of cotton in Kishinev or Kamenets Podolski, and at least in the poor working-class markets of Ancoats or Grey Mare Lane they didn't run the risk of being pelted with stones by superstitious peasants or drowned by Cossacks with no better way of passing the time.'

Isaac didn't sell stockings; he sold clothes pegs, candles and cutlery: cheap household goods. But the principle was the same: catching the attention of hard-up northern mill-workers for enough time to sell them something. 'For most of the punters,' Jacobson wrote, 'it would have been their first encounter with a Jewish comedian, though they wouldn't all have known that since it would also have been their first encounter with a Jew.' That might have been true in places like Glossop or Shaw, but not in Manchester, where the Jewish population was substantial. Robert Roberts wrote of the casual anti-Semitism he witnessed around the time of Benny's birth in 1911. 'Down Zinc Street, whatever one's social or economic position, everybody was "Christian"; therefore none of us liked the Jews. Not that we knew any: we detested them on principle.' He described a Jewish dealer opening a second-hand clothes shop in the district, 'only to see his goods pulled out on to the pavement and burned openly by scuttlers while a policeman stood by to see fair play' – 'scuttlers', with their donkey-fringe haircuts, being the gangs of bored and sometimes violent youths that were a feature of late-nineteenth-century Salford and Manchester.

By the mid 1930s, when Benny was a young man, the situation had darkened to night. There were by then 35,000 Jews in Manchester, three times the number of the 1880s, most of them from Eastern Europe, most of them escaping persecution. These immigrants weren't being driven home in carriages from Hallé concerts; they were fighting for survival. At the same time, the depression was heaping pressure on poorer districts in Salford. The antifascist campaigner Aubrey Lewis recalled: 'I remember vividly the effects and so many people in the area out of work, people literally dropping from starvation. People tried to commit suicide in the area where I lived.' The British Union of Fascists, formally established a few months after the Kinder Mass Trespass, opened its northern headquarters in the Salford district of Broughton. Blackshirts were soon marching through Cheetham singing, 'The Yids, the Yids, we've gotta get rid of the Yids'. Rosa Rothman, Benny's younger sister, went into the rag trade like so many young Jewish workers from poorer backgrounds. Well into her nineties, she could still remember applying for a job at a department store in the city and being told, 'Actually, we don't employ Jewish people'. To which Rosa replied, 'Then I don't want to work for you'. She remembered seeing Oswald Mosley walking down Deansgate. 'I said to hell with Mosley,' she told me. 'Keep the Salford grime out of Cheetham Hill.'

Isaac Rothman was not especially religious but he did join Jewish societies in north Manchester. The family went to the Romanian *shul* on Waterloo Road, before it moved to Lower Broughton. Religious observances were somewhat different among the Romanians, which is why, Rosa remembered, the children thought of themselves as a higher class than the Lithuanians. 'I don't know why, it's not like we dressed any better.' The family would stop at the grocer Maypole's for a quarter of raisins on the way home. Freda was more observant and didn't like working the markets on the Sabbath, although she would at a pinch. If they went off on the train to Glossop together, they'd leave the children sleeping, bread cut and buttered so they wouldn't have to touch a knife, the toasting fork hidden so they weren't tempted to get too close to the fire. Rosa could remember their cousins, the Ackers, throwing mud at the window to wake them up. Then Benny would take his young brother Gersh and a gang of them would walk the two miles to Heaton Park for adventures.

In 1923, on the day his oldest son turned twelve, Isaac died, plunging the family into a crisis that affected the rest of their lives. Benny was by then on a scholarship at Manchester Central High School for Boys, a grammar. He'd learned a little Hebrew in Cheetham, but was now excelling at sciences. He might have been a doctor. But the family were in far too much trouble for Benny to stay on at school after he turned fourteen and was legally permitted to leave. A neighbour put in a word about a job going at a Manchester garage, Tom Garner's, and Benny spent the next two years as an errand boy, collecting parts from motor factors. He borrowed a little money from his grandmother and built his own bicycle from spares. Having a bicycle was liberating. He could reach Hayfield; he could even reach the Lake District. For his sixteenth birthday he cycled to North Wales and walked up Snowdon. The view from the summit, the far horizon, was like a vision of the future. He joined the National Clarion Cycling Club, booming in those years. Benny was in the East Manchester branch, which sent three rides out every Sunday: slow, medium and fast. Benny was medium, and on busy weekends there'd be a hundred of them, so that they had to split into three so they didn't become a hazard on the road.

Above all, Benny was likeable, he made friends and could persuade people to do things. It occurred to him that he could make a decent living as a car salesman so he took courses at the local YMCA in advertising and marketing, which led to courses in economic geography, which brought him into contact with communist activists, one of whom persuaded him to join the Young Communist League. His developing interest in politics came at a time when the Communist Party of Great Britain was fighting its 'class against class' campaign, trying to find space for itself on the Left by dismissing the Labour Party as 'social-fascists'. This created tensions in the rambling movement, a powerful lobby on the Left of British politics, and explains in part, but only in part, the hostility Benny Rothman faced when he announced in the newspapers that the British Workers' Sports Federation was organising a trespass on Kinder Scout on 24 April 1932. At his trial afterwards the judge would draw the jury's attention to the two factors that characterised Benny as an outsider: his politics and his foreignness, his impoverished Jewishness. Yids didn't belong on a grouse moor.

The heritage industry primes us to see rural life in England as one of seamless continuity. It's all about rootedness. Similar types of people do similar types of things from one generation to the next. Families stay in one place for generations. But just as in the city, rural life is often seamed and fractured by pressures that spring from the rights of property, by our innate sense of fairness and anxiety about outsiders. Except that, in the country, outsiders have faded from history more quickly. They don't suit the narrative. One example in Derbyshire is the Irish migrant workers who dug railway tunnels through the High Peak in the nineteenth century – and suffered for it. The fatality rate among navvies working on the Woodhead tunnels, begun in 1839, was higher than that of British soldiers at Waterloo, prompting a parliamentary enquiry that, like so many, changed little. Working conditions had improved by the time the Cowburn Tunnel into Edale was dug in the late 1880s, but there was a smallpox outbreak at the Totley end of the line, killing navvies and locals alike. The deaths of some Irish went unrecorded and certainly weren't mourned; their semi-permanent camps were notorious for hard drinking, gambling and prize fights. The magistrates were kept busy.

There were Irish farm labourers too. Hannah Mitchell recalled how, because her parents had taken out a loan for their tenancy, 'no labour could be hired, except the Irishmen who came over in summer and who for so many shillings an acre and so many gallons of beer would cut the meadow grass, which we children had to make into hay. I loved these Irishmen who were always kind and gentle to children, and had a vast repertoire of songs and fairy tales … My mother had a fixed idea that all Irishmen were potential murderers, forbade us to sit in the barn with them … We grew familiar with the beauty of Killarney and the sorrows of the Irish emigrant.' When one of Bert Ward's ramblers, on the inaugural Clarion walk, the circumambulation of Kinder Scout, told an Irish joke, a navvy standing near threatened a little shillelagh law and there was a frank exchange of views. The Edwardian word was 'chafing', the modern equivalent of the disingenuous 'banter'.

Louis Jennings, on his tour around Kinder Scout, witnessed the same tension in the late 1870s. He'd spent a day exploring Woodlands from the inn at the now-submerged village of Ashopton, walking up Fair Brook on the north side of Kinder Scout before returning to the Snake Road turnpike as dusk gathered. He saw people preparing to spend the night by the road and suddenly felt anxious. These were not the sorts of people who now feature in rustic prints on the walls of themed country pubs: 'Presently I came to a horse hobbled, grazing the grass which fringed the road.' He saw a pot hanging over a fire, and a 'dark woman', code for a gypsy, with a child. The woman spoke and a man appeared out of the darkness.

'"Good evening," said I.

"Good evening," said the man, concealing something in one hand behind him, and looking very distrustfully upon me.

"I see how it is," said I; "you take me for a keeper. But if nobody interferes more than I shall do with what you have got cooking in the pot there, your supper will be safe enough."'

The traveller is defensive, but Jennings reassures him with a coin.

'This at once soothed the ground, for keepers are not in the habit of giving beer-money to gipsies.' The ice is broken, and the traveller shows him around 'their little house on wheels', which Jennings romanticises, before being contradicted with the difficulties of the roads and the hardships of winter. They part on good terms: 'I hope you will enjoy your rabbit,' he tells his new friends before returning to the inn at Ashopton.

Jennings had touched on a fault line in rural life that had overshadowed country life for more than a century: poaching. The exclusion and violence experienced around and on Kinder Scout in the years leading up to and including the mass trespass sprang from the broader context of game preservation: in this instance, keeping the numbers of grouse high. That conflict stretched back to the period immediately following the English Civil War, when poaching had been part of resistance against the Crown. At the Restoration, Charles II introduced legislation on the rights to game that replaced the old forest law William the Conqueror had introduced and that applied when the High Peak was a royal hunting preserve. According to Charles II, game now belonged only to the wealthiest landowners; lords of the manor could appoint gamekeepers to protect their interest by seizing guns and dogs. In the absence of a police force, gamekeepers became the law, and not just for the human population. Which species of animal or bird prospered or was expunged was wholly within their control. Nature had been privatised. And if game interests needed new powers, then a legislature dominated by landowners could provide them; an Act of Parliament prohibiting the burning of heather in the breeding season was passed as early as 1693.

Thirty years later, after the South Sea Bubble prompted an economic downturn and a consequent need for cheap protein, the notorious Black Act came into force. This was the first in a series of shockingly punitive poaching laws. A sentence of capital punishment became available for over fifty offences, including standing in a forest at night in disguise. Legislation around game and shooting rights became one of the most contentious areas of public life, especially in the early nineteenth century. Blood was routinely shed on both sides. Sydney Smith wrote in the *Edinburgh Review* in 1819: 'There is hardly now a gaol delivery at which some gamekeeper has not murdered a poacher, or some poacher a gamekeeper.' Hanging, transportation and flogging were regularly applied. The countryside saw a kind of low-grade insurgency against this oppression, which was mixed up with demands to increase the franchise. There was a poaching arms race: man traps and spring guns on one side, safety in numbers or subterfuge on the other.

In 1862, having left the issue of enforcement to keepers for 200 years, parliament established new county-based police forces, along with sweeping powers of stop and search. At a stroke, a new alliance between gamekeepers and police was forged, something many senior officers at the time resented: prosecuting poachers wasn't popular. The provision of the Act for stopping people on the public highway, aimed at cutting off the retreat of poachers, was particularly resented. The police could now stop anyone without cause, and did so, causing bitterness among local labourers and farm workers. With mills across Lancashire closed because of the cotton famine, a consequence of the American Civil War, there had been a predictable rise in poaching. Conflict was inevitable; there was almost immediately a riot in Blackburn when eight unemployed cotton operatives, caught poaching on the estate of a prominent landowner, were sentenced to three months in gaol.

So the fear Jennings sensed in the travellers on the Snake Road was real and justified. They were outsiders, hungry and vulnerable. The countryside was a place where people could be watched, suspected and restricted, where the preservation of game was enforced, often violently, and where a parallel system of authority – gamekeepers – worked with the law of the land. Although much had changed by the time of the mass trespass on Kinder Scout in 1932, there were direct links to this history of bitter antagonism in the establishment's reaction to demands for increased access in general, and to the mass trespass in particular.

The severe economic depression that began with the credit crunch of 1873 was still being felt across the north of England – and would be throughout the 1880s – when Louis Jennings explored the area. Austerity ruled. Walking up the Snake Road linking Sheffield and Manchester, when Hannah Mitchell was six years old, he wrote: 'Trade is still in a sorry plight in each of those towns, and whole families are constantly on their way from one to the other in the hope of bettering their condition.' He found himself stopped a dozen times by tramps begging, much to his annoyance, but felt sorry for those 'respectable artisans' and their families obliged to share the road with such flotsam. 'One man and his wife and six children were toiling wearily along the road, no fewer than four of the children being unable to walk.'

Jennings's book is full of acute observations of economic life in the Peak District, not surprisingly given his track record as one of the leading journalists of his day. Born in the down-at-heel London suburb of Walworth, the son of a tailor, he learned his craft on provincial papers, got a job on the *Saturday Review* and was then hired by *The Times* as relief for the paper's India correspondent. Jennings's lively reporting style impressed the editor. In 1865 he sent Jennings off to the United States, where he was responsible for repairing the paper's reputation, damaged from its support for the Confederacy in the Civil War. An interview with President Andrew Johnson was a major scoop, boosting his reputation among American journalists. He returned to London for a spell as a leader writer, at around the same time as Mrs Ward's rather plodding husband Humphry. Jennings's career would be more glittering.

Offered a job on the *New York Times*, he returned to the United States and within months was editor, leading a famous investigation into corruption in the city, the so-called Tweed Ring. But he failed in his attempt to buy the newspaper with the support of Republican politicians. Forced out after this failed coup, he returned to London, finding work with John Murray, the publisher. The account of his walking tour of the Peak District, published by Murray soon after this crisis, is shadowed with the sense of time passing and life's missed opportunities. After meeting the gypsies under Kinder Scout he sits in his room feeling miserably lonely: 'It is at such moments that we go once more over life's journey, and see how chequered, yet how brief, it has been.'

The prospect of climbing Kinder Scout cheered him up. 'If the Kinderscout range were in Switzerland scores of books would have been written about it, and "Sanatoria" without number would have been established on its hillsides. As it is, not a dozen tourists thoroughly explore the Peak in the course of as many years, and the very people at the local inns which are nearest to it – and they are all some miles distant – seem to know little or nothing about it.'

For his first attempt on Kinder Scout, Jennings stayed at Castleton and crossed Hollins Cross, perhaps the best vantage point from which to see Edale. ('Fresh from a visit to Switzerland, it seemed to me that I had seen nothing there more beautiful and attractive.') Then he walked up Edale to Barber Booth, where he got directions from an old woman, before continuing to 'Measter Shirt's fearm' at Upper Booth: 'A wilder or more romantic spot the heart of man could not desire.' Mister Shirt's farm was the last in the valley on 'the very borders of civilisation', and Jennings decided to stop for a glass of milk. He sat in the parlour while the farmer's wife fetched his drink, talking to her two 'young ladies' while four children looked on, much as Hannah Mitchell had done with Hans Renold, excited at this exotic man, an explorer meeting a forgotten tribe. The only person they usually saw who wasn't a relation was the postman. Jennings made enquiries about climbing the hill above the farm but was told there would be objections. Shooters were out. He would have to go around to Hayfield. Louis Jennings had stumbled on the gathering fight for access.

Before the acts of enclosure and the Industrial Revolution, freedom of access to the moors had been much wider. It needed to be, since most journeys were on foot. The access campaigner Howard Hill was one of many to argue they weren't asking for anything unprecedented: 'The struggle for the right to wander freely over these vast expanses of uncultivated moorland was not to establish a new freedom but to regain an old one.' With the coming of the canals, the turnpikes and the railways, packhorse trains on the old roads across the High Peak, like that up Jacob's Ladder and over Edale Cross, disappeared. People no longer needed to walk from village to village in the way that they had for centuries. And while acts of enclosure caused hardship and injustice in many parts of the country, much of the High Peak, although not Kinder Scout, had been conglomerated into large estates centuries ago. There were common rights, like cutting peat, but these extended only to those who farmed the tenancies. It was the growth of sporting estates that returned the moors to a near-feudal state, jealously guarded against incomers.

The High Peak holds a special place in the history of grouse shooting. Until the mid-nineteenth century, grouse had been shot 'over dogs', the dogs startling the birds into the air as the shooters walked across the moor. Guns were heavy muzzle-loaders, keeping the rate of fire down. The number of birds shot was consequently low. Several factors conspired to change this: the invention of the breech-loading shotgun in the 1850s upped the rate of fire, and getting other people to scare the grouse over your head meant you could shoot more of them. The development of grouse butts can be traced to Dunford Bridge on the north side of the High Peak. The landowner Sir Walter Spencer-Stanhope recalled his father in the 1830s using a sandy hole beside the Snailsden Road, a borrow pit for repairing its surface, which offered good cover. They dug some more sandy holes across the moor and the success was repeated. At first driven grouse shooting was regarded as cheating, but when the dukes of Devonshire and Norfolk took it up, and then the Royal Family, the practice became wildly fashionable. Working people would come out of Sheffield on to the moors to watch the sport, even if they could approach no closer than the public highway.

Driven grouse shooting quickly became a lucrative new business. There was a huge increase in the numbers of birds shot; bags mushroomed from a handful of birds, to scores, to hundreds, creating an urgent need to grow more birds. As sheep farming struggled in the face of foreign competition, grouse shooting offered a new and more lucrative alternative on marginal land. Management practices were stepped up to create an environment that was about as natural as a field of rape, although in this case the crop was grouse. Moors were drained, burned and grazed to boost the growth of young common heather shoots, the preferred food of adult grouse: today's motley pattern of the moors became established. Wolves were long gone, but other predators – foxes, stoats, corvids or hen harriers – were persecuted remorselessly. What was the point of investing money in boosting grouse numbers if they were eaten before they could be shot? In these ways, gamekeepers increased the density of grouse exponentially. And the fact that the strongest cock grouse reached the butts first meant their mortality was higher, creating more opportunities for new breeding pairs. Lord Wharncliffe at Wortley Hall claimed in 1873 that there were fifty times the number of grouse on Yorkshire's moors than there had been twenty years before.

Kinder Scout had been surveyed for enclosure in the 1830s and the common land allotted to existing landowners in Kinder's Act of 1840. This didn't immediately remove access; a member of the Manchester Geographical Society wrote in 1897 of how thirty or forty years previously they had still been free to roam. But when the boom in grouse shooting reached Kinder Scout, everything was in place to keep the public out. A century and a half after Daniel Defoe had dismissed the moors as a howling wilderness, Kinder became one of the most exclusive landscapes in Britain. In 1876, the Duke of Devonshire, acting on behalf of a shooting tenant, closed the route linking Hayfield and the Woodlands Valley, used by pilgrims and drovers for centuries, up William Clough and under Mill Hill, across Ashop Head and down Ashop Clough.

Local people were outraged. They set up the Hayfield and Kinderscout Ancient Footpaths Association, but lacking money it struggled to make headway. Then, in 1894, with support from Manchester, a larger, better-funded and more vigorous organisation was founded: the Peak District and Northern Counties Footpaths Preservation Society. Luke Garside of Hayfield, a great chronicler of Kinder Scout and part of the original campaign group, brought out his old research into the route's long human history. Had they been better funded, he wrote to the *Manchester Guardian*, they would 'have tested the matter in a court of law. Let us hope that the supine-ness of that day may not be repeated now'. The new group, still active more than a century later, raised £1,000 and hired Richard Pankhurst as counsel. Luke Garside served on its committee. Within two years the old path over Ashop Head was open to the public again.

Debates in the 1890s about the best tactics to use in regaining access offer a fresh perspective on the more famous campaign that followed the Great War. In 1894, in the renewed public surge of enthusiasm for the campaign, the old Chartist William Henry Chadwick, a man who had gone to jail for sedition in 1848 at the age of nineteen, announced he was ready to trespass on the plateau and go to jail again if necessary. (In the intervening years he'd worked as a phrenologist and mesmerist, and toured the country giving seances. *The Spectator*, reviewing a short biography of Chadwick, called him 'a hot-headed man and not over wise, but single-minded and sincere'; given a pension by Joseph Chamberlain, he was still speaking publicly for the Liberals at the general election in 1906.)

Given how the 1932 mass trespass touched on the injustices of enclosure, it's ironic that enclosure hadn't turned Kinder into a single, exclusive estate belonging to one member of the aristocracy, as it had on the Eastern Edges outside Sheffield. When Louis Jennings arrived in Hayfield in 1880, for his second attempt on Kinder, he discovered that while Kinder Scout was strictly private, 'it is divided up among numerous holders, almost all of whom are at loggerheads with each other and with the public'. The owners of the moor, Jennings discovered, 'are jealous to the last degree of their rights, and quarrel over the few birds which by some accident are still left as though the cause of empires were at stake. This arises from the foolish way in which the district has been parcelled out among a number of small holders, in patches not much larger than a table-cloth.'

High numbers of grouse were being shot in the High Peak, but not on Kinder Scout. One miserable sportsman, Jennings discovered, had just two acres, and the only chance he had of shooting a bird was if his neighbours were out and sent one over. Another paid fifty pounds – £4,000 in today's money – for his bit of moor and in the previous year had killed two grouse. Jennings joked that soon you might as well declare a lobster shooting season on Kinder Scout. 'The stranger in these parts would naturally pay very little heed to local troubles and bickerings if he did not speedily find that they materially interfered with his freedom. If you go to the right you are liable to be warned off, if to the left, to be threatened with an action for trespass. You get permission from three or four different holders, and find that there is still another who bars the way.' Happily for Jennings, as a gentleman, he was welcomed everywhere and had little sympathy for those 'who delight in fussing and flourishing about, and butting their conceited heads against local prejudices'. Those people, he thought, should stay at home.

Rambles among the Hills, whose illustrations were engraved by the father of mountaineer Edward Whymper, helped restore Jennings's fortunes. He went on to write influential political attacks on Gladstone in the *Quarterly Review*, returning north as Member of Parliament for Stockport as a free-market, pro-Randolph Churchill Tory before dying unexpectedly at fifty-seven following surgery. Readers familiar with Kinder Scout, like John Wilding of the Rucksack Club, described him as among the first and best travel writers to understand the appeal of walking in moorland scenery, rather than the more familiar British mountain districts: 'it has quite a Borrovian flavour'. The book came to the attention of Mrs Humphry Ward, most likely through her brother Willie at the *Manchester Guardian*. She drew on *Rambles* for local colour in the opening book of *David Grieve* and, thanks to the two of them, public interest in Kinder Scout was given a boost, although, despite Puttrell, walking and climbing on the plateau itself were rare events until the Edwardian era. The peak itself remained forbidden ground. As the Manchester campaigner Edwin Royce said: 'No sacred mountain in Tibet is more strictly guarded. It must not be walked upon without permission given in writing; it must not be photographed without permission of the owner; even to print its name may be an infringement of his rights.' (Ironically, half a world away, British Army officers were sneaking across the border from India into Tibet to trespass on holy Lake Manasarovar and shoot game.)

The restitution of one footpath wasn't going to meet demand from urban centres where incomes were rising and new legislation guaranteed time for leisure. Just as the fashion for grouse shooting took off among the rich, a fascination for wild country developed among the general population, starting largely with the professional classes, but extending across society after the Great War. Eric Byne and Geoffrey Sutton described this process better than anyone in their 1966 book *High Peak*, a kind of social history of the outdoors, identifying the different tribes with their contrasting rituals, and the stratification of those tribes. They write, for example, of Lehmann J. Oppenheimer: 'A lovable character, a shy man who looked on all lovers of hills as his friends.' With his talent for friendship, Oppenheimer knitted together many of the leading climbers and 'bog-trotters' before the Great War. He climbed with Jim Puttrell and Ernest Baker on Kinder in 1900, Puttrell leading them up a first ascent on the Downfall, the route *Zigzag*. Afterwards they got lost on Kinderlow as they tried to reach Edale. ('There was little scope for going wrong,' Baker wrote, 'but they made the most of it.') When they finally popped out of the mist they saw below them the village of Hayfield.

Oppenheimer had deep reserves of stamina, legs that took him from Eccleston in Lancashire to Eccleston near Chester and back in a single day, a distance of eighty miles. But he was no taciturn eater of the ground. He had studied art and architecture in Italy and ran the family mosaic firm in Old Trafford. His father was from Hanover and an Orthodox Jew, disowned when he converted to marry a Quaker. Their commissions included Notre-Dame de la Treille in Lille and the exquisite floor of Honan Chapel at University College Cork. Oppenheimer was climbing on Arran when war broke out but had trouble leaving the island on account of his German name; he got home to discover the family works had been stoned. Despite this, and even though he was forty-six years old, he joined up as soon as he could, just like his young climbing friend Siegfried Herford, writing to Herford's parents when he was killed. A few months later, Oppenheimer was gassed at Vimy Ridge. He took weeks to die, slowly drowning, cared for by his wife and daughter who travelled to the military hospital in France. His name is on the Fell & Rock memorial on Great Gable, alongside Herford and Jeffcoat. His son Eric, who changed his name to his mother's maiden name of Newton, also fought in the war. Afterwards he was art critic for the *Manchester Guardian* and a noted art historian.

Byne and Sutton also give us Cecil Dawson, a Manchester cotton merchant with a full Prussian moustache, long-legged but with a light frame, marching across the moors with metronomic precision, uphill or on the flat, without varying his speed. He drew a band of like-minded hardies around him, who acquired the nickname 'the 94th', more light cavalry than heavy infantry, and Dawson became their colonel. He walked fifty weekends a year, stopping only to wet his shirt, in all weathers, to cool down. The 94th watched the new Rucksack Club with a sort of cool antagonism, but relations warmed and most of them joined. It was the colonel who developed the Marsden to Edale walk, in Eric Byne's view the finest bogtrot in the Peak, best done in winter when it's frozen. The walk, sometimes done there and back, is a staple of the Rucksack Club. By the 1950s members of the club were doing it in less than thirteen hours. Then they extended it from Colne to Buxton: fifty miles. No tougher band ever walked the Peak.

That two recreational groups, walkers and grouse shooters, should emerge at the same time and come into conflict was no coincidence: the railways brought them all to the moors while the acts of enclosure created both an injustice and a hindrance. But the growing tension was about much more than a challenge to landowners; it would raise profound questions about an individual's freedom of movement.

James Bryce was a titan of late-Victorian public life: jurist, academic, a Liberal cabinet minister, ambassador to the United States and, with Alfred Toynbee, investigator of the Armenian genocide. Bryce was a mountain lover, a member of the Cairngorm Club, the more radical end of Scottish mountaineering, and a founding member in 1865 of the Open Spaces Society with Octavia Hill and John Stuart Mill. He was also, in 1884, the first person to introduce access legislation to parliament with his Access to Mountains (Scotland) Bill. It was the first of many. These bills were a concerted effort to turn back the rising tide of exclusion from sporting estates in Scotland, an exclusion led by the Royal Family at Balmoral. Vast tracts of the Highlands became game reserves in the nineteenth century, as wool prices fell in the face of cheap imports. That process eroded customary freedoms of access. Bryce's argument was simple to understand and based on a clear principle: that freedom of movement is a human right. During one of his attempts at legislation, in March 1892, Bryce told parliament that 'land is not property for our unlimited and unqualified use'. For Bryce there was no such thing in 'law or in natural justice' as 'an unlimited power of exclusion'. It was Bryce's vision that was finally realised with the Scottish Land Reform Act of 2003, and to a lesser extent with the Countryside and Rights of Way Act 2000 in England and Wales.

Despite the justice of his cause, these bills had no chance of passing through a House of Lords stuffed with Tory grouse moor owners and other shooting interests. The arguments against, recorded in *Hansard*, rehearse the same arguments that would be heard repeatedly over the next century: damage to property and disturbance of stock or game. The weight of those arguments was, from the outset, grossly exaggerated. Sir John Kinloch, Liberal member for East Perthshire, where there is still much grouse shooting, wasn't fooled: 'With regard to the disturbance of sheep grazing, I think it is a most extraordinary argument to be brought forward, especially by sportsmen. Ask any farmer whether he would not have a tourist in preference to a sportsman. People who live in glass houses should not throw stones, and that argument should not have been used.'

Bryce's bill of 1892, like his previous bills, referred only to Scotland; it was widely held that the issue wasn't so great a problem in England. Then again, wealthy mountain lovers in England were more inclined towards Snowdonia and the Lake District than the grouse moors of the Pennines and so barely appreciated such places were forbidden ground. But Bryce's seconder for the legislation was the Liberal member for Eccles, in Lancashire. Henry John Roby had been a Cambridge 'Apostle' and an educational reformer. He was now in the cotton business, and married to the daughter of Peter Albert Ermen, partner in what had been Ermen & Engels, the firm Friedrich's father had part-owned. 'In a populous part of Lancashire, not far from Rochdale,' Roby told parliament, 'I have been stopped from going over a hill in May on the ground that I might interfere with the grouse, and on my remonstrating with the gamekeeper on his keeping the inhabitants from going over a wild part of their immediate neighbourhood, the only answer I got was that if I went at Christmas time I should not be able to disturb much … I do hope that any legislation upon this subject will have regard not only to deer forests in Scotland, but to all moorlands and uncultivated hills in England and Wales, so that people may not be prevented from enjoying a harmless recreation, and one which can do no injury to the rights of the landowners.' Roby's demand was prescient. The Pennines would become the critical focus for access campaigners after the Great War; Tom Stephenson, among the most able of those campaigners and the originator of the Pennine Way, saw Kinder Scout as 'the cockpit' of that battle.

In 1908, England was included in proposed access legislation for the first time. This bill was introduced by James Bryce's brother Annan, and like James's bills, it had support across the political divide. A leader in *The Spectator* put the argument succinctly: acknowledging trespass was not a criminal offence, agreeing with Bryce's arguments, and prefiguring the unanswerable sacrifice shortly to be made by the people of Britain: 'At present the liberty of the public to walk on unenclosed land exists, not by law, but on sufferance. A stupid landowner may forbid all access, and no one can question his right. And yet it may be said with equal truth that he holds his land on sufferance. In a crowded country private preserves are necessarily held on uncertain tenure. If a democracy is denied a reasonable liberty, it is apt to go too far in its assertion of freedom. It is because we are so strongly opposed to anything like land nationalisation that we want to see the people given a full share of the amenities of their own country. We are constantly talking about patriotism and exhorting others to a keener sense of civic duty, but how is a man to be patriotic when he has no sense of personal interest in his country? It is worth remembering that by far the larger proportion of our voluntary forces, and almost the whole of our Army and Navy, are recruited from the working classes. Are we to exclude those who bear the burden of our defence from some enjoyment of the soil they are defending? Can we expect a soldier to fight passionately for a high-road?'

In the aftermath of the Great War, there was a lull before walking and climbing recovered their pre-war impetus. The Rucksack Club wasn't the only major British climbing organisation to experience stagnation. Many key figures in pre-war climbing and walking were gone: Siegfried Herford, Stanley Jeffcoat and Leonard Oppenheimer. John Laycock had gone abroad to escape his overbearing sense of loss. But then the social upheavals the war had caused were revealed as walkers and climbers returned, now not just the bourgeoisie but the proletariat too. The enemy was at the gates; things were about to get ugly.

On New Year's Day 1922, Henry Fowler Martin arrived at the Snake Inn early in the afternoon having walked over the old Roman road of Cut Gate. He told people there that the wind had been so strong he'd been blown off his feet. (This isn't uncommon. Thomas Graham Brown, one of the few significant British mountaineers of the 1920s, was once blown off his feet on Kinder's plateau. He said he hadn't experienced such a wind in all his years in the Alps, Alaska or the Himalaya.) Without saying where he was going, Martin left at about half past three, with an hour of daylight left. It was the last time he was seen alive. Local rambling groups organised scores of walkers to join the search, including prominent figures like Bert Ward, and Eustace Thomas of the Rucksack Club. All agreed that Martin couldn't be on the Hayfield side of Kinder. No one would be so foolish to go that way in fierce wind and driving rain. But on 8 January that's where they found him, a few hundred metres south of the Downfall, as Ward and Thomas were resting in the Nag's Head in Edale having spent another fruitless day looking on the wrong side of the plateau. Newton had perished from exposure. 'The whole attitude of the body suggested the story of a man who had struggled on to the last,' was how one newspaper report described it.

A month later they were back, looking for a second lost walker, Edwin Newton, who had set out from his home in Ashton on 11 February to visit the grave of Henry Martin, now buried in Hayfield cemetery. Harold Wild, among Manchester's best-known ramblers, wrote an account of the search: 'Edale has never seen quite such an assembly before. Some 250 persons assembled in front of the Nag's Head. In addition to the ordinary ramblers from Manchester, Sheffield, and Ashton, the party included a number of Scouts, Red Cross men and several persons who, unfamiliar with the moors, had turned out to give a hand.' Wild explained that many thought Newton had gone on to Kinder Scout first to visit the spot where Martin had perished before continuing to Hayfield. They were proved right. A rambler called Joseph Lloyd from Reddish spotted the body on a ledge fifteen metres from the top of the Downfall. Newton was lying on his back with his arms outstretched, legs crossed, his purse and stick lying near him, his hat still at the spot on the rim of the plateau from where he had fallen. He'd died, probably quickly, from a severe head injury that had knocked his false teeth out and broken his jaw. 'Kinder Scout is gradually gathering to itself a grim reputation,' one newspaper said, 'and the very name begins to have a sullen, sinister sound.' These accidents, so close together and so intimately linked, were reported widely. The public interest focused attention on the limited public access. 'He who goes there,' explained another background piece, 'does so by the permission of Mr James Watts or by stealth.'

James Watts, born in 1845, was the son of the drapery magnate and former mayor of Manchester Sir James Watts, who had acquired a chunk of Kinder Scout just as he had acquired a grand new house in Cheadle. For an enterprising man who started life as a weaver in Didsbury, the opportunity to take Prince Albert shooting on his own estate must have felt like some kind of crowning glory. He was the archetypal Victorian industrialist, one of the new rich taking his place among the establishment, as though stepping from the pages of Anthony Trollope. Elizabeth Gaskell wrote in 1856 that Watts, like most Manchester mayors, was a 'risen' man, 'willing to give two or three thousand [pounds] for the privilege'. But she admired his wit: 'on rummaging up a crest just lately, he was asked for a motto [and] gave: What's in a name?' Then again, Watts did rename his new house Abney Hall, after a familial connection to the Abney family in Stoke Newington, and in the space of a very few years had it remodelled twice, first by the architects who built his warehouse on Portland Street, and then, in a bold statement of fashion, by the leading architecture and design company of Augustus Pugin. 'A man has to look after himself and his own,' as Arthur Birling, J.B. Priestley's version of the Victorian patriarch, says in *An Inspector Calls*. And Sir James was very conscious of the dynasty he had founded, handing his name, if not his baronetcy, to three succeeding generations.

Yet his son James Watts was no Arthur Birling. He had a reputation for treating his workers well and was among the first employers to offer them Saturday afternoons off. He was also not averse to breaking the law in defence of his principles. The Watts were devout nonconformists, so James opposed the incorporation of Church of England schools into the national system, withholding a proportion of his business rates. The bailiffs were sent in, and bolts of cloth sold at auction to meet the debt, but not before his protest had been made public. James Watts wasn't, as some in the district were, against hillwalkers in principle. He served as a vice president of the Peak District and Northern Counties Footpaths Preservation Society until his death in 1926. During the fight to reopen the path over Mill Hill in 1896, he helped provide early maps that supported the access claim, and offered the society the use of a pick and shovel to erect a metal signpost when they won. Yet his attitude to the mountain seems strangely conflicted. Throughout the Edwardian period he made it difficult even for those from his own class to visit the plateau and guarded it jealously. After the Kinder reservoir was built, he moved his shooting lodge from Farlands in Hayfield to the more isolated farm at Upper House, where Mrs Ward had stayed researching her novel. Watts invested heavily in rebuilding to create a vision of Old England. The interior of a disused Cheshire church was transported to Kinder to create a great hall, and a castellated tower built. It was a kind of ersatz continuity.

After the Great War, life as a landowner was less congenial. Watts wanted the place off his hands. He tried to sell Kinder to the War Department and then Manchester Corporation. Thwarted in his attempts, Watts didn't miss a chance to use the fatalities near the Downfall in 1922 as an excuse for restrictions on access to be tightened. 'Kinder Scout,' one Manchester newspaper reported, 'is likely to be closed to the public, except for one or two roads, which take the safest routes. The mountain is the property of Mr James Watts, of Abney Hall, Cheadle. For some years he has freely granted permits to visit the Downfall and other interesting localities on the Scout, but he is now likely to refuse, in order to prevent people risking their lives on these dangerous places.'

But the accidents had alerted the public to the notion that Kinder Scout was forbidden ground. One reporter wrote: 'It may sound incredible, but it is none the less true, that Hayfield people have lived and died without ever setting foot on the summit of the Scout, or seeing the Downfall except at a distance. They pay much more respect to the gamekeeper than do the Manchester people, who imagine that Kinder Scout is only a glorified Heaton Park.' Other journalists argued that in allowing access, James Watts would be adding to the prestige of the nation. 'At present Kinder Scout is merely a game preserve. If the path suggested [from Kinder Low to the Downfall] were allowed it would open to the public one of England's most beautiful spots and give joy and pleasure to thousands. We sincerely hope Mr Watts may see his way to do it and make Kinder Scout as are all other mountains in our island home, a thing of beauty and a joy for-ever to all lovers of Nature.'

Such appeals did not mollify old James Watts. On 30 April 1923, an advertisement appeared in the *Manchester Evening Chronicle* showing two photographs of walkers on Kinder Scout under the headline 'Kinder Scout Trespasses'. The copy promised a '£5 reward will be paid for the name, address and occupation of any of the persons represented in the photos'. Anyone who thought they could was invited to apply to a firm of solicitors, Cobbett, Wheeler & Cobbett. (Cobbett's also prosecuted the Independent Labour Party for holding pubic meetings at Boggart Hole Clough. The radical William Cobbett, father of the founders, would have been spinning in his grave.) The advertisement caused outrage among Manchester's ramblers, not least because another rambler must have shopped them. Harold Wild from the Ramblers' Federation sent a stiff letter to the paper; it wasn't published but the adverts weren't repeated and the culprits never caught. This was partly because the men came from Sheffield, not Manchester. One of them was George Willis Marshall, a silversmith during the working week and one of Bert Ward's Clarion ramblers at the weekend. Willis started walking as a teenager in the early 1920s, recording his rambles in elegant copperplate in a journal headed with Ward's famous epigram, that a rambler made is a man improved. He would go on to the moors in collar and tie: his Sunday best. His photographs conjure youth, friendship. Freedom. The line of moors George Marshall walked towards was always a new horizon. He was never concerned to go elsewhere. Kinder for him was no prelude to the Arctic or the high Himalaya.

Nationally, the number of gamekeepers at the turn of the twentieth century climbed to 17,000, a pattern followed on Kinder Scout as much as anywhere. The coming of the Chinley to Dore railway brought more and more walkers and climbers to Edale and after the twin disappearances of 1922 the Watts family posted more keepers. 'Some were rogues,' Eric Byne wrote in the 1960s. 'Others, like keeper John Carrington of Barber Booth, were respectable men possessing a profound knowledge of the country and its wildlife. The modern climber and walker will have difficulty in realising how few people knew the wild country around Kinder Scout in the closing decades of the last century, and how the gamekeeper and his autocratic "Mester" completely dominated the locality.'

James Watts kept six gamekeepers on the plateau at weekends to chase off any walkers who dared to approach. The Clarion Handbook warned: 'Gamekeepers in Sunday clothes are watching at Edale Station the arrival of Sheffield and Manchester Sunday morning trains, and to see if ramblers attempted to climb any part of Kinder Scout … there are men fixed at various points on the stop to signal and intercept and turn men back – as though they were thieves.' A keeper threatened Bert Ward with a stick: 'This is the way to deal with fucking socialists.' Watts also served Ward with a writ to stop him trespassing and because Ward was a civil servant, he was made to apologise and promise not to do it again.

A few walkers relished these confrontations, for the cat and mouse across the moors. According to a friend, the bogtrotter Cecil Dawson 'was known, hated and hunted by all the Bleaklow and Kinder Scout keepers, but was never caught, although on one occasion after a day on Bleaklow we were followed to the Miller's Arms near Hazlehead and only managed to escaped by climbing through the window while the keepers were waiting for us in the passage.' The early Clarion rambler Bill Whitney was an amateur boxing champion and wrestler who enjoyed baiting even the most aggressive gamekeepers, safe in the knowledge they wouldn't take him on.

For most ordinary walkers, though, encounters with gamekeepers were intimidating experiences, exacerbated by the knowledge that the situation might get seriously out of hand. 'Practically all were armed with guns or heavy cudgels, and they were often accompanied by dogs,' Eric Byne wrote. Some of the gamekeepers were courteous, and engaged in conversation. 'Many,' according to Byne, 'were nothing but hired bullies who would attack without provocation anyone who seemed easy prey.' Including, in one notorious incident, an older woman walking along Stanage.

Protection from the criminal justice system was patchy; rural magistrates, often friends of the landowners concerned, weren't predisposed to crack down on acts of violence committed against ramblers. In 1927, a Derbyshire farmhand opened fire on a group of ramblers from the Hans Renold Social Union, wounding two of them. The farmhand was fined and told to apologise through the local paper. In August 1930, a nineteen-year-old was smashed in the face with a rifle butt by one of Lord Scarborough's gamekeepers. The keeper was convicted of grievous bodily harm and fined four pounds. The keeper's next appearance in court was as a complainant. A miner was charged with assaulting him and stealing seven rabbits. The miner got a week for the assault and a hopping-mad two months for the rabbits.

The ghost of the poaching wars haunted the Kinder trespass; that was certainly reflected in the attitude of the police. Harvey Jackson was one of those who joined the trespass in 1932, as an eighteen-year-old apprentice. Later he joined the police, and was interviewed by the chief constable James Garrow, who had commanded the policing of the trespass. Garrow noticed on his application that he had a passion for hillwalking. 'Jackson,' the chief constable said, 'we do not like hillwalkers in Derbyshire, they are not welcome.' In this context, prison sentences handed out to Benny Rothman and others after the Kinder trespass of 1932 weren't exceptional; hillwalkers, at least for some in authority, came under the heading of poachers, Irishmen and gypsies. A few months after the Kinder Scout trial, members of the Cheshire Hunt were arrested on charges of trespass and assault, after whipping a farmer who had remonstrated with them for coming on his land without permission. Yet because several members of Cheshire's judiciary were also members of the Cheshire Hunt, the charges were dropped.

National park status didn't end the confrontations, not immediately. The climber Dennis Gray was at The Roaches in Staffordshire in the mid 1950s with the Salford anti-hero Don Whillans, as famous for his laconically aggressive wit as he was for his considerable mountaineering ability. The Roaches was part of the Swythamley estate, belonging to the family of Sir Philip Brocklehurst, and jealously keepered. The grapevine had warned them of a new gamekeeper, 'a cross between King Kong and Big Daddy'. And so he proved. This titan confronted them, ducking, feinting and jabbing the air. 'I'd better warn you,' he shouted, 'I'm a judo man. A judo man.' Whillans narrowed his eyes. 'Ay, well fuck off back to Judo-land then.'

I had my own confrontation on Kinder Scout, a confused, muted exchange, more in keeping with the passive-aggressive twenty-first century. The last private landowner on the plateau was shooting in the old style, over dogs, as I arrived with my wife and young children along its southern edge one weekend. Either the warning was lacking or we had somehow missed the temporary signs that a day's shooting was taking place. I remember an out-of-breath woman approaching and glancing ahead to see a man also striding towards us, breaking a shotgun, others looking on. We had friends in common, spoke in the same manner, with the same accent, maintaining that icy politeness the privately educated rely on to indicate they despise someone. He told me of the importance of grouse shooting to the rural economy and that we must continue our walk below the plateau's edge, out of his line of fire. I knew the ground, knew how rough it was and how long it would take, especially with small children, and considered how best to turn him down. Perhaps I'd offer him the opportunity to shoot me in the back. Then I glanced behind me and saw my wife and daughter crouching on the ground, in terror at the sight and noise of shotguns. So down we went. It was like being ordered round the back of Abney Hall. Struggling through the heather, weighed down by humiliation, I caught the musty scent of the 1930s on the breeze.

When old James Watts died in 1926, his son James inherited the estate. A childhood at Abney Hall, staring at all that cloying Pugin, and an Oxford degree furnished him with a very different outlook to his grandfather's, the weaver made good. The new James was solid, quiet and hugely wealthy, a safe bet for his sparky young wife, Margaret Frary Miller. She was known as 'Madge', and then 'Aunt Punkie' in her old age, when she took to dressing up. Her sister Agatha Christie was, in the 1920s, making her reputation. The world of James Watts, his houses and friends, their brittle, moneyed self-absorption, would make regular appearances in her novels. Christie's biographer Laura Thompson described Madge as 'magnetic, sexy, quick as a fox'. A talented writer as well, she preferred the ease of marrying a plutocrat to make her money, but the marriage curdled as the years passed. Watts was just a bit too dour. 'They are an unhappy lot at Abney, I think,' Christie wrote in 1930. Her judgement was clouded a little with sibling envy, but Christie's second husband, the archaeologist Max Mallowan, described Watts as having a 'strange respect for money as a token of man's merit'. Even so, he was kind to Agatha, wrote cheques to her feckless brother and later gave her the germ for her most famous detective novel, *The Murder of Roger Ackroyd*.

Contrast the glamour of Christie's world with the rising tide of down-at-heel young ramblers from the cities swarming over the ramparts of paradise. Living in Hayfield or on isolated farms, such anonymous crowds must have held the threat of a marauding horde on busy weekends. The law had given them time, now they needed space and were minded to take it. Reports filled the local papers of rowdy behaviour, of walls being torn down and eggs stolen from the moors. Money was tight; the British economy hadn't recovered from the Great War before the effects of the Depression were felt. Sleeping rough on walks was a necessity for many ramblers, who dossed in barns and shooting cabins. It was hardly surprising if farmers and villagers looked doubtfully at these ragged youngsters. Hayfield began to get a bit of a reputation: 'We have all heard how those awful people, the ramblers, have turned the village into a sort of Blackpool of the Peak. The newspapers tell us about it every summer; local councillors denounce the rambler generally for the misdeeds or boisterousness of a small minority; and doubtless those of you who have never been to Hayfield have made a mental note that here is a place to be avoided.' The author was being ironic, but perception is often enough, and that small minority could do real damage. Shooting cabins were easy targets for vandalism, being often empty. Four Jacks Cabin in Grindsbrook, said to have been the highest in the Peak at 600 metres, was dismantled during the war and burned as firewood. A cabin on Grindslow Knoll suffered a similar fate. Photographs of rallies at Winnats Pass above Castleton show stalwarts of the access movement, the 'fucking socialists', speaking sternly into elaborate microphones before crowds numbering thousands, patiently building a democratic battering ram to overturn the status quo. To those landowners and locals determined to resist change, they must have all looked the same.

Even among those leading the fight for access and the preservation of the countryside there were private fears about what might happen should the broad mass of people gain the right to wander at will. One of the best liked and most colourful was Phil Barnes, famous for his brown velveteen suit. An outstanding photographer, his 1934 book *Trespassers Will Be Prosecuted* was both a beautiful evocation of what was denied the British people and a distillation of the campaign to gain access to it. (His epigraph was Walt Whitman: 'O to realise space! / The plenteousness of all, that there are no bounds.') But even the great Barnes had misgivings, writing to Bert Ward: 'I am afraid I care for Kinder so much that I am perhaps taking a rather selfish view but, frankly, I would rather stay away from the hills myself and leave them to the tender mercies of the shooter and keeper, than see the delicate beauty of these cloughs vulgarised by picnic parties, as for instance the Conksbury Bridge end of the Lathkill, or the Thorpe end of the Dove are today.'

That anxiety about the outsider, about those who don't belong, or hold different values, fed into the political unease the established access movement felt about Benny Rothman's proposed trespass. It had been almost half a century since James Bryce had first introduced legislation. Progress had been made, fighting piecemeal for every threatened footpath, arguing about enclosure legislation, but it was trench warfare. The wider world had had enough of trenches. The sacrifice had been made. Where was the reward? Not footpaths here and there, but a change in the fundamental philosophy? Where was the New Jerusalem? In April 1925, the *Manchester Guardian* repeated the same argument of principle *The Spectator* had made in 1908: 'There is something wantonly perverse and profane in a society in which the rights of property can be used to defeat the emotions in which mankind has found its chief inspiration and comfort. If ever any truth lurked in the phrase the "rights of man", those rights surely include the right to climb the mountains, and the right to dream beside the sea.'

As ever, it was the young who articulated that frustration most clearly and the Kinder trespass was the most notable example. Tracing through the names and ages of those involved, it's apparent how youthful the demonstration was, the prime example being Benny himself, who wasn't yet twenty-one. There was a fear among campaigners that negative headlines about young ramblers vandalising property would be conflated with the political campaign if the trespass went ahead. A 'well-known Manchester rambling official' told the *Evening Chronicle* that 'those who organise these trespasses should take care that they do not allow themselves to be confused with hooligan elements who do wilful damage'.

Benny Rothman was at the time secretary of the Lancashire branch of the British Workers' Sports Federation. This had been set up by the National Clarion Cycling Club in 1923 and had been closely affiliated to the Labour Party. But by 1932 it had drifted left to become a wing of the Communist Party of Great Britain, with Labour setting up a new competing organisation. That tension underpinned the reaction of many in the access movement who had deep links with the Labour Party, which was minded to support access legislation. They feared that Rothman would hand the Tories a stick with which to beat them. The local Ramblers' Federation secretary wrote to the papers wholly disassociating his organisation from the proposed trespass, the indignant bristling of the old guard. Who did these people think they were?

Some of them would become celebrated and admired. Among the trespassers that day was the composer Michael Tippett, then in his communist phase, and the historian A.J.P. Taylor, then teaching at the University of Manchester, where students were threatened with expulsion if they joined the demonstration. Jimmie Miller, later known as Ewan MacColl, was also there, at sixteen a precocious activist. His song 'The Manchester Rambler' became a cultural touchstone for the outdoor movement, although it was likely written later.

For all its mythology, the history of the Kinder Mass Trespass has been laid out before; the facts, once contentious, are now more or less agreed. What the trespass meant – and means – is another matter. Benny Rothman had led a BWSF camping weekend over Easter 1932, with many members up from London. Keepers turned them back from walking on Bleaklow and the group agreed that had there been more of them they could have ignored the keepers' threats. The idea of a mass trespass was born. It was proposed for Sunday 24 April at 2 p.m., and Benny, with his marketing nous, visited the *Evening Chronicle*. Despite the opposition of rambling organisations in Manchester, Benny and his friends found that the leaflets they pushed into the hands of ramblers coming off trains from Derbyshire were welcomed.

Apart from the principle of greater access, the leaflet made other demands: against war preparations within rambling organisations, for cheaper fares and the end of petty restrictions on organised walks. The sideswipe at middle-class campaigners was coded but easy to read for working-class ramblers. 'We doubted that they wanted us on the moors any more than did the landowners,' Benny Rothman wrote in his account of the trespass.

Rothman frequently acknowledged that he and his fellow organisers were young and naïve, but if their tactics were instinctive, they wrong-footed the authorities. The police tried to serve him with an injunction to stop him travelling to Hayfield. Rothman was never at home. They waited at Hayfield train station on the Saturday to intercept him. He went there by bike. The police had no knowledge of the route the trespassers would take, because Rothman didn't choose one until the morning. Hayfield parish council had a few days earlier banned public assemblies on the village recreation ground. Benny and his friends didn't know this, but, thinking they might be trapped there before they could leave for Kinder, chose a disused quarry on the Kinder road, much closer to the mountain, to congregate. They also alerted the crowds of ramblers gathering in tea shops and elsewhere that they would meet earlier than advertised. There were around thirty police under the command of the then deputy chief constable James Garrow, but they were focused on the recreation ground and consequently found themselves trapped behind around 400 ramblers making their way along the narrow Kinder road to the quarry. Rothman was lifted on to a high promontory of rock overlooking the other ramblers. He told them the trespass was to be disciplined and non-violent, and gave instructions for how they would continue.

The group then left the quarry, a cut-price crowd, in their military cast-offs and cut-down shorts, to walk along White Brow above the still-new reservoir into William Clough. (The recalcitrance of water authorities when it came to public access would occupy campaigners as much as shooting interests, but this was one fight Benny avoided, at least for the time being.) The ramblers stuck together, shielding Benny from any danger of arrest; the ground made it difficult for the police to intervene more generally. At a blast on a whistle, the ramblers left the path, whose right of access had been so hard won thirty-six years before, and crossed William Clough, their Rubicon, moving on to the moor below Sandy Heys where gamekeepers were watching them. The distance trespassed was small, partly because some of the trespassers immediately encountered opposition. There were around twenty keepers supplementing the police presence, armed as usual with sticks, representing several local landowners. Where the trespass took place was actually owned by Stockport Water Works. The Duke of Devonshire had offered his head keeper and James Watts's head keeper John Watson was also present, overlooking the scene from the ridge of Sandy Heys. There were scuffles and one special keeper called Edward Beever, who worked for the water company, was injured, although not badly. A Sheffield newspaper showed a photograph of him sitting up being offered a glass of water by a rambler, which rather undercut the later charge of grievous bodily harm.

Benny Rothman and a group of ramblers then continued up William Clough and at or near Ashop Head met a smaller group of ramblers from Sheffield, where there had been more 'official' support from rambling organisations for the trespass than in Manchester. (That contrast continued throughout the twentieth century; there was always more appetite for trespass in Sheffield than Manchester.) There had been at least two groups that set off from Edale. One came over Edale Cross to Hayfield to join the Manchester ramblers, the other came over Kinder Low towards the Downfall. George Marshall was one of the Sheffield contingent, just one of a number of Clarion ramblers. Bert Ward himself was not present, the rumour being that his earlier injunction and civil service job made him vulnerable. Other organisations were also represented, including the Woodcraft Folk, a pacifist version of the Scouts founded by Leslie Paul and deeply influenced by Edward Carpenter. The crowd was also swelled by Manchester ramblers who had either come late or had stumbled on the trespass and offered spontaneous support. Rothman and one of the Sheffield ramblers made a speech and then the meeting dispersed.

Rothman and his Manchester group retraced their route towards Hayfield where they were intercepted by a line of police who had returned to Hayfield before the trespass took place. Five people, including Benny, were then arrested. How those men were identified is disputed: most historians and Benny Rothman say gamekeepers picked them out in the presence of police. John Watson claimed it was a plain-clothes policeman who had marched with the ramblers. Either way, gamekeepers and police had worked hand in glove, just as they had in the poaching wars.

The five were taken to a lock-up and when ramblers protested outside, moved to the police station in New Mills and held overnight. Next day they were charged with unlawful assembly and breach of the peace. They couldn't be charged with trespass because there was no such offence. A sixth man, John Anderson, was also charged with grievous bodily harm for the assault on Edward Beever, despite the keeper's relatively light injuries. None of the keepers were arrested, although they had initiated what little violence there was. Harvey Jackson, the future police officer, recalled how he and his friends were met on top of Chunal Moor leaving the trespass 'by a group of so-called keepers, more like hired thugs, who set about us with sticks and boots, gave us a savage beating then pushed us into a bed of nettles. We did not dare complain.'

There was a hearing in New Mills on 11 and 12 May and the six were committed for trial at Derby assizes on 21 July. The sixty miles from Manchester stopped defence witnesses from being called. At their trial, the six defendants discovered the charges had been altered from unlawful assembly to riotous assembly, a much more serious offence. John Anderson's charge of grievous bodily harm was reduced to actual bodily harm. The jury was hardly one of their peers, consisting of two brigadier generals, three colonels, three captains and two aldermen. On the first day, the judge, Sir Edward Acton, found Rothman and his friends in contempt for arriving back from lunch ten minutes late – they had struggled to find a cafe in an unfamiliar town and didn't have legal representation. They spent the night in the cells as punishment.

Most of the accused were Jewish and working class. Harry Mendel, for example, was the son of Russian immigrants. Tona Gillett was neither, a Manchester university student preparing for entry to Cambridge and from an affluent Quaker family. (The prosecuting counsel, fancying himself a wit, asked him about being menaced by a keeper with a pickaxe handle: 'Did you quake on this occasion?') The prosecution used the fact Gillett had in his possession a book by Lenin as part of their case.

'Isn't that the Russian gentleman?' the judge archly enquired. Acton, in his summing up, warned the jury not to allow the 'extreme views of some of the prisoners' to influence them, or that they should be 'prejudiced' by the names of some of the accused 'which sounded perhaps strange to members of the jury'. Was this a sly wink or a genuine appeal for balance? Acton came from a Liberal background. His grandfather was a noted Unitarian preacher, his father a senior editor on the *Manchester Guardian*, until he was sacked to make way for Willie Arnold, Mrs Ward's brother. Acton himself showed the family's drift towards the establishment: Uppingham, Wadham College and the Inner Temple. He thrived on the northern circuit before becoming a judge: a quiet man, solid and unspectacular but reliable. Perhaps he knew his jury well enough to be genuine in his warning. Perhaps he wanted to avoid the suggestion his court was partial.

Acton did direct that Mendel, who had avoided the camera's eye, be acquitted since there was insufficient evidence against him. The others were convicted. Anderson was given six months, Rothman four, Jud Clyne and Tona Gillett two each, while David Nussbaum got a month extra for selling the *Daily Worker*. With expensive counsel and an aura of respectability, Gillett stood out from the convicted men and the judge asked him if he was not ashamed of his actions. Gillett might have escaped a custodial sentence with an apology, but chose solidarity instead. 'No sir, I would do it again.'

The prison sentences, which were widely reported, proved a clumsy own goal by the establishment. Rather than agreeing that the courts had acted against some kind of existential threat to the British way of life, there was public outrage. Edwin Royce described 'a revulsion of feeling'. Several rallies were organised in protest, and at the Winnats Pass meeting that June the crowd swelled to 10,000. Speakers deemed too weak were heckled. The Manchester Ramblers' Federation, despite its opposition to the trespass, wrote to the home secretary asking for the sentences to be reduced. But ramblers' federations hadn't changed their mind. Many leading campaigners dismissed the trespass as either insignificant or damaging – or both. Rothman and his cohorts were mocked by experienced ramblers for their claim to have been on Kinder Scout when they'd barely left a legal path that was still some distance from the plateau. The Manchester rambler Harold Wild claimed that access negotiations with landowners ground to a halt after the trespass. Stephen Morton, a well-known Sheffield rambler, said the trespass had set the campaign back twenty years. Tom Stephenson, intimately involved in the legislation that established national parks and access after the war, wrote a history of the access movement in which he made it perfectly clear that he judged the trespass to be immaterial. Even a serious social historian like David Hey dismissed its relevance.

Rambling stalwarts were quick to observe that Benny Rothman didn't remain part of the access campaign, as though your contribution only counted if you stayed with the tribe. As it happens, Rothman spent much of the 1930s fighting fascism in Manchester, which rather lets him off the hook, and anyway, he returned to the scene in later life. In 1982, when the National Trust acquired the plateau, on the fiftieth anniversary of the trespass, Benny helped set up a committee advising the trust on recreational interests. When water privatisation threatened access nationally, he once again became an effective access and environmental campaigner.

John Watson, James Watts's gamekeeper, gave his own account in later years. In the weeks after 24 April, he said, members of the Ramblers' Federation and Rucksack Club came to 'offer their hand and apologise' for the actions of the trespassers. Like Stephenson and his friends, the idea the trespass impacted on the national parks movement or improved access was wholly wrong: 'Why this senseless and stupid affair warrants so much publicity in the papers and [on] television and a plaque fixed in the quarry to the memory of the mythical "Mass Trespass" is beyond comprehension.'

Yet here I am, like so many others before me, still turning over the events of almost ninety years ago. The trespass is still fertile ground, growing fresh and nutritious perspectives. John Watson might have found it beyond comprehension, but 1932 has stuck in the outdoor public's memory. A chief executive of the Peak District National Park has praised the trespass as being a major landmark in the park's long gestation and birth in April 1951, an idea that would be flatly contradicted by those were there at the time. The Ramblers' Association now downplays its opposition to the Kinder trespass, even though their first employee, Tom Stephenson, was dismissive. It has remained stubbornly on the horizon, emerging from the mist as a landmark to head towards. There have been anniversary events, plays, histories, poems and Ewan McColl's song, whenever it was written. The mountain itself, thanks to the trespass, has become permanently associated with the long struggle for access. Both versions of the story can't be true, so where does the truth lie?

Some of the antagonism towards the event depends on perspective. Campaigners like Stephenson, a courageous and thoughtful man who, as a conscientious objector in the Great War, spent much more time in prison than Benny Rothman, were steeped in the access movement, knew its history and spent decades in public service preparing the way for national parks. The notion that an event coming from outside that mainstream could have had a bearing on it was intolerable. But it doesn't mean it wasn't true.

That attempts to widen access in the 1930s failed had nothing to do with the Kinder trespass. Despite their best efforts, the Ramblers' Federation looked on helplessly as Arthur Creech Jones's 1939 access bill was gutted at the behest of landowners. As Phil Barnes put it: 'Our leaders were too ready to accept defeat and the necessity to compromise.'

The Kinder trespass was also viewed through the prism of the hard left-wing politics of many, although not all, of the participants, politics that were too much for some access campaigners let alone landowners, who feared the trespass was the thin end of a wedge that might lead to land nationalisation. Reform of land ownership had been a powerful Liberal idea in the late nineteenth century, an idea that gathered momentum when agricultural workers got the franchise in the Third Reform Act of 1884. The Labour Party's appeal had always been, and remains, more urban than rural, industrial labour versus capital, although the Labour chancellor Philip Snowden, admittedly more a Liberal in his economic views, put land valuation and taxation in his 1931 budget. What stuck in landowning minds was how Vladimir Lenin had nationalised land in 1917, linking the idea irrevocably with Marxism and the Soviet Union, an entity Benny Rothman admired until its collapse in 1991. The idea of nationalisation haunted landowners deep into the twentieth century and the trespass has often been portrayed as part of a wider class war, an expression of hate against landed gentry: the politics of envy.

The reality was more nuanced. Plenty of local people in Hayfield watched approvingly as police marched the ramblers out of the village, even though Hayfield had a long industrial heritage and was then working class. Their antagonism had more in common with modern tensions between rural and urban life than some kind of feudal reverence for social superiors: a resentment that their concerns and culture were being overlooked in favour of more cosmopolitan cities. At one time the cities had been full of former country-dwellers. Now they were distinct breeds, and many left in the villages didn't like urban outsiders shouting the odds. Even now, perhaps especially now in the wake of Brexit, the subject of the Kinder trespass can still reawaken those tensions, like pressing on a scar.

The wider public knew little of local opinion. They certainly didn't understand the trespassers had barely made it off a legal path; had they known about it, I doubt they would have cared. They certainly wouldn't have shared the derision this prompted among experienced walkers. All they saw was a group of people with a perfectly natural desire to go for a walk in the countryside being treated harshly by a police and criminal justice system that was often, in their experience, skewed against the common man. Chief constables recognised this point very quickly, even if some landowners did not. The principle of trespass had been firmly established as a campaigning tool for decades, even if the Ramblers' Federation had opposed the trespass on Kinder. There would be another one later that year in September when a group of Sheffield ramblers attempted to reach Abbey Brook from the Duke of Norfolk's road north-west of Sheffield. Yet its impact would be negligible in comparison.

The Abbey Brook demonstration couldn't be dismissed by the establishment as a Bolshevist plot;

it had the support of many, though not all, Sheffield Ramblers' Federation members, as well as progressive organisations from across the Left. Two hundred ramblers were faced with many more 'gamekeepers' than had been on Kinder Scout, many of them armed with heavy cudgels. There was consequently much more violence against the ramblers than on Kinder Scout, despite Abbey Brook being advertised as a non-violent protest. The Duke of Devonshire's head keeper made repeated demands from the police present that they arrest the ramblers, but the police weren't making that mistake again. Once the officer in charge had got the protestors off the Duke's property, he bid the ramblers a good day and retired. There were no arrests, and no martyrs to make a fuss about. As a consequence, very few walkers now know anything about the Abbey Brook trespass, let alone the general public, even though it revealed even more starkly the aggression and hostility ordinary people faced for simply wanting to go for a walk.

Had the Kinder trespass not been organised by working-class communists, and Jewish communists at that, it might not have provoked the same level of tension or prejudice. As a consequence it would not have made the impact it did. It was the clumsy policing of the event, and the harsh response of the criminal justice system, that gave the event its potency and longevity. But there's more to it than that. Most of the other trespasses, including that at Abbey Brook, focussed on particular paths, giving those demonstrations a kind of tactical narrowness. They appeared, to the general public, as rough and tumble between opposing groups of hobbyists, ramblers against grouse shooters in a game of British Bulldog. The principle of freedom that Bryce had articulated so clearly in his bills to Parliament was somehow lost. The Kinder trespass wasn't like that.

It was about *leaving* the path, abandoning the familiar, striking out across the moor, assuming a right to roam. By accident or design, the Kinder trespass, unlike those other events, did – and does – feel like an appeal to a wider ideal: freedom of movement.

The way Benny Rothman and his friends conceived their protest had more in common with later radical environmental organisations like Greenpeace or Friends of the Earth than other rambling groups. Rothman was able to generate media attention that caught the public's attention in a way that dry letters to the editor from bigwigs in the rambling movement hadn't, just as young protestors scaling chimneys used to do. No matter if some people were outraged: the issue was now being discussed and that was all that mattered. On top of that, the notion that the children of immigrants might try to change British culture has great potency, especially now, in an age dominated by identity politics and deep-rooted changes to the nation's sense of itself. We can say that the Kinder trespass went viral, worming its way, for a multiplicity of reasons, into the public consciousness. Many of the most influential access campaigners who worked towards the access legislation that finally passed in 2000 took inspiration from the trespass and from Benny himself. Perhaps that's why this moment in history still speaks so clearly to us. It was ahead of its time.

The air-venting chimney of the Cowburn railway tunnel, built in the late 1880s high on Rushup Moor.
The railway between Manchester and Sheffield heralded new prosperity for Edale.

Nether Tor. Dense afternoon mist sinks into the Edale Valley below Broadlee-Bank Tor.

Fair Brook waters flow off the northern slopes of Kinder Scout into the River Ashop in Woodlands Valley, thence to the North Sea via the Derwent and the Trent.

118 Kinder Scout

Between 1840 and 1851 a well-appointed gritstone cabin known as the Shooters Refectory was built below The Three Knolls, Kinderlow End. The Refectory Stone, a handsomely engraved slab, has lain face down in the debris for a hundred years.

The red grouse *(Lagopus lagopus)*, a familiar bird and a characteristic call of the Kinder moors, relies on heather and peat bog habitats to survive. Identified as threatened and requiring protection due to its declining numbers, this species was included on the UK Biodiversity Action Plan priority list in 2007.

Jacob's Ladder is an ancient track joining Edale to Hayfield. It is a familiar path for walkers gaining access to the Kinder plateau.

Steep ground above Black Ashop Moor on Kinder's northern edge provides an exciting winter scramble.

Upper House, hidden above Kinder Reservoir, was refurbished by James Watts, the son of
a wealthy Kinder landowner and Manchester draper, using edifices from a Cheshire church.

Top right: The eightieth anniversary of the Kinder Mass Trespass was celebrated in 2012 at the Moorland Centre in Edale village. Speeches were made by representatives of all interested parties, including the president of the Ramblers, Kate Ashbrook; then director-general of the National Trust, Fiona Reynolds; broadcaster and writer Mike Harding (who led the singing of Ewan MacColl's 'The Manchester Rambler') and BBC radio broadcaster Stuart Maconie.
Bottom right and left: The seventieth anniversary was held at Bowden Bridge car park in Hayfield, the site of the start of the first trespass of 1932.

The Colley family and friends with the local gamekeeper relax during a 'walk-up' shoot above Grinds Brook in Edale. Walk-up shoots are a sporting form of grouse shooting where no beaters are employed to flush out the grouse.

Details from a grouse shoot around the skyline of Grinds Brook.
Top left: grouse bracelet; *top right:* Richard Colley (left), landowner Tom Noel (centre) and gamekeeper Shane Townsend (right); *bottom left:* beneath Ringing Roger; *bottom right:* award-winning gun dog Roy.

The abandoned Lower Ashop Clough shooting cabin.

Chris Harding pounding the miles across the tortuous snow-filled peat hags of the headwaters of Fairbrook Naze.

The top of Sandy Heys ridge above Kinder Reservoir is a spectacular vantage point for viewing the entire western aspect of Kinder Scout.

Kinder landscapes. *Top left:* Crowden Tower; *top right:* Beneath Jacob's Ladder; *bottom left:* cairn above Rowland Cote Moor; *bottom right:* finale on Kinderlow End.

The precipice of Kinder Downfall.

A pre-restoration ascent of the trig point at 590 metres between Blackden Brook and Oller Brook, one of three trigs on the Kinder plateau. Robin and Jodie Beatty clinging on.

Top left: Alice and Robert Helliwell, Upper Booth Farm; *top right:* Robin Wood, master woodturner and craftsman; *bottom left:* Gordon Miller, who developed the Peak Park Ranger Service for over forty years and went on to found the International Ranger Federation; *bottom right:* Andy Evans with Meg and Smudge at Kinder Downfall.
Opposite: The annual New Year's Eve celebrations on Lantern Pike above Hayfield. Every fell runner carries a fiery torch to the summit bonfire. Here, Andy Howie brandishes the first flame.

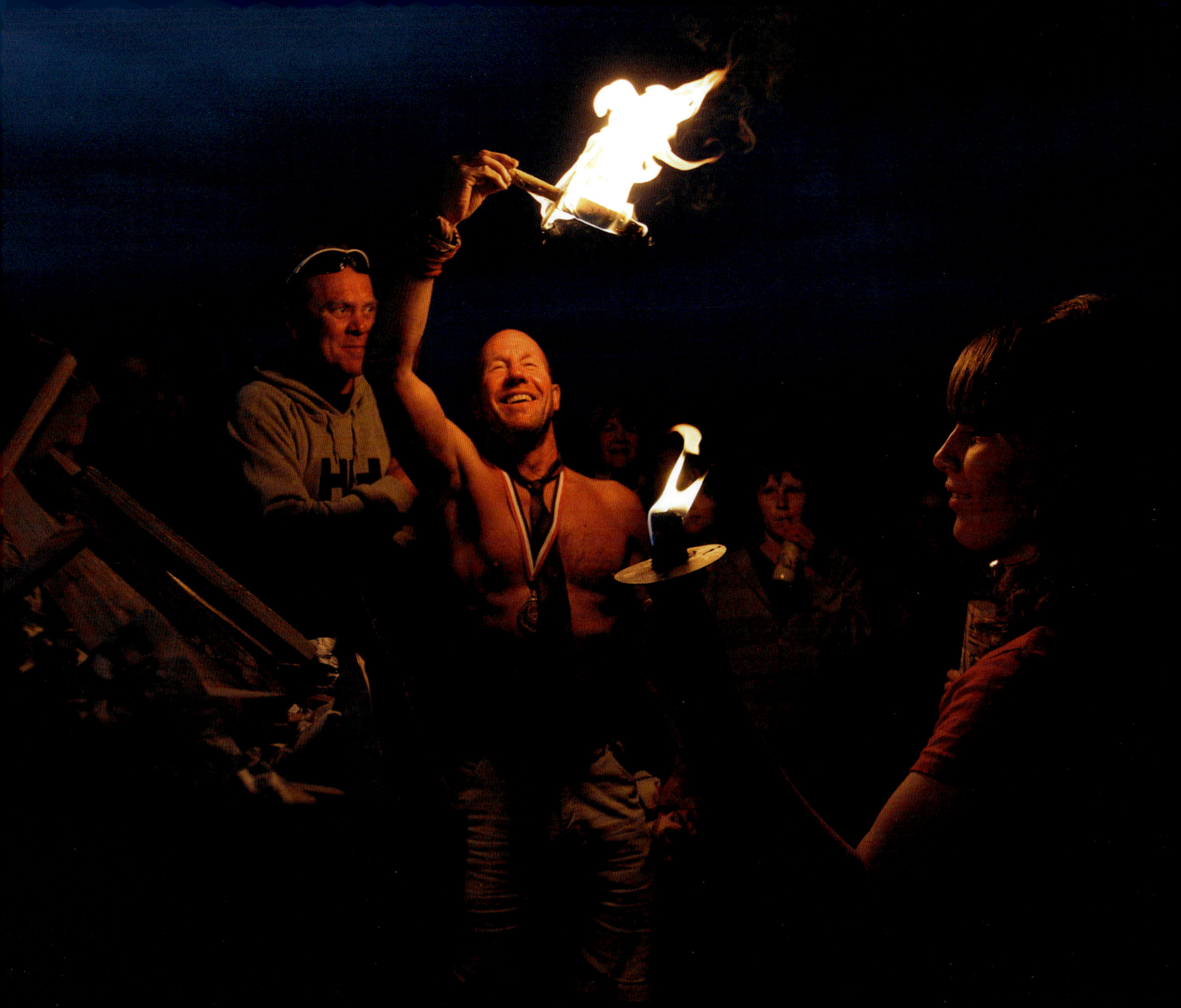

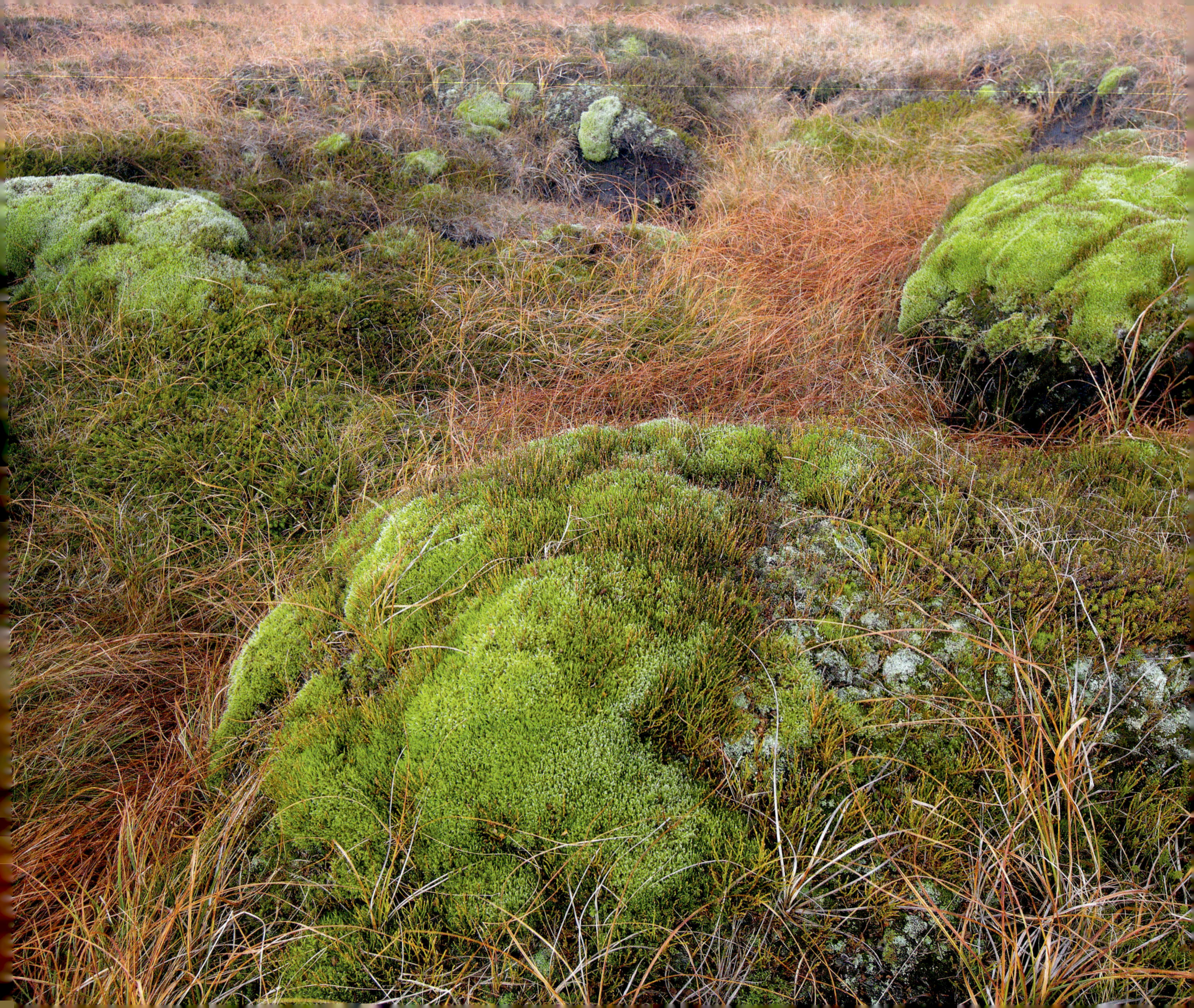

Moss

I am on dangerous ground. Down from the moors I'm sitting in a lecture hall in central Manchester. I have nothing against university buildings. This one is generically institutional, but that's fine. The issue is being in a crowd of people who know a great deal about subjects I'm interested in but know far less about than I would like. When you start stitching expertise together, into a sort of epistemological patchwork quilt, you get a fleeting glimpse of the vast scale and complexity of human knowledge, and how little of it you have fully understood. That can feel dizzying, even dispiriting. It's why people delight in experts being wrong; it's an excuse to trust our instincts.

Today's subject is moorland ecology. The moors are a world I profess to love but how much do I really understand them? At the lectern in the conference hall, ecologist Richard Lindsay is giving an overview of the importance of peat, not just in the southern Pennines, which is the subject of today's gathering, but around the world. Globally, peat holds more than three times the carbon that rainforests do and is the largest carbon store in Britain. Against the backdrop of climate change, that makes peat and the condition of peat mires and bogs of immense significance. Yet they rarely feature in the public's awareness of the challenges the world's environment is facing. Black, squidgy peat is a hard sell to the media when you've got polar bears and collapsing glaciers to look at. We don't have the attention span for our own survival.

Lindsay moves on to the ecology of bryophytes, and in particular sphagnum moss, and those species that form the basis of peat. When moss dies, and is soaked in water, it doesn't decompose, but instead provides material for the formation of peat bogs. After the end of the last ice age, 12,000 years ago, sphagnum began to form, but was checked by the growth of dense forests at lower altitudes, and above around 500 metres by birch and hazel scrub, and alpine plants. With the arrival of humans, the High Peak lost much of its tree cover; hunters burned clearings to attract game and sphagnum moss took over again on higher ground, thriving in the wet cloud that often spreads over Kinder like a blanket. While the slopes of Kinder, once wooded, became pasture, the high plateau became a bog. The archaeological record shows Kinder's plateau saw much more human activity in the Mesolithic and early Neolithic than later on. Having exploited what was available, we moved on to new ways of making a living. We're still doing it.

Over thousands of years the peat bogs deepened and compressed to form carbon-rich humus that burns very well if you can dry it out. With timber a rare commodity, and often owned and controlled by elites, religious or temporal, communities on Kinder Scout often relied on peat for fuel, cutting turfs and dragging them down from the moor on sleds. You can see the tracks the sleds gouged in the hillside over the centuries, like the holloway in Grindsbrook still known as Sled Road. Edale in the medieval era would have been suffused with the sweet, tangy aroma of peat smoke that speaks more of western Ireland than Derbyshire.

Opposite: Cushions of the moss and lichens growing through ancient tussocks of heather and bilberry are scattered across the plateau of the Fairbrook Naze promontory. Between the moss hummocks, the common cotton grass dominates the vegetation on this part of the acid upland landscape.

Like the packhorse trains, peat cutting ended with the construction of the turnpikes and railways; coal was cheap and didn't require the effort cutting turfs did. Acts of enclosure also deprived a few Derbyshire farming communities of their rights of 'turbary', the right to cut peat on what had been common land. Perhaps it's best peat fires are left in the past; burning it releases more carbon than coal, even though it has never been classified as a fossil fuel. Peat is still burned in power stations in several European countries.

Richard Lindsay is now describing sphagnum's elegant cell structure, a matrix of empty spaces, key to its unique qualities but also its fatal weakness. Its leaf has evolved to store and release water, and in death, the holes that permeate its cell structure matched with the surface tension of water contrive to keep it wet. This extreme absorbency allows sphagnum to draw water from the clouds that typically obscure Kinder Scout, vegetation intercepting air moisture, a process known to science by the gothic phrase 'occult precipitation'. It also explains why sphagnum itself, rather than peat, its sticky black corpse, has also proved a useful commodity throughout human history. Surgeons used it to staunch wounds in 1914, just as Irish warriors had in 1014 at the battle of Clontarf. Native American mothers once carried their infants in sphagnum nappies; Laplanders would line an infant's cot with sphagnum, and change it in the morning. The Vikings wrapped fish in it. These days it's been relegated to hanging baskets.

Drying sphagnum takes a concerted effort because when wet, ninety-eight per cent of its weight is water. That's more than milk. When you imagine a peat bog spread over an area miles square, you can appreciate its impact on a mountain's hydrology,

which is why water companies are represented at this conference. They are investing millions in both research and restoration of peat bogs, because bogs act as a giant sponge storing water and because bogs in the southern Pennines are rapidly falling to pieces, dumping peat into the water supply that has to be removed, at great expense, before we drink it.

When I first began writing about peat, many years ago, I called Richard Lindsay for an interview. My subject wasn't Kinder Scout but the peat under rainforests in Indonesia that was burning out of control after trees were cleared to grow palm oil. Smog from these fires blights cities in South East Asia, and the problem has exacerbated climate change; as much as five per cent of all human carbon emissions have come from draining and burning peat. In trying to explain the function of a healthy bog, Lindsay brought the subject round to the southern Pennines, since this was a landscape I knew well he could use for an example. The picture he drew was of a landscape devastated by pollution, in many areas biologically ravaged and even destroyed. It sounded, in his description, to be a hateful place. I felt suddenly disappointed. I had taken this place at face value, spent much of my life here. I believed the evocative descriptions I read in books. It dawned on me I had as little idea of what Derbyshire had been like in the past as I had of what it might be in the future, as though the landscape of Kinder was some timeless precious artefact at my disposal. I had fallen for somewhere that turned out to be raddled and broken: what did that imply for my relationship with landscape? Like I said, dangerous ground.

John Hillaby, crossing Kinder in 1967, understood this very well. Although he started his working life on local newspapers straight from school, he soon gravitated towards science writing. One obituarist wrote:

'He was passionate about the natural world and thrilled to its diversity.' His dismissal of the southern Pennines as 'depressing' was one thing. These judgements are so often a matter of taste, and come down to preconceptions. Lots of people believe landscapes beautiful or not because they grow up in a culture that deems them so. And anyway, Hillaby was barely there and doubted he'd ever go back. But what he had to say about Kinder's natural world, as somewhere sunk in 'biological penury', was more disquieting, echoing what Richard Lindsay had told me.

'From the botanical point of view,' he wrote, 'they are examples of land at the end of its tether. All the life has been drained off or burnt out, leaving behind only the acid peat. You can find nothing like them anywhere else in Europe. Here is the end-product of what botanists call a succession. The ancient woodlands that flourished after the ice melted degenerated into boggy patches of land, wet certainly, but rich in flowers. But as a result of burning, tree felling and overgrazing the land became more progressively sour. It lost its capacity to sustain more than a handful of plants, such as the bilberry, the mosses and the liverworts. On the summit of Kinder, even the bilberry has gone. The heavily-dissected peat is bare. The faint cheep of pipits sounds like the last ticks of a clock that has almost run down.'

For Hillaby, the southern Pennines had become no more than catchment grounds, whose bleak reservoirs reminded him 'of moulds into which molten metal has been poured. If Longdendale were turned upside down it would leave, you would imagine, a mountain of solid silver.' Beyond that, the High Peak was barren, 'the pasturage scanty, the moors acid and ecologically dead'. The mountain I'd grown up on was a hollow, defeated place, used up.

In the conference hall in Manchester, Hillaby's dismal sketch of the southern Pennines' ecological implosion is being fleshed out by a succession of ecologists and environmental consultants. Calculating the cumulative effect of acid rain on the western flank of the southern Pennines, downwind of the cotton mills and other coal-burning industries, one speaker concludes that a litre of concentrated sulphuric acid fell on each square metre of moorland. Another points out that while lemon juice has a pH value of 2.4, the denuded peat on the west side of Kinder Scout has a value of 2, making it more acidic. Sphagnum moss, the key species on a peat bog, needs soil with a pH value of 3.4 or 3.5. With a cell structure peculiarly vulnerable to air pollution, it's hardly surprising the peat-forming sphagnum species collapsed.

With no new peat being formed, the forces of erosion got to work on Kinder Scout's peat bogs, and the rest of the southern Pennines. Denuded peat was broken up by frost and washed into the spreading network of groughs, stripping the mountain of its topsoil at the rate of several centimetres a year. The white trig point on the north-west corner of Kinder's plateau has been left high and dry on an ebbing black tide, like rusting trawlers on the lost shores of the Aral Sea, an unanswerable gauge of what has been and what is now lost. As the peat is drained and dries out in the summer months, it becomes exposed to oxygen, microbes go to work, carbon oxidises and joins the other greenhouse gases we are busily pumping into the sky. Dried peat is also vulnerable to wildfires, which burn deep within peat hags and are consequently as difficult to put out on Kinder Scout as they are in Indonesia. One such fire, in September 1976, burned a metre of peat from parts of the bog. Had a similar catastrophe robbed the Peak District of an equivalent amount of deciduous forest, its impact on the public would have been emotionally wrenching. But we're not evolved to see the natural world objectively. We're built to see what we know, and these days, when it comes to nature, for most of us, that's not so much.

Growing up in his Salford slum, Robert Roberts was told by his mother about a lost forest of ghostly trees, a 'poisoned wood', and he set off to look for it, roaming Kersal Moor, now mostly suburbs, searching in vain for clues. Years later, reading *Essays and Sketches*, by Abraham Stansfield, one of that breed of working-class Lancashire naturalists Elizabeth Gaskell celebrated in her first novel *Mary Barton*, Roberts found the source of his mother's legend. In a woodland near Kersal Moor, on the edge of the borough, Stansfield reported how 'noxious vapours from Manchester and Salford attacked the trees, mostly full-grown beech. Twelve hundred giants of the forest had to fall. Every year they are dying in great numbers.' He had the melancholy task of condemning the decaying specimens. That kind of impact from the Industrial Revolution is easy to get our heads around.

As Roberts put it, Manchester was 'the first colossus born of a force that was changing the face of the world', but it was soon the same story on the other side of the High Peak. A report in the late nineteenth century on air pollution counted around 1,800 chimneys in Sheffield discharging smoke from metal furnaces and steam boilers, and that ignored smaller furnaces and domestic fires. The Yorkshire-born journalist and crime novelist Joseph Smith Fletcher captured Sheffield's squalid environmental collapse at its smoggy worst in his 1899 book *A Picturesque History of Yorkshire*: 'The aspect of the northern fringe of Sheffield on such a day is terrifying, the black heaps of refuse, the rows of cheerless-looking houses, the thousand and one signs of grinding industrial life, the inky waters of river and canal, the general darkness and dirt of the whole scene serves but to create feelings of repugnance and even horror.'

The poisoned air and toxic water, the dislocation from villages, the snapping of old social bonds could dehumanise Sheffield's working poor, shrinking them psychologically as well as physically. Reading crime reports from the mid-nineteenth century, you see in Sheffield the kinds of predatory sexual crimes that made headlines in Delhi a century and a half later, and for similar reasons: rural populations moving to the city, young men growing up with almost no education and not enough social structures to check violent impulses. J.C. Symons was the government commissioner who contributed material on Sheffield for *The Physical and Moral Condition of the Children and Young Persons Employed in Mines and Manufactures*, published in 1843, an important influence on Friedrich Engels: 'The child instinctively feels that it is used as a mere bit of machinery,' he concluded, after detailing a world of family breakdown, child labour, young teenage drinking, gambling and sex in the street. 'Juvenile prostitution is exceedingly common,' he reported, while reassuring nervous readers that there were 'many well conducted families' in the city.

'Very few questioned the right of industry to ruin our health and environment,' Robert Roberts wrote, 'in pursuit of profit the poor were expendable.' Edward Carpenter was among the first to link the need for access to nature with the idea of conserving landscapes, the latter idea gaining momentum from the national park movement in America. The Labour Party was built around the principle of defending the rights of labour, but nature, the wider environment beyond the provision of safe water and air people could breathe, was never taken up as an issue of social justice in the same way that health and education were, or even access to the countryside. Like Abraham Stansfield walking through his poisoned forest, the naked peat hags melting in front of our eyes reveal an unspoken pact irrespective of political allegiance: we'll keep taking because most of us feel that everything is not enough. If the modern world, like Dorian Gray, kept a self-portrait in the attic, it would look a lot like Kinder Scout.

It would be a mistake, in the story of this stubby little hill, to assume all its ills can be laid at the door of the Industrial Revolution. Sitting in Derbyshire's public record office, the parish accounts of the village of Hope spool past me on a brightly lit screen. From the late seventeenth century onwards, different record keepers come and go. Some have pedantic, crabbed handwriting, meticulous and accurate. Others are more slapdash, rushing through an unwelcome chore. Sometimes the accountant begins in earnest and finishes his final entry in a rush, glad to be free of it. The men – always men of course – who hold parish posts are drawn from familiar Derbyshire names: Eyre, Bocking, Greaves.

There are payments to bell-ringers and clock-winders, timber merchants and booksellers, for smithy work, for a silk mill in Derby, for laundry, 'for loading stone on Abney Moor' in 1691. A fascinating matrix emerges linking different building projects, church walls for example, to long-abandoned quarries around the High Peak that I've come across over the years. (This particular church wall was built by Joseph Eyre in 1702 for three pounds and seven shillings.) There are oblique hints of the outside world, of affairs of state, of wars in faraway places.

In 1759, for example, there's a lot of maintenance on church bells, this being Britain's *annus mirabilis*, which started with fears of a French invasion but ended in national celebration following victories all over the world, in North America, the Caribbean, India and Europe. Horace Walpole claimed, 'Our bells are worn threadbare with ringing for victories'. The song 'Heart of Oak' was written in celebration, the British liking trees best when they're turned into warships.

War of another kind is recorded in more detail in Hope's parish record: the war on vermin, as enacted under what are known as the Tudor vermin laws, the first being the Preservation of Grain Act 1532, the start of an official campaign against wildlife, prompted by poor harvests, that would last for two centuries and see the near-eradication of all sorts of species that we now regard as treasures to be protected. Preservation of crops was only part of the motivation. Folklore was another. Legend held that hedgehogs, known also as urchins, suckled milk from cows at night. Other targets included familiar Derbyshire species like dippers and kingfishers. Nationally, the red kite was almost eradicated.

Bounties for this extermination were paid out by parishes, and Hope was no exception. In 1687 for example, a record is made of a payment for twenty-five raven heads of one pound, one shilling and a penny, almost a shilling a piece. Another one pound, fourteen shillings and seven pence was paid for 205 'urchin' heads. The following year there's another entry for seventeen raven heads. The biggest bounties were for foxes, unsurprisingly. In 1704 the parish paid out one pound, thirteen shillings and four pence for 'four old foxes and two fox cubs'. Given average agricultural wages in the Midlands were around a shilling a day, extermination was lucrative work.

There's little remarkable about these records. It was a pattern broadly repeated across the country. And the records from this period are no historical aberration. They form part of a continuum, a ceaseless, sustained effort to take economic advantage of whatever the natural world has to offer, and the eradication of anything that stands in the way.

We are in love with our rural past: the centuries of patient effort, the near-forgotten lexicon of a more rooted way of being. The industrial culture of shepherds is venerated – and subsidised – in ways that are unthinkable for steelworkers or shipbuilders. We also have an apparently insatiable appetite for nature as entertainment. But the history of nature in Britain has been one of inexorable decline more or less since we arrived, a process that even national park status has failed to address properly. Our treasured landscapes capture a rich human story but an impoverished natural one. And the two are inextricably linked.

Just as Hope's parish accounts record the persecution of foxes and ravens, urchins and moles, earlier documents capture a still-richer ecosystem on the brink of disappearing from Kinder Scout. Royal expenditure records in the pipe rolls of Henry II contain, for the financial year ending 1161, a supplementary payment of twenty-five shillings to wolf hunters in the High Peak. Such was their reputation that a few years later they were paid expenses to travel to Normandy to get rid of wolves there. The earliest reference we have of Kinder as a surname is an application from one Philota de Kender to kill wolves and wildcats within the Peak Forest. Wolves around Kinder were present well into the thirteenth century; there are records of a wolf killing a horse in Edale in the 1250s. While the High Peak remained royal hunting ground, there was still space for wolves, but as the punitive forest laws were relaxed and sheep farming took over, that was that. No one on the margins of survival would tolerate another apex predator. You can still find wolves in the Peak District, but only in art: the carved relief on the Saxon font at Ilam church, recording the death of St Bertram's young Irish wife and their infant. We like cultural depictions of wolves, not so much the reality.

Sheep changed nature and changed the landscape, creating the sharp visible divide between open moorland and enclosed pasture, called 'intake', that characterises the charm of Edale. Some of these intakes failed; the land was simply too poor to be worthwhile. Some of these walled enclosures represent the tension between landowners and tenants taking the chance to expand their tenure at the expense of common land. It was an exercise in testing the margins, of the law and the environment. But the expansion of sheep farming meant the end of natural regeneration of forest cover, confirming the High Peak's bald appearance. A Czech friend visiting local rock climber Adam Long, driving from Ringinglow to Stanage Edge, looked out across the moors and said: 'What do you people have against trees?' (On the other hand, the Peak hasn't suffered so very badly from tax-break conifer plantations. The grouse shooting lobby often claims credit for this, but it was more reform of the tax regime in the late 1980s by the chain-smoking free-marketeer Nicholas Ridley.)

The surge in sheep farming had deeper systemic consequences. Damage to the bog on top of Kinder Scout predated industrialisation. In 1300, sphagnum dominated the High Peak. But sheep don't eat moss, and so to improve grazing, the same influx of farmers that finished off the wolf began to burn the moors; parts of the Upper Derwent were still being burned for grazing in the twentieth century. This sparked profound changes in the ecosystem. Burning increases nutrients in the short term. There was more grass and heather for sheep to graze. But burning creates a bituminous skin on peat, and water simply runs off it. The bog began to crack and fissure; the gullying that so offended writers like Hillaby was underway by the late sixteenth century, exacerbated by the hard winters and bitter frosts of the little ice age that continued until the early 1800s. As the gullying spread, like fractures on a car windscreen, the peat dried out more, hastening the process. Then came industry.

There is now cause for optimism. A concerted effort between all sorts of agencies has begun to patch up the leaking hulk of Kinder Scout, helicopters flying in materials like missions of mercy to the front line of a war to block the gullies and staunch the wounds. The species of moss stripped from the moors, leaving the hags dissolving blackly in the rain, are being replanted. Water coming off the plateau is slowly clearing. Native tree species are being planted on Kinder's skirts, another piece in a jigsaw of restoration that will help reduce the threat of flood. It's encouraging where our ingenuity can take us. Even so, the toxic inheritance of 200 years of industrialisation still poisons the substrate, still claws at recovery.

The chimneys on the horizon marked a step change in Kinder's history; it wasn't just an acceleration of consumption but a shift in perspective. You can see this shift from Hollins Cross, on the ridge that divides Edale from the Hope Valley, a vantage point as familiar to Neolithic hunters as it was to the Romans and as it is to us. It was also a coffin route, whereby the dead of Edale were brought to the Hope Valley for burial. Drag your eyes away from the ruggedly indented shore of Kinder's southern rim and turn a half circle. In front of you is the Hope Valley, with the medieval village of Castleton on the right, overlooked by Peveril Castle, first known as Peak Castle, dating back to the late eleventh century, and the towering, alien chimney of Hope's cement works with the vast quarry that feeds it sprawling behind.

The tourists come to see Peveril, safely located in the sentimental past, a crumbling, romantic ruin perched with a kind of elegant geomantic aesthetic on a plug of rock, folded into the dale above, overlooking the village. Never mind that it was for a time the locus of power in the High Peak for an authoritarian and punitive system of law and government. It's picturesque. The Hope cement works, a moment of abject planning failure in the mid-twentieth century, does at least provide jobs for the people of Bradwell, arresting the slow drift of the High Peak in the direction of commuter belt. It's more the scale of the contrast that is revealing. A tiny little castle running a large chunk of northern England on one side, and nine centuries later, a vast structure producing a million and a half tonnes of cement each year, which is in fact barely 0.03 per cent of world cement manufacture. That's quite a shift in humanity's metabolism.

The presence of such a large industrial plant in the middle of a national park is still a contentious issue. There are those who see the tall chimney as an iconic landmark itself; on a day when mist settles in the valley, its tallness piercing the white has an ethereal beauty. But its presence does have a distorting impact on the landscape, simply because of its scale and the rock it is gobbling up. When permission was given to expand the site, after a two-day public enquiry in April 1948, the landscape campaigner Edgar Morton said: 'Posterity is certain to view such a materialistic decision as an act of pure expediency on the part of a ministry with apparently no conception of the vast potential resources of raw materials available for cement manufacture in the country.' For Morton, 'the preservation of the Peak as an area of scenic value, whose rural nature should be permanently safeguarded and its farming encouraged, was of equal importance'.

It could have been worse. Failed planning applications rarely stick in the public's memory, but contemplating what people wanted to do in the High Peak before the national park was established in 1951 is a sobering reminder of the fragility of these besieged landscapes. Permission was granted in March 1937 to prospect for oil in Edale and Ashop Dale, as well as the Eastern Edges above Sheffield. Preliminary drilling was done at Barber Booth, although happily it became clear there was no oil before too much damage was done. (In the 1980s, a company called Moray Petroleum was given permission to try once more, again with no success. These surveys may prove useful to those who wish to frack natural gas under the park.)

Worse, much worse, was to follow. In 1939 Sheffield steelmaker Brown Bayley announced plans for a works to be built in Edale on land adjoining the valley's disused cotton mill, built in the late eighteenth century. The cotton had been brought by packhorse over Edale Cross; the workers, mostly women, walked the path each day from Castleton, a cottage industry in comparison. Planning authorities in Chapel-en-le-Frith, believing that a steelworks in Edale was just what the government wanted, gave permission, prompting an impassioned defence of the valley from what was then called the Council for the Preservation of Rural England, backed by prominent ramblers whose campaigning nous had been sharpened by their long and frustrating battle for access. There were letters in *The Times* and resolutions against it from 200 MPs as well as Sheffield City Council, which regarded itself as the best location for any new steelworks, thank you very much.

The CPRE was in the 1930s and 1940s at the heart of the growing campaign for national parks; its Sheffield branch, which predated the national organisation, saw the Edale steelworks as 'the ruin of the heart of the Peak, and thereby the Peak itself. It would shatter all hopes of a National Park, and virtually undo the fourteen years' efforts of the Branch.' The Sheffield branch was led by Ethel Haythornthwaite, an indefatigable trailblazer in conservation, recently married to the branch's new assistant secretary, architect and town planner Gerald Haythornthwaite. Together they formed one of the most effective and enduring partnerships in British conservation history. They oversaw and engineered the purchase of the Longshaw Estate and Blacka Moor on the west side of Sheffield, securing some of the finest landscapes within walking distance of a major city. They expended immense effort educating the public about dropping litter. At the Cutlers' Hall in Sheffield, they organised an exhibition called 'Save the Countryside', with lantern slides by Clough Williams-Ellis and a glass case containing 'What Sheffield left at Stanage last Bank Holiday'. Perhaps someone should do that again.

In 1932, the Sheffield branch published a hugely influential polemic, *The Threat to the Peak*, beautifully illustrated by the photographer and access campaigner Phil Barnes, laying out in clear detail the case for conservation not just of landscapes but architecture and nature too. The book had an introduction from the historian George Trevelyan, who had carried the heavy plaque commemorating Siegfried Herford and the other members of the Fell & Rock killed in the war up Great Gable: 'The tide of public opinion is moving with great rapidity in the direction of a new demand for the preservation of natural beauty. The young, on average, feel it more keenly than the old. Outrages cheerfully perpetrated twenty years ago "and nothing said," would be impossible today. Outrages possible today will be impossible twenty years hence. The future is on our side in no small degree, if we can hold the fort for another generation.'

Trevelyan was right. If the battle was won by a small number of heroic activists, their campaign drew on a sometimes ill-defined but deep-felt public attitude that Britain's finest landscapes were important to the nation's sense of itself, that what they offered, a sense of space and natural beauty, was worth defending, and that urban populations should have the right to access those places. England's national parks were formulated along these lines. The immediate problem was addressed. The incoming tide of development was turned back. Conservation was enshrined in law. Improved access was agreed, if not wholly won. But the degradation over thousands of years of the High Peak's environment was left, like a high-water mark, the few remaining fragments of complexity pushed to the margins. Nature was safeguarded in the legislation establishing the national parks, but, in an era before Rachel Carson's *Silent Spring*, it didn't have the same radical edge as other aspects of the bill. The notion of restoring a landscape, of recreating biodiversity, wasn't yet on the agenda.

In the course of my life on Kinder Scout there have been some powerful encounters with the natural world, moments when I was drawn wholly inside nature's dimension. Watching a peregrine stooping over Featherbed Moss as I crossed boggy ground below the crest of the moor, its yellow legs flashing in a shaft of sunlight piercing broken clouds. One winter's day, lying in deep snow on a flattening of ground, a 'bench', on the hillside above a clough on Kinder's southern flank, peering around a gritstone boulder at half a dozen mountain hares a few feet away scraping at the snow to reach the white grass below. It was dusk, the sky fading to mauve, the white of the snow deepening to indigo on the fringes of my vision. I was lying alongside John Beatty, and he widened his eyes when I glanced at him, as if to say: 'now, here is something'.

I recall too a day in early January, raw, the sky hard and grey, a fierce wind, and above our heads three dozen ravens tumbling against it, 'copping off' as John put it, each delighting in their flight, and delighting their partner. On the hillside above Glossop, driving up the Snake, I look hopefully each spring for lapwings looping above the enclosed fields of pasture, on their broad, finger-tipped wings. In summer, tying up the laces of my climbing shoes under the crags above Grinds Brook, I watched a lizard, mocking my ambitions, flowing across blank gritstone like mercury. Best of all, on the boggier ground off Kinder's northern rim, I remember almost stepping on a curlew, which thrummed into the air, wings blurring with speed, surprisingly large set against its bubbling song, before the wings were stilled, pinned out as she turned her head from side to side, tracing a deliberate arc with her hooped bill, in Ted Hughes's phrase 'a wet-footed god of the horizons'.

Despite these glimpses of treasure, there is nothing exceptional in the Dark Peak's wildlife. It contributes little in the hard fight to retain what we can of the planet's rich biodiversity, against the tide of all those people wanting stuff: all those cement factories, all those steelworks. Walking one day on Derwent Moors with a Peak District zoologist who spends his working life as a consultant to environment ministries around the world, I asked him what he thought of the park's nature conservation status. He drew his arm across the horizon in a broad arc. 'I think,' he said, 'that if you lost all this, there's one species of moth that would disappear from Britain for good.' Much of the Peak District is a beautiful factory floor, the web of life swept to the corners or down the cracks where it clings on. The place nature holds in the Peak is reflected in how the International Union for Conservation of Nature categorises Britain's national parks: under category five of its designated areas, 'a protected area managed mainly for landscape/seascape protection and recreation'. That is the least natural of the IUCN's six designations for protected areas.

This is often a surprise for those members of the public who aren't riveted by the subject of conservation. They assume the label 'national park' means wildlife is at some level better off inside one than outside. For conservationists who argue national parks should be reservoirs of biodiversity, it's even more disheartening. As far as the future goes, there is evidence, like Janus, pointing both ways. More hopefully, there is the patient restoration of moss and other moorland plants on Kinder's plateau and the rest of the southern Pennines, with funding from the European Union. Less hopefully, there is the parlous state of birds of prey in the Dark Peak. Kinder has a number of European conservation designations, like the Special Protection Area, created under the directive on wild birds. Such areas commit their governments to protecting the endangered birds that live there, which in the case of the Dark Peak the UK government has failed to do.

In 2012, alarmed at the stagnation or decline in numbers of three species that were named under the designation – short-eared owls, peregrine falcons and merlin – five land-management and conservation bodies, including the National Trust, the pro-shooting Moorland Association and the Peak District National Park Authority, launched the Bird of Prey Initiative to boost numbers on Kinder and elsewhere in the Dark Peak. The initiative also planned to support goshawks and encourage the return of hen harriers, birds which used to breed routinely in the High Peak until the development of driven grouse shooting, an industry that takes place within the SPA and is, like moorland anywhere, subsidised with environmental grants under the Common Agricultural Policy of the European Union. Subsidies are paid despite the practice of burning moorland to create young shoots for grouse, a method implicated in worsening flooding below grouse moors. Both environmental protection and subsidies are, of course, now up for discussion following the United Kingdom's decision to leave the EU.

The Bird of Prey Initiative ran for three years but was, even by its own estimation, a failure. At its start there were six breeding pairs of peregrines in the Dark Peak SPA. Conservationists hoped that by the end of it there might be fifteen. By 2015, despite good numbers for 2014, there were four breeding pairs, a drop of two. There were sixteen pairs of short-eared owls, when the number should have been more like twenty-five. The number of merlin actually dipped the year after the initiative started but recovered to record an increase of one by the end of the project, short of its target by eight. Goshawks were doing as badly as ever, and while a pair of hen harriers bred in 2014, they failed to do so in 2015. Although ecologists behind the initiative's report described the results as 'disappointing', they couldn't give definitive reasons for why the Dark Peak is so short of raptors. Decline in the numbers of peregrine falcons was, they said, especially baffling since they have been doing much better in limestone areas of the Peak District. The initiative's report did praise the working relationship between those doing the study and shooting interests. All parties agreed to redouble their efforts. All of them agreed they would not tolerate the persecution of birds of prey.

In February 2016, a man with a shotgun was filmed on National Trust moorland placing a model of a male hen harrier prominently above the ground and then hiding in heather nearby. His intention was clear: luring a real male so he could shoot it. When the man realised he was being watched, he removed the lure and drove off in his Land Rover parked nearby. Police interviewed local gamekeepers, but as happens so often, there was insufficient evidence to pursue enquiries. This was not the first time persecution of raptors on National Trust land in the Peak District had attracted the interest of the police. In 2010 a gamekeeper called Glenn Brown was filmed in the Upper Derwent Valley using a live pigeon as bait to trap raptors. He was convicted of seven offences under the Wildlife and Countryside Act 1981 and the Animal Welfare Act 2010. Brown appealed, but his convictions were upheld. Six years before that another gamekeeper in the Upper Derwent Valley, John Cripps, was convicted of smashing goshawk eggs. He also appealed, at some financial cost, and also lost. It was reported that when interviewed, he had claimed there were too many goshawks in the area killing too many grouse.

The National Trust leases the shooting rights on three areas of moorland on its estate in the Dark Peak but it didn't intervene after these convictions. Its tenants were left, in public at least, in peace. Yet when the image of the hen harrier lure and the man with the gun was published, it acted. The period of one of its tenancies was cut. The proximity of the failed Birds of Prey Initiative was one reason. But it's also true that the idea of the Dark Peak not being the special place for nature it should be is being challenged more and more vigorously. The conservationist Mark Avery has organised successful rallies in Edale and elsewhere for an end to the persecution of hen harriers with powerful support from television presenter Chris Packham. Most people aren't even aware of such a thing as a hen harrier, many won't much care about the parlous state of the Peak District's wildlife, but the radical edge this space has carried in the past is being sharpened again.

Star moss or haircap moss *(Polytrichum formosum)*, growing in profusion in the dank and poorly drained Snake woodlands. Filaments of spider gossamer threaded in the moss attract beads of moisture from condensation in the cold morning air.

The eroded peat hags of Kinder plateau underwent a huge restoration programme which began in 2007 with the Moors for the Future Partnership. In 2012 work started on Kinder. Sheep were excluded from the plateau by fencing. Water run-off was depleted by gully blocking. Native plant species and sphagnum mosses were reintroduced over a vast area.

The National Trust in conjunction with the Moors for the Future Partnership began work by introducing propagated sphagnum, and planting common cottongrass *(Eriophorum angustifolium)* and purple moor grass *(Molinia caerulea)* in a five-year-long project aimed at restoring the water table and stabilising the eroding peat.

The transformation of Kinder Scout plateau: from degraded peat to a habitat that will support increasing biodiversity.

The trappings of land management. For centuries the natural world has sustained enormous pressure and loss from the effects of agriculture, industry and entertainment.

Peveril Castle, one of England's earliest Norman fortifications, built in 1176 by Henry II.

Hope cement works in the Hope Valley emerges from the cold November mist.

Hawthorn or May tree *(Crataegus monogyna)* growing on the slopes of Horsehill Tor above Upper Booth, Edale. The May blossoms are pollinated by insects and develop into the red berries, a favourite winter food for migrant winter birds like fieldfares and redwings.

Top left: mountain hare leveret *(Lepus timidus); top right:* curlew *(Numenius arquata); bottom left:* ravens *(Corvus corax); bottom right:* speckled wood butterfly *(Pararge aegeria).*

Right: An impromptu partnership of conservation groups took part in a nest watch and wing-tagging operation of juvenile hen harriers in 2006, at a time when raptor persecution on active grouse moors was at its peak. *Opposite:* Wildlife presenters and conservationists Chris Packham and Mark Avery speak at a 'Hen Harrier Day' rally in the Peak, in support of biodiversity in moorland habitats.

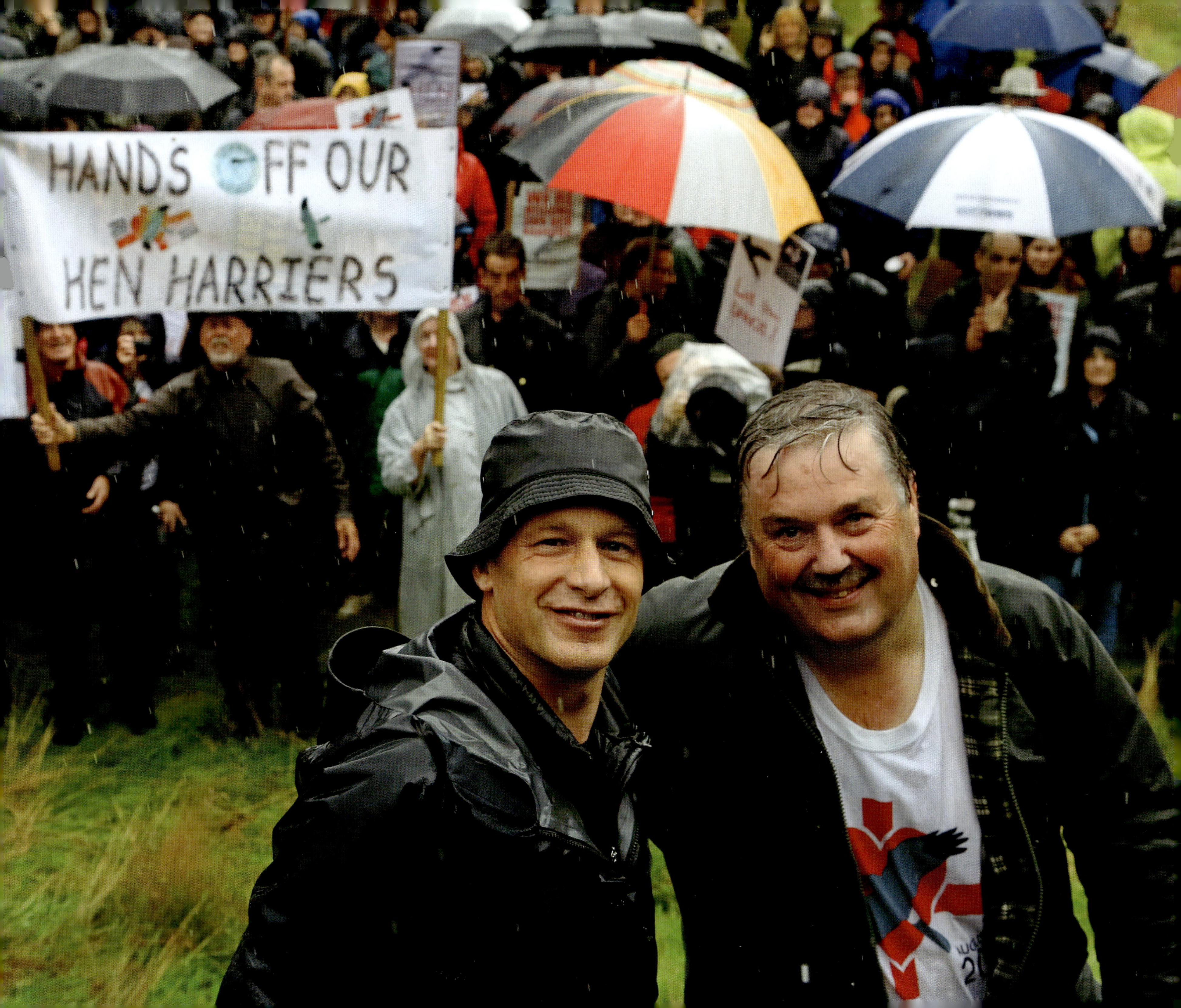
HANDS OFF OUR
HEN HARRIERS

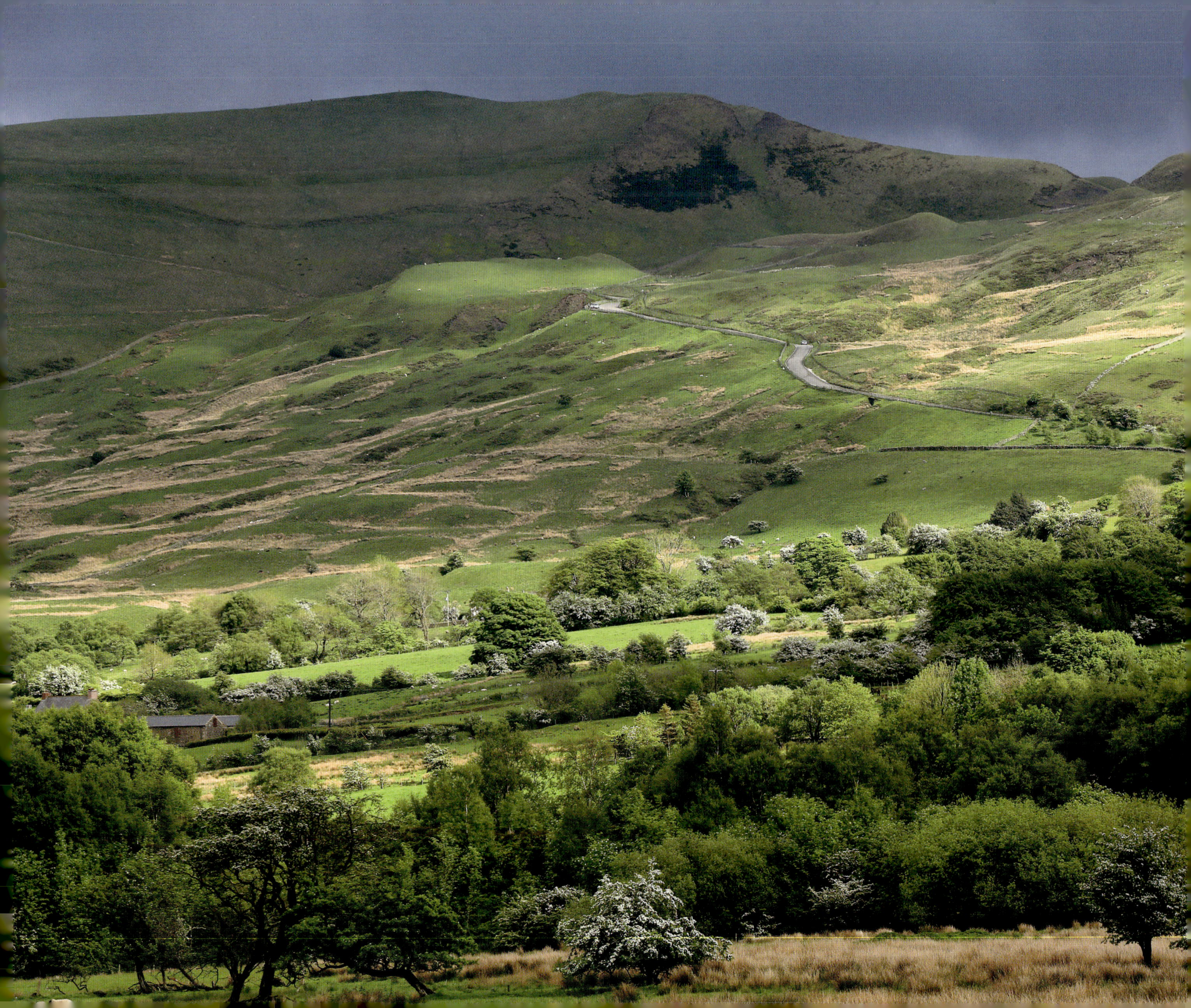

Hare

On the road up to Mam Nick, with Kinder Scout at our backs, we pulled off the road to eat our sandwiches, enjoying the view of paragliders gathered like mountain vultures over the summit of Mam Tor, soaring on the warm air of summer. After a while I noticed an older man sitting in a car ahead of us, facing the other way. He was looking out across Edale, sipping from a mug with the photograph of someone printed on it. I squinted hard but couldn't tell who it was. Neither could my wife. We talked animatedly about who it might be, and settled finally on Princess Diana. And then, having finished lunch, as we pulled out on to the road, both of us glanced across to where he was sitting, still musing on the view, still sipping from the mug. The person in the picture was himself.

It wasn't just the image that struck me: presumably the mug was a gift from his grandchildren. It was that we had both been so engaged in solving the mystery of who it might be, speculating about who an older man would put on a cup, theorising about what was in the mind of someone we had never met. This speculation, this making up of stories, this projection of possible truths is a deeply human habit, a defining one even. It makes us adroit, aware of change and its possibilities, even if we don't always like it. It makes us an accommodating species, able to flip our understanding of the world around to suit ourselves.

There was a good example overhead, in the shape of the paragliders. Nothing could persuade me to hang from a canopy and swoop around the sky, beyond a guarantee that I would survive. Then I'd try it, because I'm curious and wonder what it must feel like. But the mere fact of it is extraordinary: what won't we do? How far can we go? Beneath their feet was Mam Tor with its Bronze Age hill fort, its oval rampart circling the summit to enclose an area of around six hectares. This rampart varies in height and width, partly depending on the slope's angle. Where the ground was steeper, the position was easier to defend and something so tall or wide wasn't deemed necessary. At its most robust, construction involved layers of soil and clay mixed with stones and rubble, all raised to a height of three metres and a width of over five metres on a ledge dug into the slope. A retaining wall was built on the uphill side, and a much stronger one, of boulders, on the downhill, above a ditch two metres wide and marginally less deep. That's shallow for this kind of earthwork, but again, Mam Tor is a steep hill: there was no need to overdo it.

When a University of Manchester team of archaeologists, led by David Coombs, excavated the site in the 1960s, they found postholes, evidence of a palisade, although it was impossible to say whether the palisade had been built at the same time as the walls. In places, they also found a layer of turf sandwiched in the rocks of the rampart, suggesting that at some point it had been raised. Either the band that lived within its protection had an unusually cautious chief, or else they found out its shortcomings in the heat of battle. The Manchester team also excavated several of the hut platforms dug into the slope within the protection of the rampart. The huts had walls either

Opposite: Mam Tor (517 metres) and Mam Nick viewed from Upper Booth, Edale.

of turf or stone, postholes for timber, and hearths. They found bracelets made from fragile, pretty shales like those in Grinds Brook, whetstones and lots of pottery sherds that gave radiocarbon dates of a phase of occupancy starting early in the first millennium BCE. One hut gave up a fragment from a bronze axe, dated to around 600 BCE, suggesting the hill fort was still in use 500 years later. That's roughly equivalent to the gap between us and Michael Drayton, the Elizabethan poet.

There are two barrows on Mam Tor, held within this rampart. One was said by the nineteenth-century barrow-digger Thomas Bateman to have been excavated in the early part of his century, when a bronze axe was found with bones and pottery, but that's uncertain. The second has never been excavated. During the Second World War the site was partially levelled to accommodate a searchlight battery, to pick out German bombers on their way to the aircraft factories of Manchester. It is now topped by Mam Tor's trig point. Stand on top of it and look across at the south-west corner of Kinder Scout and you can see another barrow at Kinder Low, 'low' from the Anglo-Saxon *hlaw*, meaning hill. There are four such barrows on the plateau, dated roughly between 2,500 and 1,500 BCE. Taking the earlier date, when whoever left that axe on Mam Tor looked across at the barrow on Kinder, they were looking at a structure that was similar but 2,000 years older. To put it another way: there is almost as much time between the end of the Bronze Age and now as there was between the Bronze Age and the construction of Kinder's oldest barrows.

The year 2,500 BCE was towards the end of the Neolithic, but we know from stone tools and other finds that hunting parties were moving across Kinder during the Mesolithic, on Chunal Moor for example, where Lieutenant Houpt crashed his plane. In fact, during this period, there were more people on Kinder than there were later on, cutting timber, hunting game, passing through. Small bands, perhaps family groups, roaming across the landscape taking what they needed, their right to do so negotiated with similar groups also in the area, people, archaeologists suggest, they most likely only met infrequently at ritual gatherings.

It's a commonly held belief that our passion for mountains is a modern obsession, acquired after our material situation was secured, part of the Romantic fashion for the sublime. Until then, the myth runs, mountains were hateful places, to be avoided, just as Daniel Defoe wrote. But for most of human history and prehistory that simply wasn't true. The Peak is soaked in archaeological reminders that for millennia we had a deep connection to high places, to nature, to plants and creatures. We needed that connection to survive, to orientate ourselves in a hostile environment, to gather enough calories for our children. That relationship lasted much longer than many suppose, deep into the second millennium. Pay close attention to medieval graffiti scratched on old shepherd's shelters in wild corners of the High Peak, and you'll find symbols chipped into the gritstone invoking the Virgin Mary, symbols best defined as apotropaic, for warding off evil, the response of ordinary working people to the hazards they faced in the hills, a place where the natural could become the supernatural with a simple change in the weather. It's a way of seeing the world that's more animist than Christian. St Augustine would not have approved, but Hannah Mitchell's grandmother, with her medicinal garden and contact with the spirit world, was in touch with a way of seeing that stretches back millennia. Now we're back, in our strange, self-absorbed way, flying parachutes or climbing rock faces, because the wolves are gone and we like a whiff of danger, the smell of cordite, for the stories if nothing else. The high places are once again in tune with our culture.

The Mesolithic in Britain ended around 6,000 years ago, with the arrival of agriculture from Europe. That extends our Bronze Age axeman's perspective further back into humanity's past than he could have looked into the future. For almost all that time, more than six millennia, Britain's upland landscapes were sacred ground. Kinder Scout wasn't just a place to go hunting, it had a spiritual significance for the people who lived there, a relationship that enriched their lives, glued them together. Barrows were a scarification of the landscape: ritual marks on its face that bound people to their land and to each other. Travelling in the Himalaya, I've seen the same thing: chortens and prayer flags high on ridgelines, a current, lived relationship.

The barrows on Kinder are similar to the chortens, evidence of a profound connection to landscape. But it's a connection that has now largely melted away, like peat off the plateau. History comes and goes from Kinder Scout. One tribe leaves, packing up the concerns of their day in their rucksacks, and a new lot arrive, brandishing their own. Paradise is a place before history, and Kinder seems to offer each new arrival of the 'dying generations', as Yeats had them, a fresh blank page on which to leave the invisible ink of their lives. In that sense, the plateau of Kinder Scout is a palimpsest, scraped clean, making no demands, simply offering space to be – whoever. This seems to me an important quality for a hill with several million city-dwellers living within a short drive.

'Everybody needs beauty as well as bread,' the Scottish-born American conservationist John Muir said, 'places to play in and pray in, where nature may heal and give strength to body and soul.' That sentiment, that kind of muscular Romanticism, has truth in it, but seems rather obvious now, a bit superficial. A few years ago, discovering the Chinese novelist Yiyun Li, I came across something she said that struck a deeper chord: 'When I grew up, privacy as a concept was not present in China, and if you were hiding anything from your mother, or the party, you were in trouble. I was a very sensitive child and I reacted strongly to the lack of psychological space. These things grow in you.'

Psychological space is a valuable commodity, and not one to put a price on, something those arguing for national parks in the 1930s, against the backdrop of fascism's rise, understood well. The right to roam is for our brains as well as our boots. If this book has been about anything, it's been about the 'other' – the outsider, the immigrant, the despised, the refused, the oppressed – and their place in the world, a tide that ebbs and floods in our crossbred island and just now stands particularly high. Growing up in an era when a Jew could be beaten in the street while a policeman looked on must have sharpened Benny Rothman's keen mind to a razor's edge on the notion of inclusion. To be turned back from the hills, the one place you could be yourself, was something worth resisting. Whatever his politics, whatever his ethnicity, whatever his religion, or more accurately his lack of it, Benny's resistance to intimidation helped us define ourselves. The mass trespass revealed the deeper meaning of going for a walk: no labels, just a human putting one foot in front of the other. What could be more natural?

That space is vulnerable though. Put in a road or railway, bulldoze a hill track, string a cable car across the peaks, build fences, erect signs or just pile up stones and that space loses some of its power and meaning. The most egregious offenders are the *Keep Out* signs, raised against the backdrop of an empty moor, the ultimate limitation on psychological space. But we can build these restrictions in our own minds too. Mountain climbers talk about objectives. They study approaches, learn about routes and trace lines on photographs. It's exciting, challenging, but it's also limiting, this objectification, puts your mind on someone else's rails, can turn exploration – and self-exploration – into lists of mountains ticked off like a list of chores. People often want, as Nan Shepherd wrote in *The Living Mountain*, 'sensation from the mountain – not in Keats' sense. They want the startling view, the horrid pinnacle – sips of beer and tea instead of milk. Yet often the mountain gives itself most completely when I have no destination, when I reach nowhere in particular but have gone out merely to be with the mountain as one visits a friend with no intention but to be with him.'

Crossing the plateau at dusk in winter, the sun slipping weakly below the horizon, its fading light purple on the snow, I've felt the hairs on my neck prickling, as though something beyond my understanding is happening, something very deep and human, but also otherworldly. Absence gives way to presence. At times like this, Kinder Scout, this tired old hill, is transformed. The Celtic church had a name for somewhere such things happened: the thin places. Or as Eric Weiner, self-styled philosophical traveller, put it in his book *Man Seeks God*, 'those rare locales where the distance between heaven and Earth collapses'. The notion of mountains as abodes for the gods is familiar to us, but they tend to be exotic: Kailas, on the Tibetan plateau; Sinai, where Moses received the Ten Commandments. But English mountains, in their own rolling, eccentric way, have proved no less an inspiration. Pendle Hill, whose name pleasingly combines the words for hill from three languages, is famous for its witch trials in the early 1600s and also for its ascent in 1652 by George Fox, founder of the Religious Society of Friends, the Quakers: 'As we travelled we came near a very great hill, called Pendle Hill, and I was moved of the Lord to go up to the top of it; which I did with difficulty, it was so very steep and high. When I was come to the top, I saw the sea bordering upon Lancashire. From the top of this hill the Lord let me see in what places he had a great people to be gathered. As I went down, I found a spring of water in the side of the hill, with which I refreshed myself, having eaten or drunk but little for several days before.'

It's an oddly flat description for such a galvanising event, the sight of souls yearning to be saved and where in northern England they might be found. Perhaps it's impossible to capture these luminous experiences, so full of significance, into words. I've had my own share, in one high place or other, and sense they are beyond language, that words in fact only distract you from their purity. They are simply moments of being. No wonder so many turn to religion for an explanation. The circumstances of George Fox's experience on Pendle Hill are familiar to those who do such things for their own sake. The lack of food and water leaving you light-headed, the wide perspective, the world spread out beneath you, the endorphins from all that hard work and the natural high they bring, the wind and sun on your face. You feel complete, alive in the fullest sense.

Kinder has its own stories of witches and the supernatural, and its own religion too. George King was born in 1919 in Shropshire, grew up in a Quaker family with a strong interest in the occult, was a conscientious objector during the war, working instead for the London Fire Service, and by the early

1950s was a taxi driver in London. He spent most of his spare time doing yoga, more for the psychic experiences than improved flexibility, and in May 1954 claimed he was contacted by an alien he called Aetherius who had a simple if enigmatic message: 'Prepare yourself! You are to become the voice of Interplanetary Parliament.' George found himself designated Primary Terrestrial Mental Channel, and in 1955 set up the Aetherius Society 'to promote and act upon the wisdom of highly evolved intelligences from other planets,' who communicated with King for the rest of his life. Think of the Aetherius Society as like the Church of Scientology but without the movie stars or the valuable property portfolio.

In 1958, George King embarked on a worldwide mission, dubbed Operation Starlight, to charge rocks on peaks he judged significant with a kind of cosmic energy. Kinder Scout was one of them. In 1959 he moved to Southern California, which sounds like his natural habitat, just in time for the Age of Aquarius. But he often came back to Britain to meet his small band of followers. They still meet at the rock where Kinder Scout was charged, at Sandy Heys on the plateau's north-western corner, drawing energy from the Earth and a sense of direction from outer space.

I've sometimes wondered what George King saw in the mountains and hills he chose, but there doesn't seem to be a common theme. Mount Baldy, for instance, is conveniently close to Los Angeles; some of the others you imagine he just stuck a pin in the map. Kinder's proximity to Manchester, where the Aetherians still have a branch, might have attracted King: somewhere to reinvent the world spread out beneath your feet.

The rock King chose on Kinder Scout is unremarkable. Perched just below the crest of the plateau, it does jut purposefully towards the reservoir. But compared to others on Kinder it is quite dull. One morning, a forecast of sunshine and the possibility of mist in the valleys lured me up Grindsbrook Clough. Yet before I reached the plateau, the mist swirled in, obscuring the view. I told myself it would burn off, and pressed on westwards to Crowden Tower, which loomed out of the white like an apartment block. The sun appeared briefly, and squinting at it I almost stepped on a grouse. He cocked his head at me, red eye-stripe flaring in the light, and turned tail, scuttling across the heather with his familiar refrain: 'go-back, go-back'. Then, just as the mist rolled back in, I arrived at the Wool Packs.

Even in good weather this collection of wind-sculpted boulders is astonishing. Now, half-obscured by mist, they almost blew my mind. The rocks are arranged across the moor for a hundred square metres like a sculpture park. Yet they are purely the work of time and weather scouring beds of gritstone. I came at them over a slight rise, and in the flat light the rocks seemed compressed together, like a silent, brooding crowd, waiting for something to happen: waiting for me. Moving among them, touching them, my changing perspective brought features to life. One boulder suddenly became a toad, with a grinning maw and warty excrescences on its head. Two tapering juxtaposed shapes appeared like an old couple. The man was broader, almost squat, the woman slender, her graceful neck inclined away from her stony partner.

Some guidebooks suggest the Wool Packs inspired sculptor Henry Moore to produce the public art that made him famous. It seems unlikely. And anyway, the impact of the Wool Packs doesn't rely on any association with fame. Moore said: 'Sculpture is like a journey. You have a different view as you return. The three-dimensional world is full of surprises in a way that a two-dimensional world could never be.' Turning round to reappraise a boulder over my shoulder, I was amazed to see it change from a friendly dog to a blacksmith's anvil. Then the mist swallowed the vision, and I carried on towards Swine's Back.

Most of my days on Kinder have had a purpose, to climb something or see something, to fill in gaps or revisit half-forgotten corners. Maybe it was all an excuse, an inciting incident to redraw my mental maps, but now it seemed a little shameful. I began to roam aimlessly, half hoping the mist might clear, and then increasingly just for the sake of it. At first it felt a little uncomfortable, psychologically speaking, this lack of a plan, just wandering around, a blank in my own head, but I began to accept whatever came my way out of the mist: strangely shaped boulders, heather soaked in dew, half-formed thoughts. My mind dimmed into a benign twilight, a state R.S. Thomas captured in his poem *The Moor*.

Then I saw the hare: such a creature, a source of power, spiritual and temporal, a touchstone, as they have been for most of humanity throughout most of history, recorded or otherwise. Big-hearted, with twice the blood coursing through their bodies as a rabbit, their adaptation is not going to ground, but covering it, and quickly. A hare can touch fifty miles an hour for a few seconds, and then jink wildly to throw a pursuer off its tail. Their physical accomplishments push them to the boundaries of the supernatural. Hear one scream, as I did when a friend's lurcher surprised and caught one on Bleaklow, and in your imagination they will cross the threshold, as they did for William Blake: 'Each outcry of the hunted Hare / A fibre from the Brain does tear.' It's a human voice, a female voice, one of outrage and fear.

As a symbol in human culture the hare's image is one of the few that spans all cultures and all eras. I've found a hare's image on the outside of the Jokhang temple in Lhasa, Tibetan Buddhism's holiest temple, embossed in gold, stubby eared and with a doggy snout, glancing over his shoulder. Hares were a potent symbol for the ancient Egyptians, warding off demons, worn on amulets. In Ancient Greece they were associated with Aphrodite and Eros because, as Herodotus explained, of their reproductive fecundity. The Chinese speak of the image of the hare in the moon, and the curious symbol of three hares with conjoined ears made it all the way down the Silk Road to appear as motifs in Eastern European synagogues and English churches, a symbol of the Trinity immigrated all the way from East Asia. It's come with us into modernity too: a hare appears in Turner's masterwork 'Rain, Steam and Speed', chased down by a speeding train, a symbol of modernity, trapped between the narrow walls of a bridge. Even then, the hare had a chance. They were, over a short distance, faster than trains in Turner's day.

Pennant Melangell, in the secluded and remote Tanat Valley of Mid Wales, shows how the hare's meaning shifts and evolves. Pennant means 'head of the stream'; Melangell is the sixth-century daughter of an Irish king who fled before her unwanted marriage and took a vow of celibacy. She lived here as an early Christian hermit for several years without setting eyes on a man, until the Welsh prince Brochwel Ysgithrog and his men encountered her as they hunted hares. One took refuge under her skirts and Brochwel's dogs primly refused to follow. Brochwel was so impressed he gave her a piece of land to build a church.

The yews in the churchyard at Pennant Melangell are older than the church, a reminder that the deep roots of our relationship with nature are older than Christian faith. Even after the arrival of Christianity, hares were associated with sorcery, and still were in Hannah Mitchell's day; women magically transformed to run wild at night. And so an animist myth, built on magic and sex, meets early Christianity under the skirts of a virtuous saint. There was a class divide too: the Norman aristocracy wolfed them down; a taste eventually reflected with recipes for hare in early cookbooks, necessarily written for the wealthy. Ordinary country folk avoided eating them. A woman who ate hare during pregnancy would have a child with the hare's lip. What the animal itself feels about our fickle projections is difficult to say, but in *The Leaping Hare*, George Ewart Evans and David Thomson tell how one disgruntled hare turned and punched a cow on the nose after it grazed too close. So be warned.

The hare's meaning has shifted again in recent years, particularly the mountain hare – a longer British resident than the brown – whose fur, its pelage, changes colour, from the white of winter to a shimmering, multi-tonal coat that mixes russets and more muted browns with greys and whites. No longer a sorceress in disguise it has become a symbol of the wild we have lost. Robert Macfarlane wrote of encountering one in the Cairngorms: 'A few paces away, sitting and contemplating me, hunkered back on its huge hind legs, its tall ears twitching, was a snow hare. It seemed curious at this apparition on its mountain-top, but unalarmed. The hare was a clean white all over, except for its black tail, a small patch of grey on its chest and the two black rims of its ears.'

My hare was not like that. It was drenched with rain, coat matted and dull, blank eye watching my next move – the archetypal human threat: another death-dealer. Mountain hares were wiped out in this corner of the High Peak and then reintroduced for sport: not the sort of rewilding modern conservationists have in mind. Those in the High Peak form the only English population. Now they are being controlled again by the grouse-shooting industry, on thin evidence, although not on the scale they are in the Cairngorms of Scotland, where hundreds die in one day. But this hare was right to pay attention: it wouldn't be hiding itself, frightened and exhausted as it was, under my skirts. I would not be building any churches.

Even so, we shared a secret the hare and I. Someone else had put both of us on Kinder Scout. In the case of the hare this was literally the case, at least for her forebears. With me it was more complicated. I had swallowed some strong meat, stories of adventure, the Romantic idea of the wild, smelt and tasted a sense of freedom, swallowed it whole – and then discovered it was all constructed, put together in someone else's head and poured into mine. No wonder the hare looked wary. Watching our capricious species over the centuries, trying to work out how we're feeling, wondering what we'll do next, what stories we'll cook up, hoping that this time hares aren't part of the recipe.

We made Kinder Scout, not just metaphorically, or metaphysically, not just with our stories and our battles, but literally changed its shape, from the peat washing off its summit, to the drystone walls that turn the hillside into a harmonious grid, the trees that are and more often aren't there, to the creatures that we've allowed to remain and those we've done away with. It's our mountain. This hare, it seemed to me, was as much a cultural artefact as any I'd seen in Tibet, Egypt or Greece. If I catch sight of a peregrine flashing towards the ground, it feels like an insurrection, as though some sacred image has been pulled from the dirt, a glimpse of the past, a rebellion against the future. One day, for old time's sake, I'll take loudspeakers up there and broadcast the howl of wolves across the moors.

Kinder is mostly light and space, minimalist, roomy, accommodating – a church of our choice. The congregation comes and goes, its energy dissipating and then swelling again. Bert Ward's Clarion Ramblers disbanded in 2015, numbers having dwindled away from a high point of 200. The graves in Crookes cemetery of Ethel and Gerald Haythornthwaite, two of Sheffield's most productive citizens, have fallen into disrepair. The chapel with the stained-glass image of Herford closed, the window commemorating him salvaged and relocated to an outdoor centre in Eskdale. Yet Kinder is thronged with ramblers at the weekend, even if they've never heard of Bert Ward, enjoying landscapes still defended by campaigners the Haythornthwaites inspired. Climbers still follow the routes Herford put up, they still reveal his genius, even if the name means nothing, even if they just look at the date of the first ascent, and think, yeah, that was ahead of its time.

Hannah Mitchell was before her time; so was Edward Carpenter. Now he could marry George Merrill, put a ring on his finger, if they so chose. Maybe his dream of national parks for nature will be realised too. Hannah Mitchell lives on in the political think tank named for her, which argues the economic case for the north of England from a left-wing perspective. Perhaps, as a result, more people will read her memoir. Young feminists would find inspiration there. Benny Rothman is still well known in the outdoor world, although the image these days can seem a little nostalgic. That's a shame, because the trespass he addressed in 1932, full of youth, has much in common with climate change activism now, a cause Benny would be fighting for were he still alive, just as he did the process of water privatisation in the 1980s. He lived just long enough to see the right to roam enshrined in law. It's uplifting to spend time with the memory of these people, for all their faults and sorrows, for all their wrong turns and misjudgements. It feels like progress means something, and is possible.

On a summer Saturday morning, I shouldered my rucksack, closed the front door of my house in Sheffield and started walking up Abbeydale, cutting uphill through the beeches and oaks of Ecclesall Woods and then following the Limb Valley, the old boundary between Mercia and Northumbria that leads on to Houndkirk Moor. (Bert Ward argued this is really 'Ahnkirk Moor', the giant's church, but the man from the Ordnance Survey misheard its northern vowels.) Beyond Houndkirk came Burbage and then the long, rocky curve of Stanage, forbidden ground a century ago. Halfway along I cut across Bamford Moor, forbidden ground far more recently, and walked steeply down into the village, basking in sunshine. I stopped for a short while beside the mill pond to watch swallows hawking over its shimmering surface and then walked on, up steeply and then around the broad back of Win Hill and on to Hope Cross. Above me rose Crookstone Hill and beyond that the plateau of Kinder Scout.

It felt as though I was making a pilgrimage, of a kind, a deliberate acknowledgement that this little hill means a great deal to me, walking twenty miles or so to its summit. Rushing there is convenient, but the slow unveiling of the landscape added something: reverence, perhaps. Gratitude. Slowly, towards late afternoon, I wearily crested the rim and began tacking west, sun in my eyes, on a heading to the heart of the plateau and its diverging streams. At Fair Brook, I turned sharply left, inland from the airy sea of space to my right and found myself, despite the fatigue, suddenly uplifted. Far from the dismal, greasy world of chocolate peat that John Hillaby had seen, the top of Kinder appeared luxuriantly green. I came across a large patch of cloudberry – from Old English clud, meaning hill, rather disappointingly – known in Yorkshire as 'nowt-berries'. The leaves, already crisping in the mid-August sun, were lobed, their fruit shading to amber. I couldn't remember having seen a patch of cloudberry so large in the almost-forty years I'd been walking there. The wire fence put up as part of Kinder's restoration had done its job, keeping out sheep and giving the plateau a little breathing space, a chance to recover. The gradual unwinding of plans and the years of immense effort are steering Kinder in a new direction.

Most of the professional conservationists I've spoken to over the years think the kind of rewilding talked about in Britain and practised in Europe is fanciful in the context of the Peak District. For many of us, the human heritage of a thousand years of sheep farming is too precious, too potent a feature of this landscape to discard. Perhaps though, in the context of the UK's decision to leave the EU and the changing world of farm subsidies, the boundaries between nature and farming will be redrawn. Since the Peak District was established as a national park, nature has stayed where it was already put: on the margins. Burning moorland and killing predators to boost the yield of grouse doesn't seem a sustainable model for a national park. Something eventually will have to give. Perhaps instead some kind of core natural areas could be established: not a wilderness, but somewhere self-willed, giving nature some space, as well as the space we've given ourselves. It would still be all about us, of course, because it always is.

In the long run, in the context of geological time, it doesn't matter much either way. We'll be gone and something new will come flooding in. Kinder will no longer be a people's mountain; one day it won't be there at all. As Ted Hughes wrote: 'Heather is listening / Past hikers, gunshots, picnickers / For the star-drift / Of the returning ice.'

For now, I put up my tent and prepared to sleep.

The summit triangulation point on Mam Tor is one of the Peak's finest viewpoints. Sometimes known as the Shivering Mountain due to the instability of surrounding shales, Mam Tor lies at the centre of a long high ridge extending west to east from Rushup Edge to Lose Hill, neatly dividing the Dark Peak (gritstone) and the White Peak (limestone).

Mam Tor. *Top left:* winter at Mam Nick; *top right:* the summit of Mam Tor is dissected by dangerous shale cliffs – note the medieval ditch fortification at the bottom of the image; *bottom left:* Mam Tor from Rowland Cote; *bottom right:* temperature inversion on Mam Tor.

The early Bronze Age (2,000–1,500 BCE) round barrow – or 'low' – is a prominent landmark above Kinderlow End.

Greg Smith seeking much-needed energy at the enigmatic Charged Rock on Sandy Heys in 1993.

The mountain hare *(Lepus timidus)* generally lies low by day in grass forms or in bilberry and heather amongst protective rocks. Each year the brown coat of the summer months transitions into a white pelage, enabling the hare to cryptically camouflage into its environment. The mountain hare was introduced to the Peak in the late 1800s. Even though it is now established as a key moorland species, the total population in the Dark Peak remains low.

Mountain hare paw prints above Crowden Head.

The Wool Packs are wind-scoured plinths and mushrooms of gritstone bedrock between Pym Chair and Crowden Tower. In hill fog or winter conditions, this place is imbued with an eerie atmosphere, a navigational conundrum, and a highlight for every hillwalker on Kinder Scout.

Top left: male fern *(Dryopteris filix-mas); top right:* foxglove *(Digitalis purpurea); bottom left:* cloudberry *(Rubus chamaemorus)* in flower; *bottom right:* mat-grass *(Nardus stricta).*

Mature birch tree *(Betula pendula)* encrusted with hoar frost. Totley Moss, Eastern Edges.

Approaching Noe Stool at Edale Head during the big winter of January 2010.

Above: Kinder Downfall fighting a westerly gale.
Opposite: Ashop Head, Kinder Scout from Mill Hill. To the east and west, the night glow of Manchester and Sheffield.

On this beguiling hill ...

In summer months Kinder Scout is a gathering place, a natural coming together of walkers, runners and climbers on to this high hill. Although a summer hill, it is a winter mountain, and, for the unwary, a spectacular trickster that will lead you into a labyrinth and consume you in a mire. Kinder is a wild place, and the higher you climb there is a strong sense of leaving the world aside for a few hours, a place of solace and of adventure. Many of the paths are steeped in history, once walked by shepherds, brigands and traders with paths to shapely wind-blasted rocks, to beacons and prominences with outward views reaching to Snowdonia, and to lonely tracts of heather and sedge where the only horizon is the sky above. A Pennine fortress, Kinder divides the east of England from the west.

In the late 1950s my father brought me on family walks up to Kinder Reservoir. We looked out over the water to the huge sweeping prospect of the western edge of Kinder plateau with the Downfall cleft, dark and foreboding. I bought my first motorcycle at the age of sixteen and began to venture regularly to all parts of Kinder. In those early years I experienced its weather, its creatures, tors and escarpments, and grew to love this place entirely in its own right as one might be acquainted with a friend. In 1969 I bought my first ice axe from Manchester Piccadilly Army Navy store, and I tested it on the big westerly snow slopes between Kinder Low and Cluther Rocks. Above the Downfall was a huge slab known as Kinder Kitchen which could shelter at least ten people. It collapsed one night in the mid 1970s and melded into the jumble of rocks. The denuded plateau in those days, warmed by the sun, enabled me to walk for miles barefoot in a soft desert of eroded peat hags. On rare days we climbed on its ramparts and drank its sweet waters, we sank in the peat bogs and played in the snow dunes. As a young family, we brought up our children Robin and Jodie to know this place like their own garden. I come here when bereaved, to find myself again and to feel nourished by the simplicity of the land. Days out on Kinder have taught me so much and led me afar, to great ranges, to deserts and ice caps. Through privations of discomfort and endurance and the most testing navigation, I have learned to listen to a landscape reduced to its elements, stripped down into wind, rain and light. It has been a lifetime of joy to meet this mountain.

In these fifty years I have observed a slow depletion of the birds, plants and animals that once populated Kinder. The curlew, seldom seen on the plateau now, only nests in small numbers in the rough pastures of Edale, and Snake woodlands. The mountain hare, though occasional, seems to be less common and confined to a smaller range further north. The large flocks of grouse that were once often seen each winter are a rarity today. The peregrines at the Downfall are gone, the short-eared owls are gone, but the raven, although not breeding on Kinder, is frequently seen and heard in its high winter roosts on the edges of the plateau. One summer, I watched a raven seemingly dancing in the long tussocks at the head of Ashop Clough, then rise into the air carrying away an adder in its talons. In the icy winter of 2010 on Kinder Low summit, I remember finding signs of a skirmish, a trail of tiny animal footprints and bloody drops from a dead rabbit that had been dragged some distance by a hungry stoat.

After heavy rain many of the moorland streams lay down the rushes and grasses in artistic symmetry. Secret pools hidden in the quieter cloughs are adorned with ferns and cushion mosses, and if you're lucky on a summer evening, you may hear the hesitant chack-chacking of the ring ouzel or a wren's delicate stream of song. But it is a sparse landscape, one that will absorb you with both its detail and its magnificence. A landscape in which to listen, to breathe and to escape.

Notes from a night walk. Dec 1995.
To walk on Kinder on a moonless winter night, is to walk in the presence of something quite outside ordinary experiences. For me, this massive bulk of peat and rock is sentient, like a creature looming in the imagination. For those who live near or within sight of it, its compelling horizon is a place of otherness away from the city.

By night, in the small circle of light from my head torch, Kinder was reduced to its constituent parts of stone, water, sand, peat, moss and lichen. But there was more. Vague heaps of rocks were sensed not seen as I was accompanied into the darkness by the gurgling of subterranean waters, hissing wind, crunch of ice and nightcalls of disturbed living things. Navigation here was more divined than mathematic as the tracks, peat hags and frozen stream ways passed under my boots.

I felt the proximity of the arms of Kinder ravine that narrowed and drew me to the junction of rocks where Kinder river's quiet moorland journey ended abruptly at the clean precipice of the Downfall. In unbearable darkness, the swollen torrent leaped into the void filling me with a dread. Gravity and temptation joined together in this tumult of blasting water-filled air where I scrambled down compelled by abandon toward the very edge. Sheltering in a crevasse of tumbled blocks, I was completely away from the world, enfolded into the wild essence of Kinder Scout.

On most of more than a thousand days on Kinder I have carried a camera. It may or may not have been used because I rarely preconceive photographs. Instead, I have tried to connect with the landscape emotionally and with keen observation until a moment of special light or texture or shape of the landscape attracts my attention. When a deep connection to the landscape is revealing itself, other forces are at work and I am compelled into a momentary and isolating meditation. It is then that Kinder absorbs me in its thrall. It is a beguiling hill, a lost world that impinges itself in the memory. In that way, I hope you are reminded within these photographs of the great days you have experienced on this lovely hill, or inspired to discover it anew.

To my partner in life, Jan Beatty, and to the many friends who have endured my company on Kinder when I lift the camera from the rucksack, I extend my gratitude with a heartfelt thank you. These include Jerry Smith and Barry Thomas who shared those 1960s glory days. And to the legendary Gordon Miller who trained me in navigation and mountain skills back in '69. To Chris Harding for the running days and to Andy Howie who has always so willingly shared his Kinder enthusiasm. In recent years my friends Andy Towne, Mike Sharp, Stu Dale and Simon Kinnear have been great company in mostly adverse conditions, when Kinder becomes alive and treacherous. Finally, I'd like to thank John Coefield, Jon Barton and Jane Beagley at Vertebrate Publishing who have consistently believed in people and mountains.

John Beatty
Bamford, November 2017

A note on sources

There are a number of books either specifically about Kinder Scout or focusing on the High Peak that proved valuable in writing this one. *Kinder Scout: Portrait of a Mountain*, edited by Roly Smith, (Derbyshire County Council, 2002) has essays by specialist writers on different aspects of the mountain's natural and human history. I also drew on *Geology Explained in the Peak District* (Scarthin Books, 1998) by F. Wolverson Cope. *A History of the Peak District Moors* (Pen & Sword Local, 2014) by the leading academic local historian and rambler David Hey is an invaluable and accessible introduction. *High Peak: The story of walking and climbing in the Peak District* (Secker & Warburg, 1966) by Eric Byne and Geoffrey Sutton, though sadly out of print, is still a rich and rewarding source from the birth of outdoor culture, which captures that mix of leisure and politics that still underpins walking and climbing in the Peak. *Prehistory in the Peak* (Tempus, 2001) by the archaeologist Mark Edmonds with photographs from Tim Seaborne is an atmospheric introduction to the Peak District's early human history, although since that period stretches from the Mesolithic to the Iron Age, some 10,000 years, that is most of its human history. The book is rich in imagination as well as research.

There have been many travelogues from the Peak, a few of which are mentioned below, but *On Foot in the Peak* (Alexander MacLehose, 1932) by the *Guardian* deputy editor Patrick Monkhouse is a favourite and was well timed. He proposed to his wife Pamela, all too briefly a *Guardian* woman herself, on the summit of Mam Tor. There are a number of histories of the access movement that provide context as well as detail from the Kinder Mass Trespass. *Forbidden Land* (Manchester University Press, 1989) by Tom Stephenson gives an insider's view not just of access but the national park movement and the Pennine Way too, brought to press by Ann Holt after Stephenson's death. *Freedom to Roam* (Moorland Publishing, 1980) by the access campaigner and political organiser Howard Hill offers another, more supportive view of the Kinder Trespass. *A Right to Roam* (Oxford University Press, 1999) by the journalist and academic Marion Shoard is another landmark work on the subject. *Protecting the Beautiful Frame* (Hallamshire Press, 2001) by Melvyn Jones offers an overview of the struggle to preserve the landscapes of the High Peak and the growth of the national park movement, while at the same time preserving the immense contribution of Ethel and Gerald Haythornthwaite. *The Fight for Beauty* (Oneworld, 2016) by Fiona Reynolds is a wider view of similar themes by one of Britain's leading voices for conservation and someone with intimate knowledge of the Haythornthwaites' campaigns. Sheila Rowbotham's biography *Edward Carpenter: A Life of Liberty and Love* (Verso, 2009) was the principal source for details of Carpenter's life, a man who seems in the modern political context to have been light years ahead of his time.

In the section 'Sheep', I relied on Hannah Mitchell's autobiography *The Hard Way Up* (Faber & Faber, 1968), edited by her grandson Geoffrey Mitchell.

It seems extraordinary that she failed to find a publisher in her lifetime and yet her book should appear after her death from such a distinguished house. Perhaps there is a story there. I also have a copy of the slim pamphlet Hannah did see published about the Love Feast. *A Ragged Schooling* (Manchester University Press, 1976) by Robert Roberts is a sensitive and thought-provoking memoir leavened with plenty of humour. I'm grateful to Roberts' grandson, the science fiction author and journalist Adam Roberts, for pointing me at the memoirs of his father Glyn Roberts that appear on his website (*glynroberts.org*). For the life of Mrs Humphry Ward, there is an entertaining biography (Oxford University Press, 1990) by the critic John Sutherland. However, his account underestimates the amount of time Mrs Ward spent on and around Kinder Scout researching her novel *The History of David Grieve*. Peter Collister's essay 'Some Literary and Popular Sources for Mrs Humphry Ward's *The History of David Grieve*' (Oxford University Press, 1989) is better on this but hardly detailed. The diary of her secretary, her sister-in-law Gertrude Ward, held at Pusey House in Oxford, shows that Mrs Ward paid close attention to the reality of the landscape she reimagined for her novel. The *Rucksack Club Journal* for 1917 includes a paper on the literature Kinder Scout inspired and makes a direct connection between Louis Jennings' book *Rambles Among the Hills of Derbyshire* (John Murray, 1880) and Ward's work. It seems likely to me that she sought out features Jennings identified.

In the section 'Flight', I drew on Ray Monk's definitive popular biography *Wittgenstein: the Duty of Genius* (Jonathan Cape, 1990) and managed to visit The Grouse Inn below Chunal Moor before it finally closed. It is, at the time of writing, being converted into a private house. I'm grateful to Alan Clark of the website Peak District Air Accident Research (*www.peakdistrictaircrashes.co.uk*) for forwarding me the official report into the Liberator crash on Mill Hill on 11 October 1944. The disappearance of Jim Puttrell's autobiography was a great loss to British climbing heritage, but there is a biography by J.P. Craddock (Matador, 2009), *Jim Puttrell: Pioneer Climber & Cave Explorer*. For the life of Siegfried Herford, I relied on Keith Treacher's 2000 biography *Siegfried Herford: An Edwardian Rock-Climber* (Ernest Press, 2000), Treacher's background as a Unitarian and an educationalist making him uncommonly qualified. *Geoffrey Winthrop Young* by Alan Hankinson (Hodder & Stoughton, 1995) is one of several rich accounts of Edwardian mountaineering for those who want to know more of this period. For those who want to know more about Charles Edward Montague, his short stories and *Disenchantment*, his once-popular but now overlooked enquiry into the Great War, are still available, originally published by Chatto & Windus. Scott Russell wrote a brief portrait of him for the 1991 edition of the *Alpine Journal*; the critic Oliver Elton also wrote a memoir of Montague. I drew on articles and obituaries for other key players from the journals of various other climbing clubs, some of which are now helpfully online, particularly the *Climbers' Club Journal*. *This Mountain Life: The First Hundred Years of the Rucksack Club*, edited by John Beatty, is a fascinating pictorial record. I'm particularly indebted to the historian Jonathan Westaway and his paper 'The German Community in Manchester, Middle-Class Culture and the Development of Mountaineering in Britain, *c.*1850–1914' (English Historical Review, 2009).

In the section 'Grouse', beyond those sources already quoted, I drew on interviews with Rosa Rothman, Benny's sister, who was introduced to me by her nephew and Benny's son Harry, as background for a proposed biography. I also accessed the Rothman archive at the inestimable Working Class Movement Library in Salford. I also drew on the Garside family's scrapbooks, usefully put online by the New Mills Local History Society, a collection of press cuttings that reveals changing attitudes and behaviour, access struggles and dramatic rescues. Benny Rothman's own account, *The Battle for Kinder Scout*, was reissued in 2012 by Willow Publishing in time for the eightieth anniversary with additional useful material from Roly Smith, Tom Waghorn and Keith Warrender. The life of George Willis Marshall is told in *Days of Sunshine and Rain: Rambling in the 1920s* (Pickard Communication, 2011) by Ann Beedham. Harry Hopkins' well-known book on the Poaching Wars, *The Long Affray* (Secker & Warburg, 1985), gave useful background. Perhaps inevitably, books on the persecution of wildlife and the management of moors feature in this section, and also in the environmental section 'Moss': Mark Avery's polemic on grouse shooting *Inglorious: Conflict in the Uplands* (Bloomsbury, 2015) and Roger Lovegrove's magisterial *Silent Fields* (Oxford University Press, 2007). For a broad, deep and rich understanding of moorland ecology and history, I relied on *The Moorlands of England and Wales* by I.G. Simmons (Edinburgh University Press, 2003).

"I will ignore all ideas for new works on engines of war, the invention of which has reached its limits and for whose improvements I see no further hope…"

STRATEGEMATA, (INTRO., BOOK III), SEXTUS JULIUS FRONTINUS, C. AD84

....

"If the Panzers succeed, then victory follows."

HEINZ GUDERIAN

Introduction

This is the first book of a series detailing the history of the *Panzerwaffe* from the first German tanks in World War One to the end of World War Two. It is planned that each period or campaign will be described by a commisioned author with key knowledge of the subject, but this first book is very much a team effort and our thanks go to all those who contributed.

This is not just another book of photographs. Our intention is to include a comprehensive text for each book in the series – not just a brief summary on a few pages as in some other books. We have included as many previously unpublished photographs as possible to show the *Panzerwaffe's* equipment in use.

Although the emphasis will be on tanks, we will also be covering the Panzer Divisions as the combined-arms units that they were, so all their integral armoured vehicles will be covered – armoured cars, self-propelled artillery and anti-tank guns on tank chassis, and armoured halftracks as well as tanks.

Special thanks go to Thomas Jentz and Hilary Louis Doyle of Panzer Tracts for their help in providing the scale plans that have been used as a basis for the colour plates in this book. Readers wanting more information about the vehicles described here will find Ian Allan's separate series of books about tanks useful, and those wanting even more technical details will find the *Panzer Tracts* books essential – information about these can be found at www.panzertracts1.tripod.com

John Prigent
Series Editor

501, the first A7V tank to become ready, seen in the work yard of Steffens & Noelle's late in 1917. 501 was the only A7V to be fielded as a female (machine gun armed only) tank and remained so until mid-1918, when a socle mounted gun was finally installed. Because the Germans refrained from using scarce nickel, chrome or manganese to harden tank armour, their armour plates had to be thicker, thus increasing the weight of the tanks, and in the case of the A7V, further reducing cross-country performance. In this picture the covers for the towing hooks are being attached. (Mario Doherr Collection)

Beginnings – the first German tanks

by Rainer Strasheim

THE TANK was created by the western Entente powers during the Great War. In another – ultimately successful – attempt to overcome the Western Front stalemate, Britain fielded the first combat tanks and produced those machines best adopted to trench warfare landscapes, the rhomboids of the Mk.I to Mk.V series, while France eventually developed and mass-produced the first tank with a 'modern' layout, the Renault FT17.

The Central Powers, and Germany in particular, are usually described as only adopting this new means of warfare reluctantly and too late. Certainly there was no arms race to produce the first armoured all-terrain fighting vehicle. The Germans merely reacted to the appearance of the first tanks at the Somme in September 1916. This reaction occurred with remarkable swiftness, but did not result in a powerful German tank force. Only 20 vehicles of the indigenous A7V model and a total, over time, of perhaps 90 captured British Mk.IVs formed the rather modest German tank arm. Furthermore, the A7V is usually described as clumsy and inferior in published opinion, thus adding to the impression that the German tank effort was only third class.

The problem for the German High Command (*Oberste Heeresleitung* – OHL) was to determine whether tanks really deserved the expending of considerable resources, which were not freely available in beleaguered and blockaded Germany. In other words: Was the tank a decisive weapon? Could it become a decisive weapon?

The debut of '*armed and armoured English motor vehicles*' at the Somme had been alarming but not decisive. Individual machines had stunned the defenders, rendering their machine guns useless, but the general effect of the few '*monsters*' had been negligible. Nevertheless, here was a new weapon that had to be explored. In short order, a German tank construction programme was organised – which eventually led to the commission of the A7V tank.

But uncertainties soon arose. By incredible chance, it was not the A7V prototype that was first presented to the decision makers on 11 March 1917 but an awkwardly unfit vehicle, the '*Bremer-Wagen*'. Then, near Arras, another unbelievable event occurred: the combat use of British Mk.II training tanks with unhardened steel plates. On 11 April 1917, twelve British tanks attacked at Bullecourt, nine of which were put out of action by the defenders, and one, a Mk.II male (No. 799), stranded well behind the first German trench line. When tested, its flank was

The armoured hulls of the A7Vs were cut, drilled, assembled and fixed at Steffens & Noelle's, located at Berlin-Tempelhof, a bridge building and steel mast construction company. The man in the centre, standing on the right-hand side of the steering wheel, is Joseph Vollmer, the chief designer of the A7V and LK tanks. The A7V was his first experience in tank construction. Realising that the A7Vs were far too complex and consumed too many resources, Vollmer had already turned his attention to light tanks in the early summer of 1917. But his initial, resource oriented, plan to use the chassis and engines of available passenger cars as the basis for the LKs prevented a clean cut solution suitable for fast mass production. (Strasheim Collection)

PANZERWAFFE

Mk.II 799 with new owners. Within a few days after the events of 11 April, the German XIV. Reserve Corps, in charge of the Bullecourt sector, distributed a 'Tank Report' providing pictures and appraisals. Combat experience and subsequent trials led to the impression that steel core bullets were an effective remedy against tanks. The Germans remained unaware that the Mk.II tanks had only been built as unarmoured training machines. Because Mk.I battle tanks were in short supply, some Mk IIs had been pressed into combat service at Arras – over the shrill protests of the British tank personnel. (Strasheim Collection)

easily penetrated by the new steel core machine gun bullets at 150 metres distance, the projectiles also igniting the tank's fuel supply. It was realised that there was a cheap weapon that could effectively end the tank menace!

Next came the first French tank attack on 16 April 1917, a bloody débâcle – for the French. After these events, *General* Erich Ludendorff, the driving spirit of the German Army, decided that tanks would not become a decisive weapon and did not deserve the use of precious resources. (The floundering of the British tank fleet in the Flanders mud during summer and autumn 1917 did nothing to reverse this perception.) In consequence, the German tank programme lost momentum and did not show results… Dubious new projects like the colossal *K-Wagen* and the overweight A7V-U popped up – and never made it beyond prototypes.

Then, on 20 November 1917, hundreds of British tanks suddenly smashed some eight kilometres through the *Siegfried-Stellung* (known as the Hindenburg-Line to the British) in front of Cambrai. No breakthrough occurred because the amazing success of this mass tank attack surprised the British commanders as much as their German opponents, and eventually a counter-attack regained most of the terrain, but for a number of days the situation looked rather bleak. This changed Ludendorff's opinion considerably – but now it was too late. Whatever could be started at this point would not arrive in time for the big push in spring, when Germany aimed to achieve victory in the west. Moreover, German tactics had so far evolved without regard to tanks throughout 1917 and the regulations for attack in positional warfare ('*Die Angriffsschlacht im Stellungskrieg*') and for general infantry training ('*Ausbildungsvorschrift der Fußtruppen*'

While F.41 'Fray Bentos', a male Mk.IV, (on its way to Berlin) was probably demonstrated to OHL officers at Bad Kreuznach on 19 December 1917, the female F.13 'Falcon II' was presented to Kaiser Wilhelm II at Le Cateau on 23 December. Tank and Emperor are seen here in front of Palais Fénelon. A contemporary report describes F.13 as 'a grey hump'. The colours of its camouflage net are described correctly as 'brown netting with green cloth flaps'. Being a replacement vehicle, Falcon II was perhaps rushed into service at Cambrai in the dark grey factory finish without receiving a coat of chocolate brown, the normal hue of British tanks since early 1917. Both F.13 and F.41 are prominent in the movie 'Die Englischen Tanks bei Cambrai' that was shown in German cinemas starting January 1918. (Strasheim Collection)

The most dangerous enemy of the captured tank was the German soldier armed with screwdriver, wrench and tongs. Constant guarding was necessary to prevent precious parts from being 'found' and presented to some booty collection officer for prize money. In this picture, taken most probably in spring of 1918, all gun apertures have been provisionally closed to facilitate control. A number of harsh orders were issued by OHL and Chefkraft in order to protect captured tanks from being disassembled by their own troops. (Strasheim Collection)

BEGINNINGS – THE FIRST GERMAN TANKS

While Tank 506 is waiting for recovery (note the tank commander, Lt Voss, with binoculars, standing near the rear door), the inspection group is engaged in heated discussions. Chefkraft was accompanied not only by a whole echelon of personnel from the home agencies, but also by numerous motor transport field officers. Joseph Vollmer had already been with Abt. 1 since 27 January, trying to make his tanks work. On the second day of the inspection, only two tanks, 505 and 506, were still serviceable. 540 was disabled by a broken fuel pipe. (Strasheim Collection)

– A.V.F.) were now being finalised and would be the most important manuals used in training for the March offensive.

Nevertheless, tank building now became a top priority task. For the utilisation of those tanks captured at Cambrai (about 100 had been counted, with 30 readily recoverable) a Bavarian army motor transport depot (*Bayerischer Armee-Kraftwagen-Park* 20 – B.A.K.P. 20) was transferred to Monceau-sur-Sambre near Charleroi in Belgium to become the central workshop of the German tank force.

After the 1918 German spring offensive, some 300 more derelict British tanks would be captured around Bapaume, Peronne, and Bray-sur-Somme.

Learning lessons from the British massed tank assault, the Chief of Field Motor Transportation (*Chef des Feldkraftfahrwesens*, in short *Chefkraft*), *Oberst* Hermann Meyer, proposed in late December 1917, the construction of light tanks suitable for rapid mass production. This proposal was rejected by OHL because the projected vehicle (*Leichter Kampfwagen* – LK) did not even offer protection against ordinary rifle bullets. Yet the light tank idea had been placed and – development never stopping – the next proposal, to become the LK.II, would follow soon. (Initial planning had already begun in mid-1917, the LK thus was a genuine German product, not a mere reaction to the British Medium A 'Whippet' or the Renault FT17.)

The question remained of what to do with the A7Vs. Only 20 tanks were actually under construction but after Cambrai the intended numbers grew erratically, alternating between a total of 32, 36 and 38 – and finally increased to a maximum of 68 with 10 detachments envisaged of five tanks each (the remaining vehicles forming the reserve pool).

The original arrangement had foreseen detachments of five tanks, thereof four machine gun armed ('females', to use the British jargon) and only one with a cannon (thus a 'male'). Now all A7Vs were to receive a cannon to create sufficient anti-tank capability, should the enemy try something in the Cambrai style again. This required some critical rearrangements, and eventually only four of the five tanks of *Abteilung 1* carried a gun when the detachment arrived for evaluation at the *Führer- und Generalstabs-Kursus* (leaders- and general staff training course) near Sedan/France on 12 January 1918.

The assessment at Sedan soon revealed major complications! Grave doubts arose whether the A7V was usable in warfare at all. Tanks and crews were evaluated as 'Not combat ready'. While the engineers rushed to Sedan to deal with the technical side, Crown Prince Wilhelm proposed to hand the detachment over to *Sturmbataillon No.5* (*Rohr*) at Beuveille for enhanced training.

Abteilung 1 arrived at Beuveille on 26 January. On 1 and 2 February they were inspected by *Chefkraft*, *Obst.* Meyer. Meyer already had serious reservations regarding the A7V. He knew about its weak points: the 'low nose', insufficient ground clearance, weak frame, and soft underbelly – all leading to a vehicle not apt for crossing Western Front trenches and moving through heavily shelled terrain. And what he now saw and heard during the inspection convinced him that the A7V was not at all reliable enough to serve as a combat vehicle. (Meyer's preferred idea – after rejection of his initial light tank proposal – became to copy and improve the British rhomboid design, which had proven so optimal for Western Front conditions in 1916 and 1917. This idea led to some intensive planning and scheming but was finally dropped in favour of LK production.)

Abt. 1 stands ready for inspection by Chefkraft at the 'Tank Square' of the Doncourt training area on 1 February, 1918. The tanks are from left to right: 505 (Oblt. Seifert, the detachment CO), 506 (Lt Voss) and 540 (Lt Bartens). All crew members except the latter two commanders wear the field grey tank overalls, the drivers and mechanics with padded leather helmets in lieu of steel helmets. Note that 540 has a male front (i.e. no flap covered machine gun apertures) still without any vision slits. Note also the 'peepholes' above the gun barrels of the tanks. (Mario Doherr Collection)

Meanwhile, training with the assault battalion proceeded. The weapons personnel of *Abteilung 1* (the machine gunners, infantrymen, gunners and engineers) joined the training of the storm troopers. The motor transport men and signallers were still required to overcome the tanks' teething troubles and multiple defects. Although there never were more than three (on the occasion of Meyer's visit) and usually only two tanks operative, the tanks were continually tested to explore their capabilities and shortcomings. A number of improvements were identified and implemented. On 11 February the first refurbished Mk.IV tank arrived for comparison.

In theory all tank detachments were to execute joint training with an assault battalion before they joined combat, but no fixed schedule existed. *Abt.1* practised with *Sturmbataillon Rohr* up to its first combat mission. In March 1918 Rohr's battalion trained a number of future tank soldiers to be distributed between all detachments. *Abt.*11 and 12 were employed in getting their Mk.IVs ready, so only received some training with *Jäger-Sturmbataillon* 3 in late April. The cadres of Bavarian *Abt.13* were also sent to Rohr's battalion, but hardly arrived before they were called away to take over their tanks and join the attack on 27 May. The same happened to *Abt.14* who had not even fired their cannons and machine guns before they went into action on 27 May. Only when they were sent out for tank familiarisation training in August and September of 1918 did the detachments execute regular training with other arms including assault formations and close support batteries.

On 25 February 1918, *General* Ludendorff, officially first assistant to *General* v. Hindenburg, the Chief of General Staff, but factually the master of the German military machine, inspected *Abteilung 1* and *Sturmbataillon Rohr* at the Doncourt training area neighbouring Beuveille. Two A7Vs (Tanks 505 and 506) participated in the exercise simulating an attack. Firing blanks, they breached a wire obstacle, overcame some shell holes, pushed down a brick wall, negotiated a two-metre trench – and both became stuck at the next obstacle: a trench three metres wide. Obviously *General* Ludendorff was not impressed by this performance. His irked attitude towards tanks is quite astounding for a man otherwise open to all new forms of technical development. It appears that after Cambrai he had become well aware that his spring 1917 decision to neglect tank construction had been wrong. But as this could not be corrected, he was now doggedly determined to carry on and win – without tanks. Cambrai had clearly shown him that only the massed use of tanks promised success, but neither sending into battle 50 A7Vs with negligible trench-crossing capability nor employing a mere 30 captured Mk. IVs could fulfil this criterion. He did not yet realise that his own offensives would end the era of trench warfare, and that in a more fluid situation with battles fought in open countryside the A7V, by virtue of speed, firepower and armour, would be superior to any other current tank design.

With *Obst.* Meyer's negative assessment and Ludendorff's negative position, the fate of the A7V was sealed: the 20 armoured hulls already procured would be used – all other chassis (in total, 100 had been ordered in early 1917) would be finished as tracked lorries. Thus, even before they had fired their first round in anger, the A7Vs were discarded as fighting vehicles.

Of course, *Chefkraft* Meyer was right, the A7V was no trench-fighting machine, it might even be stopped by an irrigation ditch. Considering the original design task to produce a machine capable of everything the British tanks could do, the A7V was a plain failure. And yes, its mechanical reliability was poor, but that was a fact common to all Great War tanks. Yet Meyer could only judge whether technical specifications were met. As a motor transport specialist he lacked combat experience, and tactical advice on tank operations exceeded his scope.

For break-in and fighting through the trench zone the Germans had evolved an all-arms (except tanks) assault, incorporating storm troop, infiltration, and distinctive artillery tactics, which worked well enough under certain conditions - but was no blueprint for breakthrough.

The same was, nevertheless, true for the British rhomboids, which had achieved a remarkable break-in at Cambrai but no breakthrough. They had been built to overcome trenches and churned-up terrain. Once arrived on 'the green fields beyond' it was their turn to become clumsy – slow moving targets for gunnery practice, if not massively protected by friendly artillery and infantry (or by fog), and their sheer number that allowed some vehicles to get through.

Cavalry, the traditional arm for exploitation and pursuit, was out of place in an environment of wire and fire. But here was the A7V, as fast 'as a trotting horse' (to quote an Allied report on a captured machine), with a 12 km/h top speed according to the designing engineers, or 14 km/h as tested out by the crews, running across country still at 6 to 8 km/h. It had a quick-firing 5.7 cm cannon that could penetrate any existing Entente tank armour up to 2,000 metres, and six heavy MG-08 7.92 mm machine guns. Its 30 mm front armour was solid enough to resist a field cannon even at close quarters. The maximum cross-country range was 30 to 35 km. But like all tanks of the era, travelling such an – extraordinary – distance would require intensive repair and overhaul afterward, or even while en route. And the crews would desperately need rest and refit from the intolerable fumes, the infernal heat and the deafening noise inside. If a tank got stuck or went out of order, a crew of 18 to 25 men with one light and six heavy machine guns, plus copious stocks of ammunition, could either form a strong point or go on marauding as an assault party. Eighteen was the minimum crew of an A7V if all stations were to be served. Usually reserve numbers and trainees were carried in addition.

The gun compartment of an A7V showing the direction indicator above the cannon and the fire control box above the right hand aperture. The light signals were: white 'Achtung' (attention); red 'Feuer' (fire); light off meant 'cease firing'. Gun crews were not very happy with the very limited field of vision provided by the telescopic sight of the socle-mounted 5.7 cm cannon because orientation through it was almost impossible in a moving tank. They preferred instead the simple 'peepholes' seen on Tanks 505, 506, 507 and 540, equipped with a buck (trestle) mount for the gun. (Strasheim Collection)

LEFT: One of Abt. 11's tanks seen on a train awaiting transport to St.Quentin. They arrived at Essigny-le-Petit on 17 March 1918. The man with the Iron Cross 1st Class standing in front of the rail wagon is Unteroffizier Fritz Leu, serving as tank driver with Abt. 11. Leu had been instrumental in capturing the first British Mk.IV in drivable condition near Cambrai on 23 November 1917. At least two of the men sitting atop the tank wear the leather-patched trousers of the mountain artillery, also issued to assault troopers and tank crews. If this is the vehicle which Leu drove on 21 March, it is Tank 101 commanded by Lt Werner von Richter. (Strasheim Collection)

In early 1918 German tactical thinking remained indifferent to tank use. Tanks were a weapon in support of the infantry. They would flatten wire obstacles, advance together with the infantry and subdue any points of resistance that had survived the artillery preparation. They would help repulse enemy counter-attacks. They were not to lead the attack, but might surge ahead to deal with enemy strong points. They might also not accompany the infantry all the time, but stop or retire for technical reasons. In short, the tanks were added to the newly-developed doctrine without much thought about their optimal employment. And the nature of the terrain, not the tactical purpose, decided whether captured Mk.IVs or A7Vs would be used. The possible combination of Mk. IVs for fighting through the trench zone and A7Vs for exploitation was never considered.

In terms of tactical handling, the A7V had quite progressive features. There was a fire control system with coloured lights managed by the tank commander, and a direction indicator, also operated by the commander, for the cannon. This was a far cry from conditions inside the Mk.IVs, which the Germans generally crowded with a crew of twelve (while British Mk.IV crews numbered eight – or even less), where only gestures, hand signs and loud shouts were available for the commander to direct his crew – and he usually had no influence on the aims that his gunners took.

The A7V's signalling lamps were highly appreciated because they could transmit reliably over long distances through the haze of battle. Tests with radio were conducted but produced no workable solution. Runners were routinely employed, carrying a lump hammer to gain access to a tank by pounding a signal on the armour. Carrier pigeons were often used, messenger dogs never. The tanks were also equipped with signalling flags and flares.

Only one man – the driver – was required to move an A7V around. One of the most popular demonstrations was to have the vehicle rotate several times on the spot, something the Mk.IVs (where four men were required to manage movement) could not do.

Abteilungen 1 and *11* had only an A7V *Überlandwagen* (tracked lorry) each for their first combat mission on 21 March, 'organised' despite the ban on using *Überlandwagens* as recovery vehicles. In all later actions the *Abteilungen* just left immobile vehicles behind and salvage was done by the motor transport troops of the

Tank 505 did not get far on 21 March 1918. After running into a wire obstacle, its clutches burnt out and the gear wheels locked. The tank commander, Lt Voss, was wounded. Note the gaudy camouflage scheme and varying-sized Iron Crosses painted by the crew prior to the mission. According to the recollections of a former Abt. 1 member 'all colours available' (at Beuveille) were used for that purpose. As all the machine guns have already been removed from their apertures this picture was taken well after the action. (Strasheim Collection).

Abt. 11 awaits entraining after 21 March. Before the action the tanks had been hidden inside the halls of the artillery workshop at St. Quentin. Note the A7V-Überlandwagen (tracked lorry) commandeered to serve as a recovery and supply vehicle. On 26 March Chefkraft reported that only one machine gun-armed tank each from Abt. 1 and 11 remained operational. The detachments would be withdrawn to Charleroi for repair and be ready again in early April. (Strasheim Collection)

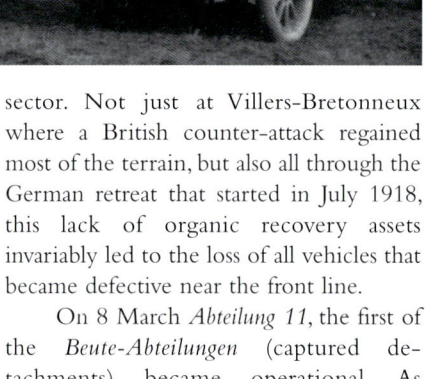

When Abt. 1 entrained at St.Quentin railway station on 27 March 1918, Tank 507 slipped from the rail wagon and fell on its left side. For recovery, Lt Bartens stayed behind at St.Quentin together with Tank 505. Note the obligatory guard. 507 still carries the makeshift markings applied by the crew. Various dots of the camouflage paints are visible on the front armour. (Strasheim Collection)

sector. Not just at Villers-Bretonneux where a British counter-attack regained most of the terrain, but also all through the German retreat that started in July 1918, this lack of organic recovery assets invariably led to the loss of all vehicles that became defective near the front line.

On 8 March *Abteilung 11*, the first of the *Beute-Abteilungen* (captured detachments) became operational. As cannons could still not be used because the telescopic sights were not ready yet, the initial strength comprised five female Mk IVs (Tanks 101 to 105).

On 21 March 1918, at St.Quentin, *Abteilungen* 1 (four A7Vs) and 11 (five Mk IVs) participated in the opening German offensive of 1918, 'Unternehmen Michael'.

Of the four A7Vs, two (Tanks 505 and 507) broke down before they even attained the British trenches, as did the recovery *Überlandwagen*. Because this was partly due to bad visibility in the dense fog, *Hauptmann* Walter Greiff, commander of *Abt.1*, stopped movement until vision had cleared sufficiently. The two remaining tanks, 501 and 506, were then successfully employed to overcome some British strongpoints that still held out.

The five Mk IVs of *Abt.11*, led by the commander, *Hauptmann* Adolf R. Koch, in Tank 103, attacked headlong into the dense fog – and all co-ordination between them ceased immediately. The vehicles roamed around – mainly behind the German infantry screen, which rapidly outran them – supporting the

BEGINNINGS – THE FIRST GERMAN TANKS

The tactic adopted for the British tanks in response to the German spring offensive has disparagingly been dubbed 'savage rabbit' (keep hidden until rushing upon the enemy). On several occasions, British tanks attacked the advancing German troops after 21 March. Usually these attacks were quickly repulsed by the accompanying batteries of the German field artillery, who – different from defence – found it easy to concentrate their mobile guns against the slow moving rhomboids. Also, the German infantry displayed no 'Tankschreck' (tank horror), but smoothly avoided the machines while covering them with machine gun fire. Those tanks that managed to retire after their 'savage' attacks were in most cases abandoned by their crews (as they could not move fast enough to escape their assailants), 40 of them completely intact (except for the parts that German soldiers passing by could easily remove). B.A.K.P. 20 established special recovery squads at Bapaume, Doingt and Bray-sur-Somme for collection of the vehicles captured after 21 March. (Strasheim Collection)

suppression of isolated enemy positions until they had to refuel. Two of them, Tanks 103 and 104, were damaged by artillery in the lifting fog.

The performance of the Mk IVs on test at Beuveille and in action on 21 March caused *Hauptmann* Willy Rohr to state: '*The captured English vehicles have stood the test worse than the German tanks. Co-operation with the infantry appears to be impossible because of their modest speed.*' This assessment was soon confirmed by *Jäger-Sturmbataillon* 3 who quickly realised that the Mk IVs of Abt. 11 and 12 could not be integrated into infantry assault training.

Already, at Beuveille, Rohr had evaluated the A7Vs and had arrived at a conclusion that was quite different from Meyer's: '*Provided the terrain is carefully reconnoitred and chosen, they can be used with success.*' The next German tank action at Villers-Bretonneux would confirm that the senior tactical authority for evaluation of war material to be added to the German arms inventory was right.

The battle of Villers-Bretonneux on 24 April 1918 was no major German offensive but a local affair intended to improve the German positions by taking the small town of Villers-Bretonneux, the high-lying forests west of it, and the village of Cachy. This would provide good artillery observation of Amiens, the major rail hub between the French and British front sectors. The terrain had been assessed as favourable for A7V tanks (no wide trenches, and few shell holes). All three detachments (numbers 2 and 3 had become operational by the end of March) were deployed.

With one tank (543 '*Bulle*') of *Abteilung* 2 out of order and staying behind at Marchienne-au-Pont, the home base of the A7V detachments near Monceau-sur-Sambre, and one (503 '*Faust*') of *Abteilung* 3 broken down after detraining, thirteen A7Vs participated in the attack. Their employment would be a nasty surprise for the British. (Since those British soldiers who had witnessed German tanks at St. Quentin were either dead or prisoners of war at the end of the day, the first German tank action had remained unseen by the Entente commanders.).

The vehicles were divided into three groups: Group I with three tanks (526, 527, and 560) from

A look into the command post of an A7V. The driver's seat – surrounded by levers – is at the right. Slight turns of the tank could be made with the steering wheel. For a full turn, on the spot, one track was put into reverse gear. While the driver had full control over the movements of the A7V, his field of vision forward was impeded by the vehicle itself, allowing observation of the ground in front of the tank only further away than nine metres. The commander's position is to the left. He had no duties other than to direct and co-ordinate his crew's activities and to observe the terrain. When travelling behind the front, the command turret's front, top and rear armour plates could be folded down for better ventilation. The front plate could be raised independently while the top and rear remained folded down. (Strasheim Collection)

Tank 506 'Mephisto' of Abt. 3 just before 24 April 1918. Note the emblem of a red devil running with a snatched rhomboid tank. It seems that during repairs at B.A.K.P. 20 (which became necessary after St. Quentin) the vehicle received tidy markings and a new coat of paint, most likely similar to that applied to the captured Mk IVs – green, red brown and clay yellow in irregular blotches. The camouflage colours were not considered permanent and weathered away rather fast, with clay yellow disappearing first. In this picture the front armour of the turret is up while the top and rear are still folded down. Being an early and not yet modified vehicle, 506 had no commander's hatch and no compass casing installed in the turret top plate, only a circular opening (for flags and flares) in the right forward corner. (Strasheim Collection)

Abteilung 1:

Group II with the four tanks (501, 505, 506, and 507) of *Abteilung 3* and two (541 and 562) from *Abteilung 1*:

Group III with the four tanks (504, 525, 542, and 561) of *Abteilung 2*.

Group I had the most favourable terrain. Despite the morning fog which (as at St. Quentin) clogged the battlefield, Tank 526, the mount of *Oberleutnant* Skopnik, advanced at high speed, ploughing through the utterly surprised British defenders with continuous cannon fire and blazing machine guns. Reaching the outskirts of Villers-Bretonneux, the tank crew noticed that the German infantry had not been able to follow, so they turned their vehicle and drove back, shooting at any British that had survived their first run. After this 526 advanced together with the infantry, assisting them by subduing strong points that still held out.

An infantry battalion commander remembered: '*Suddenly I heard a strange engine noise behind me. Expecting that an English tank had broken through, I ordered some bundled charges to be prepared. Abruptly the fog lifted and I saw a tank with a big Iron Cross. The first German tank that we ever came across. I shouted: 'Hey there, Mr. Tank, get over here!' and the vehicle turned towards me. The small iron door opened and out jumped – a very tidy First Lieutenant, with dress-boots, spurs, creased trousers, and monocle. And us? Looking like swine in the mud! 'Is the battalion commander present?' – 'Right here!' – 'I'm at the Captain's disposal. What orders does the Captain have for me?' – 'Clear the English machine gun positions over there! How long will that take you?' – 'Twenty minutes. Where will I find the Captain afterwards?' – 'In the village at my command post.' Shake hands and off went the tank. Five minutes later we advanced into Villers-Bretonneux without any losses. After twenty minutes the First Lieutenant reported to my 'office'. 'Sir, announce capture of 160 Englishmen.' - 'Where are they right now?' – 'I've already sent them toward Germany.' – 'Very good, Lieutenant. Now I need your help to take an English artillery position beyond the village.' – 'I regret, Sir, but I'm running out of fuel and have to return to base.' We were thankful to 'Mr. Tank' anyway.*'

Tanks 527 '*Lotti*' (*Leutnant* Vietze) and 560 (*Leutnant* Ernst Volckheim) sped ahead and moved back in much the same fashion. After escorting the infantry into the village they were called back to subdue resistance at the brickyards, where the defenders still held out. Here they were joined again by 526. The tanks remained in the area until noon, busily reducing points of resistance that still held out, and advancing into the village – not least to collect some booty (toast, orange marmalade, real soap and other luxuries missing from the German 'Ersatz' diet) before finally returning to their assembly area.

The terrain held more difficulties for Group II, and the British trenches were more elaborate in their area. This generally slowed the A7Vs down and the German infantry was able to follow suit, which also worked quite satisfactorily. Out of the fog the mighty tanks appeared and forced the defenders down, and before they could regain their balance the German infantry were upon them. Tank 541 broke resistance at a fortified farmyard by simply running through it knocking down walls. Tanks 505 '*Baden* I' and 507 '*Cyklop*', later joined by 541, advanced south of Villers-Bretonneux, helped repulse two British counter-attacks, and assisted the infantry in occupying their objective: the Bois d'Aquenne, the eastern part of the high-lying forests. Tank 506 '*Mephisto*', after a successful initial advance, got stuck in a large shell hole and was abandoned by its crew, which kept on fighting as an assault team.

Tank 501 '*Gretchen*', the only A7V still without a cannon, advanced south of the fortified farmyard but soon had engine trouble. The driver was wounded, and no reserve driver was carried. Only after Corporal Bönsch from '*Elfriede's*' crew got to the tank and succeeded in restarting the engines was '*Gretchen*' able to retire. Tank 562, carrying an experimental wireless set with drag antenna, experienced engine trouble as well (which impelled the commander, *Leutnant* Wolfgang Bartens, to form a temporary assault team) but finally joined 505, 507, and 541 near the Bois d'Aquenne.

Group III had a complicated task. To support the infantry into Cachy they had to circle north around two small forests and then south again to meet the infantry exiting the forests. While circling through the fog-clogged expanse Tank 542 '*Elfriede*' slipped into a sand pit and fell on her right side. She was abandoned by her crew, which now also formed an assault team. Two men, one the commander, *Leutnant* Stein, were killed in the process and Private Anders was missing, later turning up as a prisoner of war with the enemy.

Tank 561 '*Nixe*', while circling, supported the infantry of the northern neighbour division, but then – the fog lifting – the commander, *Leutnant* Wilhelm Biltz, was able to make out his objective, the spire of Cachy church, and changed direction towards that village.

Now unfolded the first tank-versus-tank engagement in history. While advancing and firing at British positions at the fringe of Cachy, 561 ran into three British Mk IV tanks that had been ordered forward to defend the line between Cachy and the Bois d'Aquenne. Two of these were female tanks, only one, No. 4066 commanded by 2nd Lt Mitchell, was a male. There are two accounts of this engagement. One by Mitchell, which is a rather lengthy affair, while Biltz' report is quite short and to the point, in fact it is his after-action report, which he supplemented by some additional information in 1938. He noted several enemy tanks, three of which were of the familiar type and rather close, with the foremost already firing at *Nixe*. Biltz immediately had the reverse gear thrown in and the vehicle turned towards the enemy, simultaneously ordering his gunners to open fire. After several rounds had been fired at the Mk IV nearest to 561, the enemy ceased shooting and moving. The gunners (and Biltz) took this for evidence that the vehicle had been put out of action and – with *Nixe* turning left again – now concentrated on the two females (commanded by 1st Lt Hawthorne and 2nd Lt Webber), which were about to escape west, hitting both of them and stopping one. Just at this moment, *Nixe's* armour was penetrated near the gun. One of the gunners was killed immediately while two more were fatally wounded. Fearing that the tank might blow up, the crew jumped out and took cover. When the tank did not burst into flames and the driver found the engines still running, they reboarded the vehicle and were able to coax it about 2 kilometres eastwards before the engines finally quit. Mitchell's central narrative basically matches this report. As there are no photographs known that show the damage to 561, we may assume that it was in fact Mitchell's gunner who scored that hit (and two further ones detonating close to *Nixe's* right flank sending splinters below the side armour, damaging some pipes in the soft underbelly and eventually leading to engine breakdown because of oil and coolant loss), although the front armour of the A7V was supposed to be proof against a calibre such as the six-pounder of a male Mk IV.

The two remaining A7Vs of Group III, 504 '*Schnuck*' and 525 '*Siegfried*', had successfully made rendezvous with the infantry but their support was not enough to help the 77. *Reserve Division* take Cachy. The 77th had only recently arrived from the Eastern Front, and had had only five days of induction training into Western Front conditions by *Jäger-Sturm-Bataillon* 3. Now they were utterly confused and irritated by the constant shelling and the tenacious resistance they met – and their left wing regiment still hung back, fighting in the forests.

When – shortly after Tank 561 had been hit by artillery (in the perception of 77. *Reserve Division*, who did not see the Mk IVs) – an infantry counter-attack out of Cachy and a foray by seven Whippets coincided, the "*weak forward elements*" of the 77th's right wing broke. Those in front surrendered to the enemy, those behind ran back for some 1,000 metres. British publications usually highlight the carnage that the Whippets allegedly caused by running over the hapless Germans, killing at least 400 of them. Looking at the German side – where an inquiry was held on the reasons why Cachy had not been taken – no indication of any such massacre can be found. However, the Whippets soon met resistance. The commander of Tank 525, *Leutnant* Friedrich Wilhelm Bitter, noticed the strange looking vehicles (he thought they might be French) and had his tank turn towards them and open fire. Simultaneously a battery of 77 mm field cannons of the right neighbour division went into firing position and blasted away at the Whippets, as did several minethrowers[1] from both divisions, while the small arms of the 77. *Reserve Division* remained ineffective because they had no steel core bullets. One minethrower took on Mitchell's 4066, which had now been identified as attacker number eight, and split the left track, after which Mitchell's crew abandoned the vehicle. In short order, four Whippets were hit and put out of action while the remaining three retired hastily. But the smoke columns from two burning Whippets were no incentive for the exhausted and bewildered 77. *Reserve Division*. They started to dig in. Cachy would remain in British hands.

The A7V attack had been an overall success, and *Hauptmann* Rohr's assessment had been confirmed in battle. But a night-time counter-attack with two pincers, one out of the Somme valley, the other out of Cachy, retook most of the ground and thus overshadowed the tank action. (Ironically, the whole affair thus resembles Cambrai re-enacted in miniature with roles reversed.) The blame clearly went to 77. *Reserve Division*, which had failed to secure Cachy thus exposing the German centre to a serious flank threat.

On 25 April three A7Vs remained on the battlefield: 542 lying on its side but completely intact behind the Entente front line (to be salvaged in May and tested subsequently); 561 blown up by a German demolition squad during the night; and 506 intact in a crater behind the German front line but soon heavily damaged by a shell hit (the only A7V to survive, salvaged by the Australians in July 1918, transported to

---

[1] These were developed by the engineer branch with the aim of delivering heavy charges (up to 50 kg of explosives) in fortress combat. Because of the lack of proper artillery ammunition, they were also used in the initial phase of trench warfare. That made them quite popular and led to an expansion of the arm. Unlike mortars (such as the British Stokes) their rate of fire was very slow, and unlike howitzers they lacked range. Their advantage was that the bombs could easily be manufactured by companies that did not have the expensive and sophisticated equipment necessary for artillery shells. As they were technically complicated, had a slow rate of fire and were cumbersome to transport, they were finally replaced by mortars (on the model of the Stokes). Yet ordinary mortars are in no way equivalent to mine throwers as they lack the 'punch'. Those used by troops around Cachy were all of the light type, which had the highest rate of fire and the least punch. These weapons were used for anti-tank purposes on a flat trajectory mount and proved quite successful as 'tank killers'.

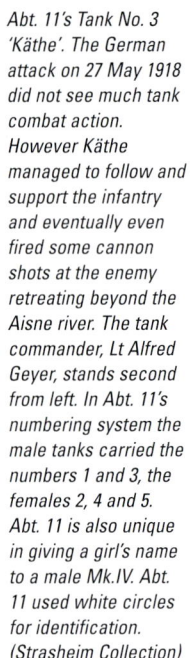

Abt. 11's Tank No. 3 'Käthe'. The German attack on 27 May 1918 did not see much tank combat action. However Käthe managed to follow and support the infantry and eventually even fired some cannon shots at the enemy retreating beyond the Aisne river. The tank commander, Lt Alfred Geyer, stands second from left. In Abt. 11's numbering system the male tanks carried the numbers 1 and 3, the females 2, 4 and 5. Abt. 11 is also unique in giving a girl's name to a male Mk.IV. Abt. 11 used white circles for identification. (Strasheim Collection)

Australia and still on exhibition in Brisbane, Australia today). Statistically, about 13 per cent (two vehicles) of the tanks broke down before the attack and 20 per cent (three vehicles) were lost due to the non-existent salvage capability.

The next tank action went to the captured detachments. *Beute-Abteilungen 11, 12, 13,* and *14* participated in the offensive at the Chemin des Dames on 27 May 1918. While the German infantry stormed ahead the Mk IVs slowly crept along, always behind the action and hardly spending ammunition. Only in *Abteilung 12's* sector did strong resistance temporarily check the attackers. The tanks (only three had negotiated the enemy's first trench line) arrived and two of them were almost instantly knocked out by French 75 mm field cannons.

The next attacks near Reims saw the A7Vs at their worst, confronted with terrain they could not negotiate and French 75s to take advantage of their immobility. One (Tank 529, Biltz' '*Nixe* II') was lost in a badly co-ordinated action on 31 May, another (527) in a badly reconnoitred diversionary skirmish on 1 June.

On 1 June, in an attempt to take the Fort de la Pompelle east of Reims, *Beute-Abteilungen 13* and *14* went into action too. *Abteilung 13* lost all three serviceable tanks, plus one each from *11* and *12* reinforcing them. *Abteilung 14* lost three of its four operative tanks. The infantry grumbled: '*The tank attack failed completely. But at least they did attract the enemy shells away from us.*' In reality only the *Abteilung 13* tanks had accomplished nothing at all, those from *11, 12,* and *14* had done what they were supposed to. The infantry was effectively supported into the fort, but proved too weak to hold it and by noon were back in their old trenches, leaving behind eight Mk IVs lost (of which only a single one was salvaged later on).

Now the pattern was set. The A7Vs would either fail because the terrain was unsuitable for their use, or achieve good results on favourable ground. The captured Mk IVs would either miss the action because they were too slow to keep pace with the infantry, or (irrelevant whether in success or failure) swiftly be knocked out if they joined combat.

The engagements to follow were:

- 9 June, at the river Matz: *Abteilungen 1* and *3*, no tank losses. *Abt.3* (Tanks 503, 505, 507, 543, and 564) supporting the infantry with overall success against an enemy ready to fall back. *Abt.1* bringing only two tanks (541 and 562) to bear, of which one (562) became stuck in a French battalion command post, after which the tank attack stalls.
- 15 July, at the Forêt de la Montagne west of Reims: *Abteilungen* 1 (Tanks 501, 540, 541, 560) and 2 (Tanks 504, 525, 563), accompanying a successful advance against a delaying screen of Italian troops, no tanks lost. The skilful use that the Italians made of well-positioned small machine gun parties was effectively thwarted where the tanks advanced.
- 15 July, in Champagne south of Somme-Py and east of Reims: *Beute-Abteilungen 11, 12, 13,* and *14* also in support of the final German offensive. No success, but heavy losses against stubborn resistance. From a total of 20 available

Tank 560 followed by 527 and (most likely) 526 on the approach march. This picture was presumably taken on 31 May or 1 June 1918. As always, as many crew members as possible try to escape the interior heat, noise and fumes. The Skulls and Crossbones are a distinctive mark of Abt.1. Only in October 1918 – after having been annexed to Abt.1 – did Abt. 2 vehicles start to display them too. The extensive use of camouflage nets as seen in this picture is also a distinctive trait of Abt. 1. (Mario Doherr Collection)

Tank 507 'Prinz Eitel Friedrich' of Abt. 3 seen near Tilleloy on 8 June 1918. Despite the ban on using royal cognomina already issued on 25 May, Abt. 3 displayed the Hohenzollern family names for identification purposes during the tank attack on 9 June. 543 became 'Prinz Adalbert' (later changed to 'Adalbert'). A regimental history mentions an A7V 'König Wilhelm'. On 505 a faint 'Wilhelm' can still be traced in early September, and 503 has a 'K..' still. Abt. 3 relied on frequently changing names for identification and is not known to have adopted the 1 to 5 number scheme at all. Also, their tanks still displayed a single Iron Cross each side as late as October 1918. (Strasheim Collection)

BEGINNINGS – THE FIRST GERMAN TANKS

A7V Specification

Weight: 30 tonnes
Crew: 18
Engines: 2 x Daimler 100 HP
Speed: 9 km/h
Armament: 57mm Maxim-Nordenfeldt and 6 x 7.92mm Model 1908 Maxim machine guns
Length: 7.34 m (24ft 1 in)
Width: 3.1 m (10 ft)
Height: 3.3 m (10ft 10 in)
Armour: 7.5 mm to 30 mm

Tank 527 of the Villers-Bretonneux Abt. 1 (an A7V type) lies abandoned east of Reims after having been hit by a French 75 mm cannon on 1 June 1918.

Although the front armour may have been proof against such hits, neither the roof nor the turret were. Note the Iron Crosses for aerial identification on the front and rear louvres. Note also that the louvres are of the second type with nine longitudinal slits instead of 45 small slots. These second type louvres were installed on Tanks 525, 526, 527, 528, 529, 560, 561, 562, 563 and 564. The ammunition box for the cannon lies besides the tank as does one machine gunner's seat. After Villers-Bretonneux Abt. 1 adopted the number-in-ring system also in use with the captured detachments. The ring colour is white. (Strasheim Collection)

© COPYRIGHT HILARY LOUIS DOYLE

PANZERWAFFE

Deutscher Tank bei Rollot

562 stuck in a French command post after 9 June. Again, a guard has been detailed to prevent equipment being 'found'. The picture clearly shows the limitations of the A7V – its 'low nose', aggravated by the 3 cm front armour and the cannon, trapped it definitely in a situation that never would have stopped a British rhomboid. Note the commander's hatch (at rear) and compass casing (in centre) of the turret top plate. 562 was later salvaged and – after repair – given to Abt. 2 where it received the name 'Herkules'. (Strasheim Collection, courtesy of Didier Guènaff)

Tank 525 'Siegfried' of Abt. 2 seen at Marchienne-au-Pont, most probably after the combat on 15 July 1918. The number '520' chalked beside the front door is not the tank number but the number of bullet impacts counted and marked with white circles. Strangely, 525 does not show the extra turret armour peculiar to Abt. 2, and did not have it fitted in action either as indicated by the hit marks on the turret, although 529 'Nixe II', lost on 31 May, already displayed that feature. There is camouflage paint applied to the vehicle, presumably again green, red brown and clay yellow in irregular patches. False apertures have been painted on the male bow. Abt. 2 used Roman numerals (initially in solid white, after Villers-Bretonneux in red with white outline) instead of the number-in-ring system. (Strasheim Collection)

This Mk.IV male was probably photographed in 1919 or 1920. The German camouflage paint has weathered away and only the Iron Crosses and a very faint identification circle remain above the former British tint (which was the chocolate brown). The semblance of an identification circle indicate that this was a vehicle of Abt. 14, who used light blue as a circle colour. This supposition is verified by the place name 'Epine de Vedegrange', which clearly lay in Abt. 14's sector of attack on 15 July 1918. The vehicle ran over a landmine that broke the right-hand track, after which the crew abandoned it without blowing it up. Note the faint 09 below the Iron Cross. This indicates that the front male tank seen in the bottom photograph on page 4 met its fate here for a second time. (Strasheim Collection)

vehicles, 13 entered combat of which 11 were lost of which four struck landmines and four more were hit by artillery.

● 31 August, at Frèmicourt: *Abteilungen 1* and *2* employed. The former did not arrive in time because all tanks broke down during the 20 km approach march, causing 30 friendly casualties when a house in Beugny collapsed due to engine vibrations. The latter conducted an uncoordinated and eventually unsuccessful counter-attack. Tanks 504 '*Schnuck*' and 528 '*Hagen*' were lost. Additionally, Tank 562 '*Herkules*' had already been hit by an aerial bomb in the assembly area.

● 7 October, at the River Arne near St.Etienne: *Abteilung 3* with four serviceable tanks providing close artillery support to another uncoordinated yet successful counter-attack, and regained possession of the town for some hours. No tank lost.

● 8 October, east of Cambrai: *Beute-Abteilungen 11*, *15* and *16* in combat with tanks of British L Battalion (12th Bn), involving Mk IV versus Mk IV, with each side losing four vehicles in the mêlée. It was temporarily a successful German counter-attack. This is the only known occasion where German tanks used 13 mm anti-tank rifles against their opponents: 10 shots were fired on two British Mk IVs, both vehicles belonging to the four that L Battalion lost. But, all told, the losses were higher. Three disabled tanks of *Abt.11* had already been abandoned prior to the encounter because salvage proved impossible in the continuous shelling. A fourth had also been hit but was extricated although remaining unfit for combat. One tank of Abt. 15 had been knocked out too but was able to retire to the railhead under its own power. And on 9 October, two more tanks were blown up because they could not be moved to the railhead.

● 11 October, at Iwuy: *Abteilung 1* – also in charge of *Abt. 2's* remaining vehicles – (Tanks 501, 525, 541, 560, and 563) supported a successful counter-attack, with one loss (560) – and Bavarian *Beute-Abteilung 13*, losing three tanks (118, 137, 142) without entering combat. Again, overall losses were higher. Abt. 1 had already left behind (and cannibalised) Tank 540 on 3 October. *Abt. 13* abandoned and destroyed Tank 127 on 9 October and 213 on 12 October.

● 1 November, near Valenciennes: *Abteilung 12* spearheaded a successful counter-attack (with three of their five tanks became unserviceable). *Abt.13* brings only one tank (coming under *Abt.12's* command) forward and lost it due to a direct artillery hit. *Abt.14* initially remained in reserve and finally moves up to cover the left flank. *Abt.14* had four serviceable tanks plus one in need of repair at the end of the day and remained with *17. Armee*, while *12.* and *13.* are withdrawn. This was the final German tank action to take place in World War 1.

In all cases there were too few German tanks to make a lasting impression. Even successful counter-pushes such as those on 8 and 11 October and 1 November only restored the situation for some hours before the enemy advance continued.

Starting in mid-August 1918, after the successful Franco-British tank attack east of Amiens, each army group on the Western Front received one tank detachment for familiarisation training

Tank 120 of Abt. 14 seen at Roux. It subsequently received the name 'Liesel'. This is not the 'Liesel' lost at the Fort de la Pompelle on 1 June 1918, but the second or even third Liesel. Abt. 14 frequently used the same name again when commissioning a replacement tank for a vehicle lost. The number 120 can be read on the inside of the escape hatch. Three of the soldiers wear leather patched trousers. The tank does not yet display the light blue identification circle on the horn but a name on its rear side armour, which indicates that it has just been issued to Abt. 14. (Strasheim Collection)

Tank 118 of Bavarian Abt. 13 stands forlorn near Chateau Avesnes-le-Sec after 11 October 1918. As Abt. 13 had been out for demonstrations and exercises since mid-August, the change to Buntfarben camouflage and Latin Crosses ('Balkenkreuze') had not yet been implemented. White squares emphasise the Iron Crosses and – if orders have been followed – a diagonal white band on the roof is added for aerial recognition. 118 was the No. 3 tank of Abt. 13 and commanded by Lt Joseph Korb. Abt. 13 used yellow circles for unit identification. According to Abt. 13's combat report the vehicle was set on fire when it was abandoned by the crew. Note the rail arrangement above the command cupola, a peculiarity of Abt. 13 tanks in the period from the end of July to early October 1918. (Strasheim Collection)

Three captured Mk.IVs – two male, one female – clad in Buntfarben ('coloured tint', a camouflage pattern officially introduced in July 1918) are seen here after recapture. Le Quesnoy was taken by the New Zealand Division on 4 November 1918. No names or numbers are visible, although the right hand tank may carry an identification circle. The tanks could be relics of the actions on 8 October, in which case they would be Abt. 16's vehicles, or on 1 November, in which case they would have belonged to Abt. 14 (the only detachment that was not withdrawn), although it is difficult to see how and why the detachment should have moved south-eastwards to Le Quesnoy. (Strasheim Collection)

The Whippet tank with Abt. 13 suffered damage on 8 September while negotiating a crater at the Lieu St.Amand training area. In this picture the vehicle has been winched up and rests on a pile of lumber. The crew watch the ongoing exercise, as do the officers to the left. In the background a male Mk.IV of Abt. 13 can be seen. Note the Iron Cross on the Whippet's bonnet. This is the only Whippet known to have carried German camouflage (again green, red brown and clay yellow) and markings. It was later briefly seen with Tankabteilung Körting in January 1919. (Strasheim Collection)

with tanks. These training courses lasted until the end of September. Only *Abteilungen 1* and *2* remained at Marchienne-au-Pont (except for their unsuccessful sortie to Frèmicourt), while at Roux (also neighbouring Monceau-sur-Sambre), the home base of the captured detachments, *Beute-Abteilungen 15* and *16* gradually became operational.

At the end of September OHL ordered a concentration for one big counter-push with all nine detachments, a force of about 45 tanks (including some spare Mk IVs). But this plan was abandoned again before the detachments could even be put on trains.

As the German *17.* and *3. Armee* were now the targets of powerful enemy attacks, both were given tank detachments on various occasions. Yet only *17. Armee* managed to use the tanks successfully in several instances, while only one of the planned missions in *3. Armee's* sector was effectively executed but utterly unsuccessful because the A7Vs of *Abteilung 3* could not negotiate the Arne brook at St. Etienne – the existing bridge had been blown up by friendly forces just prior to the counter-attack that *Abteilung 3* were to support.

17. Armee however, constantly appealed for tanks and used them – not because the individual tank actions were such glorious successes, but because of the moral support that the presence of friendly tanks gave the infantry. Even the fiasco at Frèmicourt, where co-ordination between tanks and infantry had not happened at all and one tank (504) was hit by friendly fire (the 77 mm rounds did not penetrate the front armour, but the impacts convinced the crew to abandon the vehicle), never discouraged *17. Armee*.

After the enormous force that the counter-attack at Iwuy had displayed, the infantry even asked specifically for A7Vs – in clear appreciation of what a powerful machine the fast and well-armed A7V was if employed for high-speed counter-strikes on favourable terrain. (OHL, in contrast, always warned when deploying A7V detachments: '*Transferred tanks are of the obsolete German type. Caution! Not to be used in heavily shelled terrain.*')

In terms of developing the German tank arm, the first steps occurred in late summer and early autumn. A tank training area was set up close to Monceau-sur-Sambre, a tank commanders' training course was launched (but never completed), and at home a tank-replacement detachment was about to be established at Zehrensdorf on the Zossen manoeuvre ground. New formations were also envisaged: the personnel of a Saxon and a Württemberg captured tank detachment were just gathering, and the Bavarians were planning to enhance their contribution. The German collapse of late October and early November 1918 stopped further progress.

Another fast vehicle (with a top speed equalling that of the A7V) fell into German hands in summer 1918: the British Medium A, called 'Whippet', a number of which had been captured during the German advance in late March. After intensive testing the verdict was that the Whippet was a good vehicle that might well be worth copying – if the LK. II with superior characteristics was not already under construction.

An early LK prototype arrived for field tests and comparison at *Abteilung 3's* training and demonstration area near Saarburg on 30 August 1918. Only two of the Whippets captured were restored to running condition. One was immediately sent to Berlin, where the German engineers disassembled it for comparison with ongoing LK construction.

The second runner was temporarily given to *Abteilung 13*, which undertook the tank familiarisation exercises for Army Group Crown Prince Rupprecht, but in mid-October it was called to Berlin. (This vehicle, the only one to carry German camouflage and markings, was later seen in *Freikorps* use in January 1919.) The often repeated rumour that the Germans fielded a whole detachment of Whippets holds no substance.

Several non-running tanks were also used in familiarisation and anti-tank

The first Whippet restored by B.A.K.P. 20 was immediately sent to Berlin in spring 1918. It is seen here with the armoured body removed for study purposes. With each track driven by one Taylor engine, the mechanical arrangement of the Whippet was as complicated as that of the A7V. The LK tanks used one engine to drive both tracks and consequently needed only one gearbox. (Strasheim Collection)

Captured British Mk IV (Female)

Weight: 27 tonnes
Crew: 8 -12
Engines: Foster-Daimler 105 HP
Speed: 5 km/h
Armament: 2 x 6pdr 5 x MG
Length: 8 m (26.4ft)
Width: 3.2 m (10.5ft)
Height: 2.4 m (8.17ft)
Armour: 6 to 12mm

A captured British Mk.IV, known as 'Lotte' photographed with a captured Renault FT17 Runner of Abt. 14 at a staff training ground near Sedan in September 1918

While Abt. 13 had the Whippet, Abt. 14 received a Renault FT17 runner for exercises and demonstrations with Army Group German Crown Prince. After capture, this Renault somehow lost its machine gun-armed turret (on which the tank's name 'Hargneuse' – Biting One – was written) and received a wooden turret mock up. The Mk.IV is 'Lotte', however not the one lost at Fort de la Pompelle on 1 June 1918, (which was No. 3) but a later successor (No. 2 tank of the detachment). The photograph was taken in September 1918, most probably on the former training ground of the leaders and general staff training course near Sedan. (Strasheim Collection) training (plus a huge variety of dummy tanks made from lumber and canvas).

After 27 May 1918, a number of Renault FT17s were captured as well. A running one (with a wooden turret mock-up) appeared with *Abteilung 14*, which undertook the tank familiarisation exercises for Army Group German Crown Prince.

Another runner was sent to Berlin and subjected to anti-tank tests at Marienfelde in late September 1918. The Germans dismissed the FT17 as too slow and having insufficient trench crossing capacity.

The end of the war caught the German tank force in the process of relocation. B.A.K.P. 20 was destined for the MAN factory at Gustavsburg near Mainz, but never arrived as a coherent formation. The tank detachments were transported to Erbenheim near Wiesbaden, where the tanks were parked on the terrain of the horse race course while the soldiers elected their soldiers' council, received their final pay and started for home because the war was finally over.

On 27 October *Abteilung 2* was formally handed over to *Hauptmann* Hans Thofern, Commanding Officer of *Abteilung 1*, who had already taken over *Abteilung 3* on 23 October. Now only one A7V detachment remained, with a total of ten tanks of which eight were available and perhaps four operational. On 3 November *Abteilung 1* was put on trains at Marchienne-au-Pont and travelled toward Erbenheim.

In all, the small German tank force had lost about 80 dead, 220 wounded, and some three or four soldiers taken prisoner of war by the enemy. From a TOE strength of almost 1,400 soldiers of all ranks, this amounts to losses of roughly 22 per cent.

The German plan for 1919 shows that the lesson had finally been understood. This plan was first formulated in June 1918, far in advance of the big Entente tank attacks at Soissons and Amiens, and even before the final German offensive failed on 15 July. It is therefore a remarkable piece of evidence: the early decision to mass-produce tanks was a reflection of realising that Germany was no longer able to achieve victory in 1918 – even while preparations for the Champagne offensive and the '*Hagen*' assault against the British front line were still taking place. It is also clear that once the paramount importance of tanks had been understood the problem of resource allocation was no longer held relevant.

The tank force would consist of light LK and heavy Oberschlesien tanks. For the interim period the A7Vs and the Mk IVs would be used as heavies until the Oberschlesiens became ready. The plan called for 150 heavy (Mk IVs, of which 170 were reported to be still available, and the remaining A7Vs, which were expected to expire soon) and 400 light tanks in April 1919 (the programmed number of LKs – not yet contested by reality – quickly inflating to 800 and 1,000). The total numbers of tanks envisaged for end-1919 were 4,000 LKs and 400 Oberschlesiens.

The heavy tanks would operate in detachments of 15 vehicles divided into three companies with five tanks each. The light tanks would come in detachments of 100 vehicles divided into three companies. A company would have 31 tanks and consist of three platoons of 10 light tanks each. One third of the LKs would be gun armed, two thirds would carry machine guns.

However, Germany's collapse and the subsequent terms of the Versailles Treaty put an end to these schemes. What is known about actual LK production leaves serious doubts as to whether even 400 machines could have been ready in April 1919.

A proper tactical doctrine for tank warfare still had to be developed.

While the record of the German tank detachments in 1918

Another captured Renault runner was No. 66260 'Manoeuvre', seen here with soldiers of the Württemberg mountain battalion. This tank was later sent to Berlin where – together with Mk.IV F.41 and the first Whippet – it featured in an anti-tank primer illustrating the weak spots of Entente tanks. It was most probably also the Renault subjected to anti-tank tests at Berlin-Marienfelde in September 1918. One advantage of the FT17 was that it could easily be transported on trucks or trailers, thus overcoming the dependence on railway lines which severely restricted the deployment options of the heavier designs. (Strasheim Collection)

An LK.II clad in Buntfarben on test. This one carries the 5.7 cm cannon also used in the A7Vs and the captured male Mk.IVs. The gun was found to be too heavy and its recoil too powerful for the LK. The solution envisaged was the 3.7 cm cannon under development by Krupp. However that weapon was not yet ready by the time of the German collapse. LK production therefore concentrated on machine gun armed tanks only. LK development was a continuous process in which the LK.I was improved into the LK.II machine gun version, while the LK.II gun tank provided the second line of development. The – blueprint only – LK.III finally arrived at the 'modern' layout of the FT17. (Strasheim Collection)

Two A7V (Überlandwagen) chassis had been provided to the signals branch which proposed to develop a special communication tank. These vehicles were not intended for use with the tank detachments but were to serve as communication centres for all troops, especially in attack. Only the front right and rear left barbettes had been constructed as machine gun mounts; those at the front left and rear right were designed to carry signalling lamps. Apparently Oblt. Hans von Skopnik (believed to be the second man from right) seized the two uncompleted vehicles in November 1918 and organised their completion as riot control tanks at Steffens & Noelle's. (Note the fourth and sixth man from right, also visible together with Joseph Vollmer in the picture on page 3). One vehicle showed up with Kokampf in January and May 1919, carrying the number 54 and later the name 'Hedi'. The fate of the second one is not known. (Mario Doherr Collection)

can be traced with sufficient detail, only fragments of the story of the armoured *Freikorps* units are known. The written sources are few and disconnected, and the known photographs allow only glimpses.

During November and December 1918, the German armies in the west conducted a well organised retreat and – once arrived on German soil – melted away like ice in the sun. In parallel, new voluntary formations emerged. These were called '*Freikorps*', taking up a tradition from Prussia's fight against Napoleon in 1812/13. The *Freikorps* had two important tasks: protection of the eastern borders ('*Grenzschutz Ost*') and safeguarding the internal order and cohesion of the Reich.

The German more-or-less government-controlled forces peaked with some 600,000 men in spring 1919, but downsizing had already started in June/July of that year. The last *Freikorps* were disbanded in early summer 1920, and by 1 January 1921, the size of 4,000 Officers and 96,000 NCOs and men prescribed in the Versailles Treaty had been achieved (plus 15,000 sailors in the minute navy).

One of the better known armoured *Freikorps* formations was '*Tankabteilung Körting*', also known as '*Kokampf* (*Kommando der Kampfwagen-Abteilungen* – combat vehicle detachment command) or '*Kampfwagen-Abteilung Lüttwitz*'. The nucleus of this unit seems to have been formed by *Oberleutnant* von Skopnik (not to be confused with *Oblt*. Skopnik of A7V-*Abteilung 1* who was killed in the summer of 1918), who seized the two prototype A7V '*Nachrichtenwagen*' (communication tanks) and arranged their completion, allegedly for '*Grenzschutz Ost*', which provided a good justification to persuade factory workers otherwise generally unwilling to assemble weapons that might be used against themselves or their colleagues.

On 7 January 1919 *Hauptmann* Georg Körting, former deputy commander of the assault tank detachments, took command of the unit. Within the next few weeks, *Kokampf* was created and largely expanded.

Several other tanks were added to the inventory. Those known are:

'*Imperator*', an A7V tank (most probably 507, sent to Daimler for repair in October 1918)

'*Hanni*', an ex-*Abteilung 12* Mk IV female, Tank No. 4 of that detachment

Another ex-*Abteilung 12* Mk IV female, Tank No.3

(*Abteilung 12* had received a complement of new tanks on 23 October. Some of the old, worn out machines were apparently dispatched to Berlin for overhaul. Because of ongoing relocation, B.A.K.P.20 no longer accepted repair jobs from mid-October.)

At least two more Mk IV females of unknown origin (probably earmarked for the tank training detachment at Zehrensdorf) and one Whippet (the one that had been with *Abteilung 13*).

There may have been other tanks, but photographs – so far – only show the vehicles mentioned above.

Ninety light tanks, 38 Krupp-Daimler D.Z.V.R., 20 additional Ehrhardt, and 30 makeshift lorry-based armoured cars were ordered for '*Grenzschutz Ost*' in a largely scaled down version of Plan 1919. How many of these really saw completion – and at what date – remains open.

Hungary had possessed 14 LK.IIs, '*acquired very inexpensively from demobilised materials of the German Army*' since 1920. In 1921 Sweden bought at least 10 LK.IIs from Germany. While the Hungarian LKs were kept secret and hidden in railway wagons for some time, the Swedish machines were presented to the public as indigenous *Stridsvagn M21*, allegedly assembled and completed in Sweden from parts bought in Germany and with Swedish armour plating.

The organisational set-up of *Kokampf* (for '*Grenzschutz Ost*') originally foresaw three detachments, each with one heavy (tank) and two light (armoured car and motorised Flak) platoons, plus a central workshop.

PANZERWAFFE

'Hanni', followed by Kokampf's Ehrhardt armoured car, approaches the Alexanderplatz in central Berlin in early March 1919. This Mk.IV remained in support of the drive against Spartacist strongholds in eastern Berlin for several days. Note the special 'street fighting' version of the German steel helmet worn by most soldiers in the foreground. As the visor would hinder looking up to detect snipers on roofs and in windows, it was removed by this particular unit. Note also that civilian pedestrian traffic flows unimpeded in the background. Being an ex-Abt. 12 vehicle, Hanni carried a red identification circle with the number 4 inserted, plus the Kokampf plaque ('Kokampf – 153 – Abt.') and skull and crossbones. (Strasheim Collection)

A motley array of Kokampf vehicles at the Marstall (royal stables) in Berlin in the spring of 1919. The armoured cars are from left to right:
- *Russian Fiat/15 'Strolch'*
- *Russian 60 HP Hotchkiss 'Lotta' (often misidentified as a Russo-Balt)*
- *Makeshift armoured truck 'Mausi' (note 2 cm Becker gun in turret)*
- *Makeshift armoured truck 'Schnucki' with same armament*
- *Russian Packard L-01015 (also with 2 cm Becker gun in revolving turret)*
- *Russian Packard L-0?*
- *Ex-Belgian Peugeot 'Raudi'.*

The 'L' refers to General von Lüttwitz to whose command Kokampf belonged. 'Strolch', 'Lotta' and 'Raudi' saw combat in Munich in early May. (Strasheim Collection)

The detachments were initially numbered 01, 02, and 03 – but became 101, 102, and 103 when *Kokampf* became an element of *Reichswehrgruppenkommando 1*. Detachment 104 had been planned to be a Bavarian unit but was never established. Two more detachments, 105 and 106, may have been formed or been under formation, but no further details are available.

While 01/101 remained the detachment based in Berlin and using those vehicles known from photographs, 102 had its origins in the '*Armoured Detachment of Army Command North*' (augmented by *Kokampf*), and 103 was formed from '*Armoured Detachment of Army Command South*'. (Both army commands were *Grenzschutz Ost* formations, the former based in East Prussia, the latter in Silesia.)

Detachments 102 and 103 may have been deployed in support of the planned operation against Poland (to re-take the Posen province and smash the Polish army), which was prepared but never executed after the terms of the Versailles Treaty became known in early summer 1919. Detachments 101 and 103 were finally disbanded in Berlin, while 102 was demobilised in East Prussia. *Abteilung 103* is recorded in Silesia until 19 January 1920. The photographic account of 102 and 103 for 1919 still has to be discovered.

Yet tanks were only one facet of *Kokampf*. Just one of them, 'Hanni', was used in combat during the March 1919 fighting in central and eastern Berlin. For countering internal unrest the weapons of choice were armoured cars, of which *Kokampf* possessed a motley array. Armoured cars were much easier to move around and their effect against an enemy usually armed only with rifles and machine guns was as good as that of tanks.

'Hedi' seen at Leipzig railway station in May 1919. Three tanks, 'Hedi' plus two Mk.IV females, had been given to General Maercker's Landesjäger-Korps for the pacification of Leipzig and Halle. They certainly added to the strength of the force, but saw no combat. The tall officer (fourth from right) is 2nd Lt Bornschein, a veteran of A7V Abt. 1. While the first man on the right displays the 'Grenzschutz Ost' collar emblem, four others wear the silver oak twig of 'Generalkommando Lüttwitz'. Skull badges and cuff titles marked 'Kampfwagen' are worn on the left sleeve. Note the 'Lüttwitz L' on the licence plate of the passenger car. Hedi's Kokampf plaque ('Kokampf – 151 – Abt. 01') is hardly visible behind the third man from right. The tank seems to be densely covered by soot. (Mario Doherr Collection)

The mailed fist of the Berlin-based Garde-Kavallerie-Schützen-Korps in late spring/early summer of 1919: Two ex-Italian Lancias (at left) and two ex-Russian Austins (third pattern). Normally, two vehicles were in service with Garde-Kavallerie-(Schützen)-Division and two with Division von Lettow. The vehicles display no Kokampf markings, yet the personnel serving them regularly are seen wearing 'Kampfwagen' cuff titles and skull badges. The Garde-Kavallerie-Schützen-Korps was disbanded in June/July 1919, but 2nd and 3rd Naval Brigades (previously units of Div v.Lettow) lived on until May/June 1920. (Strasheim Collection)

The man sitting in the centre is Kapitänleutnant (Naval Lt) Lothar von Arnauld de la Perière, the highest scoring submarine commander in history, seen here as commander of the assault battalion of 3rd Naval Brigade ('Marinebrigade') within Division von Lettow (also known as 'Marine-Division'). Again, a Lancia and an Austin are prominent. The Lancia shows the plaque 'S-GS-52' on its bonnet. Some months later, in April 1920, von Arnauld's unit participated in the subjection of the Red Ruhr Army. After this operation three armoured cars still belonged to the unit: a Lancia 'Enzio', a Russian Fiat/17 'Lottchen', and a Russian Fiat/15 (ex-'Strolch', no name visible). A fourth vehicle, 'Lotta', had been lost in combat. (Strasheim Collection)

The Germans had only produced a rather limited number of armoured cars during the war, which had seen very little or no combat use but had travelled far and wide, some even to the Caucasus and the Baku oil fields. And they had captured a large number of armoured cars, the majority in Russia and Italy, some of which had been used to form additional armoured car units (none of which saw combat).

In early 1919 *Kokampf* had only one indigenous German armoured car, an Ehrhardt, plus some makeshift armoured lorries of 1919 vintage, all their other armoured cars being captured vehicles. (The motor vehicle replacement depot at Berlin-Schöneberg had been the central collecting point for captured armoured cars).

After the Versailles Treaty was signed on 28 June, the Allied Military Control Commission, which finally moved into Berlin on 15 September 1919, demanded the scrapping of all tanks and decentralisation of *Kokampf*'s fleet of armoured cars. Subsequently several tanks were scrapped in Berlin. Others may have gone into hiding.

Essentially, 'decentralisation' became a thinning of *Kokampf*'s armada by giving armoured cars to some of the *Reichswehr* brigades now being formed, where they comprised the '*Leichter Kampf-Kraftwagen-Zug*' (light armoured car platoon) with two combat vehicles. The personnel (when coming from *Kokampf*) usually kept their '*Kampfwagen*' cuff title and the skull and crossbones badge, and because of which the platoons are often misidentified as '*Kokampf*'. However, *Kokampf* remained the central body for swapping vehicles and personnel – and retained the heavy detachments 101, 102 and 103.

Not all brigades had armoured cars, and those which had did not strictly adhere to the number of two, and some acquired their armoured vehicles from sources other than *Kokampf*. For example, the Bavarian Brigade 21 (former *Freikorps Epp*) possessed six armoured cars: four specially built for them, one ex-Italian Lancia, and one Daimler makeshift armoured truck.

The Württemberg Brigade 13 fielded three armoured cars for the 'liberation' of the Ruhr district in April 1920 – and had at least one Mk IV female tank "hidden at home."

The Bavarian special solution: an armoured car of Freikorps Epp. Constructed (like the D.Z.V.R.) on the chassis of the 100 HP Krupp-Daimler tractor, the vehicle had a crew of twelve and fielded a 3.7 cm gun (in the turret) and seven 08 machine guns (two per side, one rear, one in the turret rear and one reserve). Four of these monsters were ordered, but only one (licence plate: M II 619) became ready in 1919. The completion of the three others dragged on until mid-1920 as the factory workers were well aware of the potential use of the vehicles and thus saw no reason to hurry. The plaques (apparently covered with mud here) read: 'Vom Kampfwagen abbleiben, sonst wird geschossen!' (Stay away from armoured car, else fire will be opened!) Note the black flag with skull and cross bones on the bonnet. A small black rhombic dot denotes the Freikorps Epp Lion emblem below the forward plaque. The overburdened vehicles could only be used 'at moderate speed and on good roads.' (Strasheim Collection)

In early 1920 the new Krupp-Daimler D.Z.V.R. and additional Ehrhardt armoured cars started to arrive in numbers. They very soon replaced the foreign and makeshift vehicles, which must have been a mechanical engineer's nightmare in terms of spare part procurement. As the Versailles Treaty forbade armed armoured cars for the emerging *Reichswehr* (but in the Boulogne appendix of 22 July 1919 allowed 150 of them for the Germanpolice), about 50 vehicles were handed over to the police forces of the German '*Länder*' (states) until the end of 1920.

On 30 May 1925 the Allied Military Control Commission published its final paper on German arms and equipment delivered or destroyed under the terms of the Versailles Treaty. According to this report, 59 tanks had been delivered. This number, however, did not include the bulk of the tank detachments parked at Erbenheim race course in November 1919. Those tanks – and others possibly still on the railway destined for Erbenheim or Gustavsburg – were captured by the advancing Allied forces. French forces occupied the Wiesbaden bridgehead (that incorporated Erbenheim and Gustavsburg) on 15 December 1919.

Two Krupp-Daimler D.Z.V.R. of Schwere Kampfwagen-Abteilung 103 seen approximately at the time of the Kapp revolt in March/April 1920. By that time, detachment 103 was back in Berlin and re-equipped with the 'modern' D.Z.V.R. armoured cars. The vehicles had a crew of six and normally carried two 08 machine guns. Six more men could be transported for dismounted action. High fuel consumption was a limiting factor for D.Z.V.R employment. The small letters below S.Kw.A.103 read '1.Zug' (first platoon). Kokampf sided with Herr Kapp and General von Lüttwitz during the revolt, a fact that certainly promoted the rapid disbanding of the unit in early summer of 1920, not least because the industrious Hptm. Körting was relieved from his position in the wake of the unsuccessful insurrection. (Strasheim Collection)

Two Kfz 3 of the Reichswehr out on an exercise some time before 1933. These heavy cars were forbidden to be driven off hard surfaces, and were only supposed to be personnel carriers, though it seems likely that rifles could be fired through their many vision ports. Their camouflage colours are already quite subdued in comparison to those of World War I. (Prigent Collection)

Between the Wars
Rebuilding, new tactics and new equipment

by John Prigent

A S MENTIONED in the last chapter, the Treaty of Versailles imposed severe restrictions on German forces. This was not just a matter of banning tanks and slashing the size of the army and navy to 100,000 officers and men; warplanes (previously forming a part of the army) and heavy artillery were forbidden, and even the famous General Staff organisation was to be disbanded. An infantry division could now have no more than 11,240 men, including officers, and a cavalry division no more than 5,525. The Allied Commission enforcing the Treaty's provisions seized much equipment but allowed a few armoured cars to be retained by the Police. Some tanks and armoured cars were kept by the *Freikorps* as well for a short time.

The old Imperial Army ceased to exist and the new *Reichswehr* replaced it in March 1919, permitted under the Treaty only as a border guard force and to prevent civil disorder. The army was thus not immune from the turmoil of the immediate post-war years, and in fact was forced to contribute to it by discharging so many men when there were no jobs for them to go to. Inflation was rampant, with even postage stamps needing to be denominated in thousands of Marks and then hundreds of thousands. Hans von Seekt, commander of the General Staff, effectively evaded its forced dissolution by simply transferring many of its sections to other departments and maintained its heart, the Operations Section, under the innocuous new name of *Truppenamt* or Troops Office.

He also set up no fewer than 57 study groups to consider the lessons of the late war, with well-respected high-ranking officers appointed to them. Everything was to be analysed and recommendations made for the future, from basic infantry tactics to the military weather forecasting service. Tanks were not neglected in these studies; even though Germany was no longer allowed to have any, their effectiveness and tactics in the war were to be examined and future tank types and tactics considered.

As a result of all these studies new tactical regulations were issued in 1921, ignoring the absence of tanks, artillery and air power and instead setting out how they were to be used by Germany or countered if used by an enemy. The expressed intention was to provide the German army with doctrines that would apply to a modern army possessing them. Clearly it was already thought that the Treaty restrictions would eventually fall away.

Troop training in anti-armour tactics and in cooperation with tanks was obviously going to be difficult when there were no tanks to train with. The solution was to build dummy tanks. Some were very flimsy, mere constructions of canvas on wooden struts to be used for target practice and mounted on skids so they could be moved around the exercise grounds. Others were more mobile, mounted on bicycle wheels. These were probably also mainly used at targets, though they may also have been trundled around to familiarise troops with the appearance of a tank attack – almost certainly without any live ammunition being fired at them!

At a later stage of the development of these '*Panzerattrappes*' (literally 'tank mockups, or dummies') they became motorised. Many were simple constructions that could be fitted to light car chassis after removing their passenger bodies, with turrets mounting dummy machine guns. Others were more permanent, even

These very early Panzerattrappes are thought to have been photographed at Sennelager in the early 1920s. They are not very mobile, most being on skids though one has wooden wheels, and were used as targets for anti-tank rifle practice. It is interesting to compare their shapes with the Kfz 3 armoured car of the same period. (Prigent Collection)

having fixed steel bodies and actual machine guns. This type was clearly very useful for training future potential tankmen in tank tactics without using actual tanks.

The progress made in developing new unit organisation, tactical doctrine and training was quite considerable, but the manpower restriction was a great hindrance if Germany was to rebuild a significant fighting force. Conscription was forbidden by the Treaty, and minimum enlistment was required to be for 12 years, so there was no possibility of simply cycling large numbers of short-term conscripts through the training each year to build up a reserve of trained manpower. However, there was a loophole in the Treaty provisions – there was no limit on the number of NCOs. This gave the *Reichswehr* an opportunity that was seized upon, and by 1926 it had more chiefs than indians with only 36,500 privates in its 100,000 strength! These NCOs were given far more responsibility than in other armies, many being given positions such as platoon leader that in other countries would have been held by officers. When the *Reichswehr* became the *Wehrmacht* under Hitler many of them became officers in the expanded army.

Meanwhile, ideas for new tanks and other fighting vehicles were being put forward and solutions sought to the problem of developing them 'illicitly' without detection by the Allied Commission enforcing the Treaty provisions. Some vehicles were built in secret and tested in Soviet Russia, with the German designers and engineers moving abroad to do their jobs. Others were simply claimed to be intended as agricultural or cargo-hauling tractors and produced without armoured superstructures or turrets – though, oddly for use on farms, with armour hulls which would have betrayed their true purpose if the Commission had spotted them.

Tactically, however, the *Reichswehr* was following the same trail as other armies, with an emphasis on lightly-armed tanks to operate against infantry. Its officers were encouraged to travel abroad and see whatever

The dummies mounted on bicycle wheels had a very light construction, just canvas over a wooden frame, so they could be moved easily. These were photographed in Bavaria on the mid to late 1920s and their shape is now much more tank-like, with imitation tracks and turret mounting a dummy machine gun. (Prigent Collection)

they could of foreign armies' exercises – they were often welcomed as observers – and the result was that since almost everyone else was thinking in terms of the 1918 fighting, so did they. Light tanks and unturreted tankettes armed only with machine guns were the common approach to the attack on infantry, the theory being that their potential numbers could simply swamp the defences and their speed would allow exploitation of the resulting gaps in enemy lines. Heavier tanks would be needed in smaller numbers, some with anti-tank weapons to destroy enemy light tanks and some with 7.5 cm guns firing high explosive shells to attack artillery and fortified positions. The tank was still seen as merely a support for the infantry's attacks by authorities such as Volckheim (one of Germany's few officers with tank experience in World War I) and by Fuller in Britain.

A paradigm shift took place when it was realised that a medium tank with machine guns plus an anti-tank weapon could both attack infantry and dispose of enemy tanks. Far-sighted officers like Guderian in Germany and Liddell Hart in Britain expressed different ideas, calling for more gun-armed tanks and devising tactics for their use in attack and defence, and practical experience during exercises with the few 'heavy' tanks available showed the correctness of this approach. Nevertheless economic factors held sway and the cost of such tanks was too high during the depression of the 1930s so machine gun-armed light tanks continued to be built in large numbers for most armies.

Tactics

A number of standard formations were devised for the *Panzerwaffe*. Long journeys were, as far as possible, made either by rail or on trucks and trailers; the light weight of the early Panzers meant that heavy trucks could easily carry one tank and tow a trailer with a second. Long marches on tracks, such as that to Vienna during the *Anschluss* described in the next chapter, produced very high numbers of breakdowns: engine or transmission failure, suspension and wheel problems, or simply track breakages. The technology of those days was simply not up to producing long life in these stressed components, though it improved rapidly in later years.

These two Panzerattrappes were seen at Juterbog, a base near Berlin, on 12 November 1933. They look much more like tanks, but are still only mounted on skids. (Prigent Collection)

Tactical movement in formation fell into several stages. Approach marches across open country were made in company-strength columns, with the Panzers deploying into battle formation when still out of enemy firing range. Obviously this was an ideal, and long battalion or even regimental-strength columns were sometimes the only way forward when cross-country travel was impossible due to forests or marshes so an advance had to be remain road-bound.

There were several alternative battle formations; a company could deploy its platoons into line-abreast formations, into lines echeloned back to one side, or into arrowheads, either with gaps between them to extend the front or fairly close together. The company might in turn have the platoons in line, echeloned or in arrowheads, or have two platoons forward and one in reserve behind them. The same basic formations applied at battalion and regimental level too, and even to whole divisions. The actual choice of which formation to adopt was governed by the strength of an enemy position and the terrain obstacles.

There were several ways to conduct an attack: frontal assault, flanking attacks, a combination of those two with one being a feint to pin down the enemy, and straightforward envelopment if the enemy could be surrounded. Tactics for defence were primarily focussed on swift counter-attacks against any enemy penetration of German lines, using the same formations as for an attack.

In theory, Panzers were to be supported by infantry in close company – though this became a sore point during wartime combat, when escorting infantry sometimes failed to keep up or even failed to advance at all. The infantry was needed not just to hold the ground captured by the Panzers but also to spot enemy positions: vision from inside a buttoned-up tank is limited, so it was very easy for a Panzer commander to fail to see, for example, a camouflaged anti-tank gun position. Artillery was also supposed to be emplaced to support the Panzers' advance, firing from behind them and moving up later if unable to advance with them, and anti-tank guns were to be alongside the Panzers to guard their flanks against enemy tanks.

In practice, experience showed that the Panzers outran their supports in mobile warfare because men on foot and horse-drawn guns simply could not keep up with them. This led to the development of *Schnelltruppen* (fast troops) infantry mounted in trucks, bicycle infantry and motorcycle infantry. Their cross-country mobility was still limited, so halftrack personnel carriers were built that could keep up with the Panzers across most terrain. Motorised guns also had problems across country, and self-propelled guns on tracked chassis were the eventual answer for both field guns and anti-tank guns. The *Panzer Division* of the later wartime years was a far cry from that of 1939, as will be described later in this series. For now, it

PANZERWAFFE

By 1935 dummy tanks were being mounted on light car chassis. This one is seen in the Nuremberg manouvres of 1935 and seems to be simply put over the normal car body. The early 'crash hat' for crewmen is still in use but would soon be replaced by a large black beret worn over a padded helmet. The experimental tactical marking presumably indicates a tank unit, though it does not follow the rules for those applied to the actual Panzers. (Prigent Collection)

suffices to say that most of the German army was still on foot or on horses until after the end of the campaigns in this book.

Tank development up to 1939

There were a number of experimental designs during the 1920s and early 1930s, some total failures and others built as prototypes. One, intended as an armoured ammunition carrier, was rejected for that role but resurfaced during the war on the Russian Front as a radio-controlled chargelayer for destroying enemy bunkers. Although fascinating to study, none saw service as tanks so the following brief descriptions will be confined to those that did. It is noteworthy that none of the pre-1939 German tank designs were armoured to resist anything more than small-calibre amour-piercing bullets from rifles and machine guns! The theory was that they would be attacking infantry, with only a few anti-tank weapons to be worried about which would be suppressed for them by artillery. The drawbacks of this approach were to become very evident when they had to face hostile tanks and determined anti-tank gun opposition.

The production tank chassis were also used for a number of special vehicles: self-propelled anti-tank guns, self-propelled artillery and bridgelayers. Since none of these were used until 1940 their description will be left for the next volume in this series.

The Grosstraktor

The first specifications for a heavy (in the terms of those days) tank had been drawn up by 1926. Its code-name simply meant 'large tractor'. It was to have a short 7.5 cm gun and co-axial machine gun in a fully rotating turret, a second machine gun in the hull front, and a third in a small separate turret at the rear of the hull. Contracts were given to Krupp, Rheinmetall and Daimler-Benz to design and build two prototypes each in mild steel. Secrecy was maintained throughout, though if the Commission had found out about them the argument might have been made that they were only mild steel so not subject to the Treaty ban on tanks. All six were ready in 1929 and were shipped to Kazan in the Soviet Union for testing, and went through several stages of modification both there and after their return to Germany in 1933. Although they were not enormously successful designs, with faults in their suspensions and tracks accounting for a number of the changes made, they did serve to test ideas and in fact the four runners among them took part in the first exercise of the newly created *Panzer Division* in 1935 before being retired to serve as barracks 'monuments'. Photographs show some intriguing modifications after their return to Germany: one was fitted with a dummy long-barrelled 7.5 cm gun, perhaps merely to make it look more impressive, and another was modified to mount a dummy 3.7 cm gun beside the short 7.5 cm. This seems likely to have been a 'proof of concept' trial by Krupp to see if the proposed mounting of this combination in their turret for the *Neubaufahrzeug* tank, that was being designed in 1933, would actually be workable. The intention was to provide it with both an anti-armour weapon, the 3.7 cm being a good anti-tank gun at the time, and an anti-personnel and anti-artillery weapon in the short 7.5 cm with its high explosive ammunition.

This is a Krupp Grosstraktor as a barracks monument. It has been fitted with a dummy main gun, but shows the position of its hull machine gun – which is a long way forward of the hull gunner's head cover and has no gunsight opening. Thus it cannot have been easy to fire and must have been impossible to aim. (Prigent Collection)

The Neubaufahrzeug

The *Neubaufahrzeug* design, or NbFz for short, began life in 1932 as the *Mittlere Traktor* or 'medium tractor', still keeping up the pretence that tank designs were for agricultural or road haulage vehicles. A year later its name changed to *Neubaufahrzeuge*, or 'new build vehicle' which was even more cryptic. Like the *Grosstraktor* it was to mount a short 7.5 cm gun firing high explosive shells, but this time with a co-axial 3.7 cm anti-tank gun and a machine gun beside it in the turret and with not one but two subturrets mounting machine

BETWEEN THE WARS 27

One of the Rheinmetall Grosstraktors was fitted with a coaxial 3.7 cm gun beside its 7.5 cm. Both appear to be dummies, and this may have been a test for the coaxial 7.5 cm/3.7 cm mounting of the NbFz. It is in a single-colour finish, possibly feldgrau. (Prigent Collection)

A Daimler-Benz Grosstraktor seen as a barracks monument for II Abteilung, PzRegt 8 at Wunsdorf in April 1939. It is still in the three-colour scheme but has been fitted with a long-barreled gun which appears to be a dummy 7.5 cm. It is unknown whether this was done merely to make the monument look more impressive or as part of a test of possible mountings for a proposed tank gun version of the long-barreled 7.5 cm anti-tank gun that Rheinmetall had begun developing in 1935. (Prigent Collection)

This is an LaS of PzRegt 6 at Zossen, near Berlin, in 1935. Although obviously a forerunner of the Pz I Ausf A, it has air cleaners in the crew compartment and a completely different engine deck with large hoods through which the exhaust pipes ran to the silencers. It is painted overall feldgrau (Prigent Collection)

guns, one in front of the main turret and one right behind it. This time only Krupp and Rheinmetall were asked to submit designs, and the Rheinmetall hull was chosen Two NbFz were built in mild steel during 1934, one with a Rheinmetall turret design and one with a Krupp-designed turret. The Krupp turret had the 3.7 cm gun beside the 7.5 cm and the Rheinmetall one above it – not a position where loading it would exactly be easy, though it did eliminate parallax errors in sighting. The Rheinmetall turret was also quite different in appearance, being rounded rather than flat-sided, and had a very bad shot trap in its rear-hinged side hatches. In general it is regarded as a bad thing to have a hatch that opens like this. Opening such a hatch under fire will immediately let shots ricochet inside, and also force the occupants to expose themselves as soon as they try to get out, instead of having the open hatch for partial cover between themselves and the enemy. After initial tests, three more NbFzs were built, this time in armour steel and all with the Krupp turret. They were used in the 1935 *Panzer Division* exercise and also in the 1940 invasion of Norway.

THE *PANZERKAMPFWAGEN* I

The origins of the Pz I were in the 1930 concept of the *Kleintraktor* or 'small tractor', a codename used to conceal its true intended use for military purposes. At this point it was not a tank but a scouting or weapons-carrier vehicle. In 1933 it was renamed *Landwirtschaftlicher Schlepper* (LaS for short, and meaning 'agricultural tractor'), still maintaining the pretence that it was not a military vehicle because the Versailles Treaty had not yet been repudiated by Hitler, and it only became Pz I in 1936. The *Kleintraktor* design used a suspension partly based on reverse-engineering of what could be seen in photographs of the British Carden-Loyd Light Tractor, and a Carden-Loyd was bought later and used for comparative trials. The *Kleintraktor* prototype chassis was built by Krupp and tested in July 1932, and a further five with improvements were ordered. Following further tests an initial production series of 150 were ordered in July 1933, 135 from Krupp and three each from five other firms. They were now under the LaS designation and built as chassis only, without superstructures or turrets. These were used as driver training vehicles after attempts failed to fit them with both items – probably the origin of Guderian's claim that the Pz I was originally only intended for training, not for combat. Since the hulls of this first series were built of armour steel it is clear that they were intended to fight; mild steel would have been cheaper and perfectly adequate for training vehicles.

A Pz I Ausf A seen on a test run in May 1936 at Nuremberg. It is from the first production series of machine gun tanks, shown by the vision port in the superstructure rear, and carries the three-colour camouflage scheme. (Prigent Collection)

These Pz I Ausf A carry the 1937 type of tactical markings applied for exercises. Unfortunately the unit, believed to be PzRegt 4, did not follow the official specifications and the precise meanings of their variations are not known. (Prigent Collection)

PANZERWAFFE

A parade of Pz I Ausf As of PzRegt 2 at Eisenach, probably photographed in 1938

They show their grey and brown camouflage patterns, which are different on each tank. They also show a patch of new paint on the rear of each turret where the previous exercise markings have been painted out, to be replaced by a white Panzer rhomboid and small figure 2 on the backs of their superstructures. (Prigent Collection)

Panzerkampfwagen I

Weight: 5.4 tonnes
Crew: 2
Engine: Krupp M305 3.5 litre, 60 HP
Speed: 37.5 kp/h
Armament: 2 x MG13k 7.92 mm MGs
Length: 4.02 m
Width: 2.06 m
Height: 1.72 m
Armour: 5 to 15 mm

BETWEEN THE WARS

© COPYRIGHT HILARY LOUIS DOYLE

© COPYRIGHT HILARY LOUIS DOYLE

This kleiner Panzerbefehlswagen on Ausf B hull was fitted with an experimental frame aerial for its radio. It has no machine gun yet, due to a shortage of mounts for them, and carries the three-colour camouflage scheme. (Prigent Collection)

Further orders were placed for tanks with improvements that had been found necessary while the first 150 were in use. This time they were to be complete with superstructures and turrets, which were to mount twin machine guns. Nearly 1,200 were built by Krupp, Grusonwerk, MAN, Rheinmetall, Henschel and Daimler-Benz, with production ending in December 1935. But the Pz I was not completely satisfactory as it stood, even with the improvements made, because its motor was underpowered and its trailing idler wheel (that met the ground like the road wheels) allowed the track to be thrown off the wheels too easily. It was therefore decided to change the motor from the original air-cooled Krupp type to a water-cooled one from Maybach. Its radiator and fan were placed beside the motor, needing only the same space as the Krupp motor, but the hull was lengthened at the rear to let the air flow freely through them and out of a new vent in the hull top. The idler wheel was also changed to a smaller one raised off the ground. Nearly 400 of this new version were built in 1936 and 1937 and designated Pz I *Ausführung* B – the original type of course then becoming Pz I Ausf A.

A few Ausf A were converted as *kleiner Panzerbefehlswagen* (small command tanks) with the original turret replaced by a small fixed turret of about the same size, and used in the 1935 exercises that saw the first trials of a complete *Panzer Division*. Some, though not all, had 'frame' aerials fitted for their longer-range radios while others relied on the normal rod aerial. These command tanks proved useful, so over 160 were ordered to be built on the improved *Ausf*(Model) B hull. These had wider fixed turrets, extending right to the port side of their superstructures, and some were experimentally fitted with frame aerials.

THE *PANZERKAMPFWAGEN* II

In July 1934 contracts were awarded to Krupp, MAN and Henschel for prototypes of a new tank in the 10-tonne class, to be armed with a 2 cm machine cannon and a coaxial machine gun. Secrecy was still being maintained, so the codename given to it was Las100 though it soon became retitled as *Panzerkampfwagen* II. The MAN vehicle was chosen as the best design and several short test series were built between 1934 and 1937. *Ausführungs a1, a2, a3* and b were very similar, with six small wheels in pairs each side all connected with an external beam like that of the Pz I. The Ausfs a all had the same power plant, but the *Ausf* b had a new engine which meant a slightly longer hull. Then, in 1937, the *Ausf* c appeared with a new suspension of five larger, independently sprung, wheels and thicker frontal armour. These improvements were adopted for the *Ausfs A, B* and *C* built from 1937 to 1940, only small internal improvements distinguishing them from each other. Many were retro-fitted with extra bow armour, giving their hull fronts a square appearance to replace the earlier rounded bow, and with episcope-equipped cupolas to improve vision for their commanders; some were built with these features. Then, in 1938, Daimler-Benz was asked to design a new

A Pz II Ausf a. Its guns have not yet been fitted. (Prigent Collection)

This Pz II is probably an Ausf A or B. It has been back-fitted with appliqué armour on its hull and turret fronts and with a commander's cupola. It is in the grey and brown colour scheme although the boundaries between the colours are very faint and hard to see. Behind it is a SdKfz 250/8 Ausf B armoured ambulance with Red Cross markings. The photograph was probably taken in early 1940 before the French campaign. (Prigent Collection)

One of the Rheinmetall Leichttraktors was retired to serve as a barracks monument. It still bears its three-colour camouflage. (Prigent Collection)

Pz II that could maintain a higher top speed as equipment for the new *Leichte Divisionen* (Light Divisions) that were to support the *Panzer Divisions*. This had a new hull shape and a new suspension of four large roadwheels each side, and was produced in 1938 and 1939 as *Ausfs* D and E distinguished by their tracks – *Ausf* D had rubber pads on its links, while *Ausf* E had all-steel tracks.

THE *PANZERKAMPFWAGEN* III

The first glimmerings of the eventual Pz III came as early as 1928, when Krupp and Rheinmetall were given contracts to develop tanks in the 6-tonne class carrying a 3.7 cm anti-tank gun in a fully rotating turret and with a crew of three or four men. The project was codenamed *Leichttraktor* (Light Tractor) and each firm built two examples. In 1930 all four were shipped to Kazan in the Soviet Union for trials in secret (the Versailles Treaty was still in force so everything about them was top secret) and only returned to Germany two years later, in summer 1932. They went through further tests in the next few years, and a number of modifications to try out different suspension designs, and took part in the summer 1935 *Panzer Division* manoeuvres. All of this gave a great deal of useful experience in the internal layout that was necessary for successful operation of a medium tank, as well as its desirable size, and by June 1934 Krupp, Daimler-Benz, Rheinmetall and MAN had all been invited to submit proposals for a medium tank codenamed *Zugführerwagen* (Platoon Leader's Tank) – in short, ZW.

Trials chassis for two tanks were ordered from Daimler-Benz and for one from MAN, with one turret to come from Rheinmetall and two from Krupp. Two further chassis were ordered from Daimler-Benz, testing different suspension systems. The MAN chassis and Rheinmetall turret were not selected for production, but the three Daimler-Benz chassis were all ordered into limited production (with modifications after the tests of the trials chassis) as *Ausführungs* A, B and C of the Pz III. The A suspension used five roadwheels on coil springs each side, while B used eight small wheels on leaf springs arranged as two sets of four wheels each side and C had leaf springs cushioning a set of two at front and rear with a set of four in the centre. The C suspension was also produced in a slightly modified form for the *Ausf* D. All four versions were only produced in small numbers – 10 As, 15 Bs, 15 Cs and 30 Ds – but saw active service in the Polish campaign. In December 1938 the *Ausf* E went into production. This had yet another suspension version,

A Pz III Ausf A. The chassis number 60107, visible on the jack in the original print, allows its identification as a tank of PzRegt 5 in 3 PzDiv. (Prigent Collection)

Panzerbefehlswagen III D1 with tactical number B03 is seen ready for rail transport. Although most of its frame aerial is hidden, the ball-mounted machine gun beside the dummy 3.7 cm in its turret is enough to identify the type. Behind it is a kleiner Panzerbefehlswagen that has been fitted with a frame antenna as well as with a commander's cupola. (Prigent Collection)

This is a Pz III Ausf B, the only version with round hatches on the hull front for servicing the brakes. The new suspension used shock absorbers mounted close together in pairs. (Prigent Collection)

A Pz III Ausf D with tactical number 431 shows the third version of this suspension and the longer hull at the rear. (Prigent Collection)

A Pz IV Ausf C shows the construction of its hull front and the tactical sign for a Panzer unit, not often seen on tanks. (Prigent Collection)

with six larger roadwheels each side mounted on torsionbars. The improvement was so great that nearly 100 were built and this remained the suspension for all future Pz III production. *Ausf* E had the same armament as the earlier variants, but its armour was doubled to 30 mm thickness from the 15 mm of the earlier versions. Like the Pz I, the Pz III was built as a command tank; the D suspension was used so it was designated *Panzerbefehlswagen* III *Ausf* D1.

THE *PANZERKAMPFWAGEN* IV

The Pz IV had its genesis in 1935 with the *Begleitwagen* ('escort vehicle'), or BW, that Rheinmetall was asked to design. A mild steel chassis was built, but it proceeded no further. Its suspension, copied for that of NbFz, was not particularly successful so an alternative Krupp design was chosen instead for a further two prototypes, imaginatively codenamed *Begleitwagen* I and II. Prototypes of both were built by Krupp in 1936 to test alternative suspensions: BWI with eight roadwheels in spring-mounted pairs each side, the arrangement adopted for the eventual Pz IV, and BWII with three pairs of larger roadwheels each side. The BWI was successful and, after extensive detail modifications to the design, was put into production as the Pz IV in late 1936 with the first production tanks being accepted nearly a year later. It is worth noting that the BW code designation misled Allied intelligence reports into describing the Pz IV as the '*Batallionführerwagen*' or Battalion Commander's Tank, a name that has been mistakenly copied in many books.

The Pz IV *Ausführung* A was very similar to the BWI to look at, with a hull superstructure that extended almost to the sides of its trackguards and a driver's front plate with a "bay window" appearance to give him more room than the hull machine gunner/radio operator who sat beside him. The hull machine gun was in a simple ball mount and the vision port flaps were also very simple. The turret mounted a short 7.5 cm gun with coaxial machine gun in an 'internal' mantlet – the moving armour that protected the gun mount being behind an outer cover. The commander's cupola was a simple drum shape and turret vision ports were, again, very simple. Maximum armour was only 14.5 mm on the best-protected areas: the near-vertical hull front plates, the turret, and the cupola; it was intended only to be proof against armour-piercing rifle or machine gun bullets.

The *Ausführung* (*Ausf* for short) B, produced during 1938, had a number of detail changes. Its armour now went up to 30 mm maximum thickness in the vulnerable frontal areas, to protect it against 2 cm

The rear view of a Pz IV Ausf A shows how its superstructure sides come out beyond the V of the engine deck louvres. In all the later versions the superstructure was slightly narrower, so its sides were in line with the V. (Prigent Collection)

Below: This Pz IV Ausf A is very unusual. It has the expected simple drum-shaped commander's cupola and the engine air vent with four louvres of this version, but has been fitted with the hull machine gun mount of an Ausf D instead of the simple ball mount normally found on Ausf A. (Prigent Collection)

Here is a complete Company line-up of Pz IVs, IIIs and IIs seen in 1939. The closest Pz IV, without a tactical number, is an Ausf A showing its normal, simple, hull machine gun ball mount. Next to it are two Ausf Bs with two Ausf Cs beyond them. Their grey and brown colour scheme is clearly seen. (Prigent Collection)

PANZERWAFFE

A Pz IV Ausf C most unusually showing its tactical number of 412 with a dot on the hull front as well as on its turret sides. The photograph is believed to have been taken at Eisenach exercise ground in 1939. (Prigent Collection)

This Pz IV Ausf C with tactical number 432 was photographed at Grafenwohr in 1939. The armoured sleeve of its coaxial machine gun is clearly seen. (Prigent Collection)

This Pz IV Ausf B is unusual in carrying a Wehrmacht number plate. It also shows the different shape of its external gun mantlet to that of the Ausf C, visible by comparing these two photographs. Not visible is the other main difference between the Ausfs: the C had an armour sleeve around its coaxial machinegun while the B's machinegun had no armour. (Prigent Collection)

armour-piecing shot, the superstructure width was reduced, the bay-window driver's plate was straightened to give more space to the radio operator (who no longer had a machine gun but instead a vision port and a separate port to fire through with a pistol), the cupola was replaced with an improved type featuring armoured sliding shutters over its vision ports, and all other vision ports were upgraded with better armour. Both *Ausf A* and *Ausf B* were only built in small numbers and were retired to training use after the fall of France.

Ausf C followed in 1938 and 1939 and was built in much larger numbers, with 134 gun tanks and 6 chassis for bridgelayers. It was very similar to *Ausf B*, the visible changes being a minor reshaping of the top edge of the outer mantlet armour and the addition of an armoured guard for the coaxial machine gun's barrel. Like the earlier versions it was mainly used for training after the fall of France.

The last version of Pz IV designed without the test of battle was *Ausf D*, which reintroduced the radio operator's ball-mounted machine gun and the 'bay window' driver's front plate. A total of 232 were built, after the Polish campaign had ended but too late to incorporate the thicker armour that battle experience had shown was needed. It served in France, Russia and North Africa. Later Pz IVs were successively improved with thicker armour and more powerful guns, but description of them will be dealt with in later books of this series.

THE *PANZERKAMPFWAGEN* 35(T)

The takeover of Czechoslovakia yielded a fine haul of Czech tanks, including the LT35 (which went through several title changes in German service but is best known as the Pz 35(t)). It carried a 3.7 cm gun with a coaxial machine gun and another machine gun for the radio operator, and was as fast as the PzIII as well as better-armoured than that tank. Two hundred and two were taken over, with most used to equip *1. Leichte Division* (later expanded to form *6. Panzer Division*. Like the Czechs, the Germans did not regard the Pz 35(t) as entirely satisfactory so no more were built and it slowly disappeared from service during the Russian campaign.

THE *PANZERKAMPFWAGEN* 38(T)

The Czech Pz 38(t), on the other hand, was very popular. The Germans were able to seize the entire first production batch of 150 while most were still being built, since it had been ordered only shortly before the invasion, and it quickly gained a reputation for reliability. With four large wheels each side on leaf springs it had a good suspension, and with the same armament as the Pz 35(t), and higher speed and at least equivalent armour to the Pz III in the first batch, it was a godsend for the *Panzerwaffe* that was so chronically short of medium tanks. Extra batches were ordered, slightly changed from the Czech specification, so the first 150 were later designated *Ausf A*. The *Ausfs B* and subsequent Pz 38(t)s were only produced after the Polish campaign but the *Ausf As* that had already been completed were used there by *3. Leichte Division*. In fact the Pz 38(t) chassis was so good that it was later used for self-propelled guns, including the famous '*Hetzer*', and personnel carriers based on it were used by Sweden for many years after the war.

ARMOURED CARS

The *Reichswehr* was permitted to have a few armoured cars. Designated Kfz 3, they were produced before 1927 by adding a 5 1/2 ton armoured body to already-heavy converted artillery tractors. Needless to say they were essentially roadbound and retired when better equipment became available, but at least one was pressed into service during the siege of Berlin in 1945.

Next to appear were the Kfz 13 machine gun carrier and Kfz 14 radio car, armoured to protect against armour-piercing 7.92 mm bullets from the front but only against ordinary rifle fire from sides or rear. Nearly 150 were built on strengthened Adler and Daimler-Benz car chassis between 1933 and 1935. These were not roadbound but were only rear-wheel drive so had limited cross-country ability, and thus when better cars became available, they were transferred from the *Panzer Division* reconnaissance units to serve beside horsed cavalry. They saw active service in the Polish and French campaigns.

In 1933 Germany introduced six-wheeled armoured cars, the SdKfz 231, 232 and 263 built on cross-country truck chassis from three different manufacturers. Like the SdKfz 13 and 14, they only had limited cross-country ability, with only the two rear axles being driven, but they did include a rear driver's position to allow a quicker getaway from trouble than simply reversing would permit. 231 and 232 versions had turrets mounting a 2 cm gun with a coaxial machine gun, but the 232 also carried a radio and frame aerial while the 263 used a fixed version of the same turret carrying both a frame aerial and a telescopic aerial mast for its more powerful radio sets, and had only a ball-mounted machine gun for self-defence.

Then came the SdKfz 221, 222 and 223, all built with similar bodies on a rear-engined chassis designed for military use and with four-wheel drive. The 221 had a small turret with a single 7.92 machine gun, but no radio, and was built from 1935 to 1940. The 222 was more potent, with a larger turret mounting a 2 cm cannon and coaxial machine gun but still no radio, and was built from 1937 to 1944. The 223, the radio car of the series, actually appeared in 1936, before the 222. It carried a frame aerial for the radio and a small turret armed like the 221. It remained in production until 1944.

In 1937 the eight-wheeled armoured cars appeared. With eight-wheel drive and eight-wheel steering they had a better cross-country performance than the earlier designs, and they also had the rear driver's

PANZERWAFFE

An SdKFz 263 radio car being shown to children on one of the Wehrmacht's open days. It already carries the post-1935 grey and brown colour scheme. (Prigent Collection)

An SdKfz 231 6 rad is followed by Kfz 13s. The photograph was taken before 1937 and even though it bears a WH (for Wehrmacht) registration number, its three-colour camouflage remains from Reichsheer days. Like the Kfz 13s behind, it bears not only the early form of tactical symbol for an armoured car unit, apparently in yellow, but also the rhomboid sign for panzers. Unfortunately the name on its side is illegible. (Prigent Collection)

This SdKfz 231 6 rad was photographed in 1935 during the Nuremberg manoeuvres. (Prigent Collection)

A Kfz 13 and Kfz 14 of the Reichswehr seen on exercises in the mid-1930s. (Prigent Collection)

position to allow driving in reverse at full speed of 90 kph. They were rear-engined, and armed and equipped like their six-wheeled predecessors. Having been intended to fill the same roles of armoured car, armoured car with radio, and long-range radio car respectively, they were given the same designations of SdKfz 231, 232 and 263; to avoid the obvious confusion, 8 rad (8 wheel) was added to their SdKfz numbers and the six-wheeled versions had 6 rad added. The 263 (8 rad) had a fixed superstructure instead of a turret.

Like their contemporary tanks, but more understandably since they were expected to retire when opposition was met, none of the armoured cars were armoured to resist more than rifle-calibre armour-piercing bullets.

Halftracks

Four and six-wheeled trucks were unable to keep up with the Panzers across anything worse than smooth open country, so design work began in 1933 on a series of 'halftrack' vehicles to be used as gun tractors and recovery vehicles. The SdKfz 10 was a 1-tonne vehicle for towing light artillery – the 3.7 cm anti-tank gun and the several light Flak guns; it appeared in 1937. The SdKfz 11 was a 3-tonne tractor, introduced in 1934 for similar purposes. SdKfz 6 had a 5-tonne capacity and was produced from 1935, while SdKfz 7 could haul 8 tonnes and was produced from 1938 as a tractor for heavier guns such as the 8.8 cm anti-aircraft gun. More powerful still were the SdKfz 8 12-tonne prime mover used for towing heavy artillery, and the SdKfz 9 with an 18-tonne capacity for recovery jobs and for towing tank-transporter trailers.

As well as these towing vehicles there were also armoured derivatives of several of them. The SdKfz 251 was designed as an armoured troop transport capable of accompanying the Panzers anywhere, using a modified version of the SdKfz 11 chassis. With its production beginning only in mid-1939, it is not surprising that less than 70 had been built by the start of the campaign in Poland and only a few were in action, as command vehicles, with most still being in use for troop trials and training. An unarmoured version was also being produced, with a mild steel body since armour production lagged behind chassis availability, and about the same number of these were also available. All of these were *Ausf* A vehicles, with two vision ports each side of the troop compartment behind the ones provided for the driver and commander. The armoured and unarmoured versions can be distinguished by the use of cast, bulged armour for the port covers of the armoured hull, the unarmoured hulls having flat port covers. The SdKfz 8 was also built in an armoured version mounting a special version of the 8.8 cm anti-aircraft gun for use as a bunker-buster, which was used in the Polish campaign. Other armoured halfracks came too late for that fighting and will be dealt with in the appropriate books of this series.

Camouflage colours

During World War One the Germans used disruptive camouflage schemes in sand, green and brown – which were to return in 1943. It is not clear what camouflage colours were used in the 1920s, but the first series of Pz I A was ordered to be delivered in *feldgrau* (field grey), a grey-green paint used at the time for civilian vehicles used by the army so suitable for the pretended role of the 'tractors'.

By 1935 a new three-colour scheme had been introduced using earth yellow, brown and green, all three much more subdued in tone than the World War One colours (these colours can be seen in photographs of *Reichswehr* armoured cars, so must have been in use for some time before the *Reichswehr* was replaced by the *Wehrmacht* in 1935). The three colours were applied in irregular patches, every vehicle different to a greater or lesser degree, and could have a narrow black border separating them though this seems to have been very rare. The patches could have 'soft' edges, feathered together by a paint sprayer, or be hard-edged as if applied with a brush; both styles were used.

Then, in 1937, a new scheme was introduced using the famous 'Panzer grey' with a different brown applied in large soft-edged patches to cover 1/3 of the vehicle. These two colours were both very dark and hard to tell apart in photographs, even when clean and especially under a coat of dust, so it is not surprising that for many years it was thought that German tanks were painted overall grey at the beginning of the war. The overall grey scheme did not, in fact, emerge until July 1940, after the fall of France.

National insignia

German tanks carried no national markings until July 1939, when white crosses were ordered to be painted on both sides, front and rear to distinguish them from enemy tanks. They were also to have white rectangles painted on their engine decks for air recognition. The white crosses stood out very well on a battlefield, so much so that the crews believed they were being used as aiming marks by the Poles, and in many cases they were subdued with a coat of mud or had their centres painted out; opinions differ over the colours used for this, but some photographs show grey centres and others show what appears to be yellow. After the Polish campaign this high visibility was officially acknowledged by an order in October 1939 to replace the white crosses with new black ones outlined in white. Several forms of cross could be seen, with wide or narrow arms of varying lengths, and some units seem to have settled for just applying the white outlines of the arms – leaving the background grey between them.

Unit markings and tactical numbers

The first unit markings were applied for 1 PzDiv's initial exercise in 1935, when playing card symbols were used – hearts, spades and clubs are seen in photographs so diamonds may well have been used as well. For the 1937 exercises, this system was replaced by placards 420 by 240 mm – officially light grey but white seems to have been used as well – carrying various symbols to identify units and sub-units. Even these were found too limited, so a new system was introduced using white numbers on black rhomboidal placards at sides and rear. The numbering was straightforward: the first digit identified the company, the second digit the platoon, and the third the tank within the platoon. The placards were supplemented by some units during the Polish campaign by the same numbers painted large on the turret sides, and eventually dropped after the campaign so that just the turret numbers remained, and were often on the turret or hull rear as well. Sometimes the first number was replaced by a letter in headquarters units – R for *Regiment* and N for *Nachrichtung* (signals) being common, and a *caduceus* (the 'snake round a staff' symbol) for medical officers. Roman numerals I and II were also used, identifying the tanks of the first and second battalions' headquarters within a regiment.

This still left the question of how to identify the division. Symbols were used on hull sides, or fronts and rears, usually painted yellow in the early days though other colours came into use later in the war. An official list was issued after the Polish campaign, but at least some symbols were already in use during the campaign such as *4. PzDiv's* 'Mercedes star' – an inverted Y within a circle, drawn with doubled, rounded lines and a small circle at its centre. 1 PzDiv used an oakleaf as its symbol, though its official emblem after October 1938 was a single dot, but it is not certain that the oak leaf was used during the Polish campaign.

Other markings

There were official symbols for the various types of unit, usually applied only to softskins such as trucks and cars but sometimes seen on armoured cars too and self-propelled guns when these came into service. It was very unusual to see the Panzer symbol, a solid white or white-outlined rhomboid, on a tank because these were always assumed to belong to a Panzer unit.

Tanks were identified by *Fahrgestellnummern* (chassis numbers) which were stencilled on the glacis or the driver's front plate. They are usually invisible in photographs due to dust, but sometimes the number can be seen on a jack or other equipment.

Wheeled *Wehrmacht* vehicles carried number plates, showing a letter prefix and black numbers on a white background. For the *Heer* (Army) the prefix was WH, with WL for the *Luftwaffe* and WM for *Wehrmacht Marine* (the Navy). These number plates appeared on armoured cars and also on halftracks. On rare occasions number plates also appeared on tanks, mainly when they were used for driver training but also when they were undergoing tests before acceptance by the *Wehrmacht*. Those plates had different letter prefixes allocated according to the place of registration.

The creation of the Panzer Divisions that fought in Poland

1. PzDiv was formed in Weimar in August 1935 from parts of the old *3. Kavallerie* (Cavalry) *Division*. It had *Panzer Brigade 1* made up of *Panzer Regiments 1* and *2*, both formed in October 1935 with two battalions each.

2. PzDiv was formed in Würzburg in October 1935 and its *PzBde 2* had *PzRegts 3* and *4*. *PzRegt 3* had been formed in Dresden in May 1935 as motorised cavalry but converted to an armoured regiment in October that year, and *PzRegt 4* was formed in October 1935 at Ohrdruf. After the Anschluss with Austria *2. PzDiv* was stationed in Vienna until the Polish campaign.

3. PzDiv was formed in Wunsdorf, also in October 1935, and its *PzBde 3* had *PzRegts 5*, formed in October 1935, and *6* formed at Zossen also in October 1935.

4. PzDiv, like *2. PzDiv*, was formed at Würzburg but not until October 1938. It had *4. PzBde* with *PzRegts 35* and *36*. *5. PzDiv* had *5 PzBde* with *PzRegts 15* and *31* and was formed at Oppern in October 1938 although *PzRegts 35* and *6* were not formed until November 1938, at Bamberg and Schwerin respectively.

I. LeichteDiv was the strongest of the light divisions, with *PzRegt 11*, formed at Paderborn in October 1937, and *65 PzAbt*, formed at Sennelager in October 1937. It fought thus in Poland, and was transformed into *6. PzDiv* after the campaign.

2. LeichteDiv had *PzRegt 66*, formed at Eisenach in November 1938, and became *7. PzDiv* after fighting in Poland.

3. LeichteDiv had *67. PzAbt*, formed at Gross-Glienecke in November 1938, formed at St Poelten in July 1938, and became *8. PzDiv* after the Polish campaign. *4. LeichteDiv* had *33. PzAbt* and became *9. PzDiv*.

PzDiv Kempf was formed in East Prussia as an ad hoc unit as late as August 1939, with both Army and SS units including *PzRegt 7* which had been formed at Ohrdruf in October 1936. The division was disbanded after fighting in Poland.

As is clear, the effort to create Panzer units had led to a certain amount of confusion with, in some cases, regiments being formed after the divisions that were to command them.

Austria had few armoured vehicles for the Wehrmacht to take over, but one series that did create interest was the wheel-and-track vehicles designed by Saurer. They could run on roads using wheels and also retract them to run on tracks across country. These are wheel-and-track ammunition carriers parading in Vienna in 1937. (Prigent Collection)

Austria and Czechoslovakia – 1938

by Carlos Caballero Jurado

Austria – the *AnschlussPanzerwaffe*

Hitler always wanted Austria to be part of the Reich and expected to achieve this through political means, but the conservative dictatorship in control of Austria since 1934 opposed unification with Nazi Germany. However, Nazism did not cease to spread in Austria. In 1937 orders were issued to prepare a plan for military intervention in Austria, 'Fall Otto', in the event that any attempt to reinstate the Habsburg dynasty was made in that country. In February 1938 the chancellors of Germany and Austria – Hitler and Schussnigg – met but did not manage to overcome the confrontation. And on 9 March, Schussnigg called for a plebiscite that would be held on the 13th to ratify Austrian independence. The country seemed to be on the verge of civil war between supporters and opponents of unification with Germany. On the 10th, Hitler ordered the immediate invasion of Austria. Only 48 hours later, on the 12th, *General* Beck (Army Chief of Staff), who opposed the idea of the invasion, said that a large number of troops were necessary to put it into practice. But as no plan for '*Fall Otto*' had been devised one had to be improvised in a hurry, and the task was entrusted to Erich von Manstein, another genius of armoured warfare. Although a whole Army (the Eighth, under von Bock's orders) was mobilized for the operation, von Manstein saw that speed was the key factor (to abort any Austrian resistance or to prevent a reaction from the Czechs), and the main role was allotted to 2. *Panzer Division*, which would carry out a meteoric advance on Vienna.

But the base of 2. *Panzer Division* was 400 kilometres away from the Austro-German border and, as the situation had not been foreseen, it was not fully operational. The Panzer crews were not properly trained. Part of the Staff was on an exercise, too far from the base. The Division did not have fuel transport columns or mobile workshops. No suitable maps were available (tourist guides had to be bought). Nevertheless at midnight on the 11th, 2. *Panzer Division* was already on the Austrian border. Along with the units that were attached to it, it was put under the orders of the *Panzerkorps* to be commanded by *Generalleutnant* Guderian.

At the spearhead was the reconnaissance group of the Division (*Aufklärungs Abteilung* 5), reinforced by *AA* 7, and the Motorcycle Fusiliers Battalion of the Division (*Kradschützen Btl.* 2). Behind them were the two Panzer Regiments, 3 and 4. Their strength was incomplete, for they had only 184 Panzer Is and 45 Panzer IIs. As the Division had a single Motorized Infantry Regiment (*Schützen Rgt.* 2), the motorized SS Regiment '*Leibstandarte Adolf Hitler*' was attached to it (although Berlin buses and removal lorries, etc, had to be requisitioned to achieve full motorization). Anti-aircraft protection was ensured by two light groups of the '*General Göring*' Regiment of the *Luftwaffe*.

During the 11th the Austrian Government made some attempts at organising resistance, but in the end chancellor Schussnigg gave his resignation to President Miklas and a new government was formed which was in favour of the unification with Germany. The Austrian Army had a single armoured force, the Light Division, with twelve Steyr ADGZ armoured cars and 72 Fiat Ansaldo CV-33 light tanks.

Early on the 12th, Guderian's *Panzerkorps* initiated its penetration into Austria. Because of the supply problems many units had to refuel – at Austrian petrol stations! But the advance was too fast, and Vienna

Austria's Saurer armoured observation vehicles proved of interest to the Germans, and were taken into Wehrmacht service for use by artillery forward observers. Their complicated mechanisms did not stand up well to field service, so few were built. (Prigent Collection)

would have been reached shortly but for the fact that it had to be slowed down to organise security in Linz, where Adolf Hitler – who had lived there in his boyhood – entered on the 12th. Even so, at midnight the vanguards of 2. *Panzer Division* entered Vienna where crowds, surprised by their swift appearance, hailed them.

From its base to Vienna 2. *Panzer Division* had advanced over 700 km in 48 hours. For such fragile vehicles as the Panzer Is this meant serious wear, as a result of which at least 30 per cent of the tanks were out of use due to breakdowns before reaching Vienna. The most conservative German generals made good use of the occasion to criticize the *Panzerwaffe*, as it seemed that an armoured division would write itself off with breakdowns in just three or four days of operations. The old infantry, on foot and on horse, looked much more reliable. However, had the *Wehrmacht* trusted these old means it would have taken them at least four or five days to reach Vienna, thus opening a time interval in which the Austrian or international political situation could have taken an undesirable turn for Germany. It was the *Panzerwaffe* generals who were most conscious that the Panzer Is were no good as war machines. But even with such poor means a real *Blitzkrieg* had been achieved. However, in the case of Austria, the enthusiastic welcome that the German troops got made this campaign known as the '*Blumenkrieg*' ('Flower War').

THE SEIZURE OF CZECHOSLOVAKIA

Unlike Austria, in the case of Czechoslovakia, Hitler had always bet on a military solution to the strategic problem that this country posed to the Reich. It formed a deep wedge well into German territory. The fact that, when Czechoslovakia was created in 1919, over three million Germans had been included in the country against their will also raised constant tension. When the Germans living in the mountain region around Bohemia, called the Sudetenland, saw the *Anschluss* of Germany and Austria, they also started large-scale agitation to join the Reich. The Czech Government responded with repressive measures that gave Hitler the perfect excuse to act.

Since mid-1937 the German High Command had been working on '*Fall Grün*': a two-front war game, where the German main initial effort was to be made against Czechoslovakia. By February 1938 there was already a very elaborate plan: the bulk of the German troops would attack from Silesia, southwards through Moravia to split Czechoslovakia in two. Virtually all the Panzer forces available would take part in this attack, which would break through the very powerful Czech fortifications in northern Moravia. The unexpected occupation of Austria in March opened up a completely new perspective: now it was possible to carry out a pincer attack, from both Silesia and Austria. As the Czech fortifications in southern Moravia were much weaker a plan was immediately devised to exploit this possibility, by placing part of the Panzers in Austria.

But a fundamental change came on Hitler's orders, as he did not want to launch the Panzers against the fortified lines on support operations for the infantry but on an attack that would exploit their speed, starting from Bavaria and into the heart of Bohemia, to Prague. The High Command opposed it as much as

Czechoslovakia had a good store of armoured vehicles, among them these PA-II armoured cars from the 1920s. Seen here in their 1930 Czech camouflage, they were used by Wehrmacht police units in rear areas despite their lack of rotating turrets. (Prigent Collection)

These Pz II Ausf b were photographed in the Sudetenland in October 1938. (Prigent Collection)

it could, but the deployment finally adopted reflected Hitler's point of view. On the other hand, all efforts had been made to increase the power of the Panzer and motorized troops after the *Anschluss*.

The plan that was eventually approved, an attack from Silesia southwards, would count on a *Panzer Division* (the Third) and an independent *Panzer Regiment* (the 15th). Among the troops advancing northwards from Austria to meet them were 2. *Panzer Division*, 4. *Leichte Division* (which had just been established) and a motorized infantry division. But the attack that was seen as decisive was the advance from Bavaria and on to the East, to Prague, which would be carried out *by* 3. *Panzer Division*, 1. *Leichte Division* and three motorised divisions. The early Panzer IIIs and IVs, which were joining the units in very small numbers would take part in the operation.

The danger of war was now most real. The Czech Army had excellent armament, with better tanks than the Panzer Is and IIs (although in smaller numbers). But the ethnic composition of the country (with ethnic minorities of Germans, Hungarians, Poles and Ukrainians, and the Slovaks confronting the Czechs) weakened in practice the strength of the state and of its army. In the end a diplomatic solution was reached

50 PANZERWAFFE

Two LTvz 35 are seen, still in their Czech Army camouflage, being inspected by a German Army commission sent in May 1939 after the seizure of the rump of Czechoslovakia to assess what Czech equipment might be useful. The officer is belived to be Oberstleutnant (Lieutenant Colonel) Olbrich, the head of the commission. The serial numbers show that these two tanks are from the batch built by CKD. (Prigent Collection)

This is Skoda's prototype S-III-6 medium tank under test by the German commission in May 1939. It was not put into production for the Wehrmacht. (Prigent Collection)

with the Munich Agreements (29 September 1938): Czechoslovakia abandoned the Sudetenland, which was occupied by the Germans without a shot on 1 October. It was a new '*Blumenkrieg*'.

From then on Czechoslovakia entered an acute process of dissolution, which was encouraged as much as possible by the Germans with their support to the Slovak independence fighters. The *Wehrmacht* drew up a new plan, '*Unternehmen Südost*', to occupy Bohemia-Moravia as soon as there was a chance. This came when the Czech Government tried to crush the Slovak separatists, who asked Germany for help. While the Czech president was in Berlin, where he was put under pressure during the night of 14 March until he agreed to make Bohemia-Moravia into a German protectorate, nine German infantry divisions, and nine '*Schnelle Truppen*' (Fast Troops) divisions entered the country. Moravia was occupied from the North by 5. *Panzer Division* and 2nd Motorised Division and, from the South by 2. *Panzer Division* and 4. *Leichte Division*. Bohemia was occupied with a concentric advance by 3. and 4. *Panzerdivisions*, 2. and 3. *Leichte Divisions* and 29th Motorized Division. On 15 March, when the Czechs started an uprising, the 3. *Panzer Division* tanks were already in the streets of Prague. This time there was no popular welcome. But the war booty captured from the Czechs was so great that it allowed Germany to establish new Panzer Divisions, armed with Czech tanks.

AUSTRIA AND CZECHOSLOVAKIA-1938

Panzerkampfwagen II A, B or C

Weight: 9.5 tonnes
Crew: 3
Engine: Maybach HL 62 TRM, 140 HP
Speed: 40 km/h
Armament: 1 x 2 cm KwK 30 & 1 x MG34 7.92 mm MG
Length: 4.81 m
Width: 2.28 m
Height: 2.02 m
Armour: 14.5 mm basic + 20mm appliqué when uparmoured

A Pz II A, B or C seen in early 1938 in an unidentified town in Czechoslovakia after the seizure of the Sudetenland.

Its grey and brown camouflage can be seen clearly. The turret number 341 identifies it as the lead tank of the 4th platoon, 2nd company and the underlining probably signifies the 2nd battalion of its regiment. (Prigent Collection)

The Panzer I Ausf. B of the 3ª Compañía of the Batallón de Carros de Combate arrive in Santander on 26 August 1937, in the vanguard of the 4ª División de Navarra that occupied the town. (via L. Molina)

The Spanish Civil War

by Lucas Molina Franco

PANZER GRUPPE – DESTINATION SPAIN

ON 23 September 1936 *Oberstleutnant* Wilhelm Josef *Ritter* von Thoma, commanding the 2nd Battalion of *Panzer-Regiment* 4 based at Scheinfurt, was sent urgently to Spain. His mission, as outlined by the *Heer* High Command, was to take charge of an armoured training group that was to sail for Spain within a week.

Three days earlier, on 20 September 1936, a meeting had been held at the Neuruppin base for the officers, NCOs and troops of the two battalions that made up *Panzer Regiment* 6, and commanders immediately asked for volunteers for a mission abroad of some importance though Spain was not mentioned. They warned their men that these were not just exercises or manoeuvres; real fire was expected and they could be taken prisoner, wounded or even be killed on the battlefield.

Almost every man stepped forward and volunteered for this secret mission outside their homeland; it represented a romantic adventure for some, and for most it would offer a good chance to put into practice the tactics learnt over long months. None of them knew their final destination or the significance of the mission but they knew for certain that it would not be an easy task.

With the personnel thus selected, the body of troops was organised and the standard tank types in the unit at the time were prepared: *Panzerkampfwagen* I *Ausf.* As, plus the different types of vehicles, trucks, motorcycles, and armament that were necessary to fulfil the mission.

The volunteers were taken to Döberitz, near Berlin, where they were given a bonus for urgent purchases and civilian clothes. In addition, during the period of absence from Germany, they became temporarily discharged from the *Wehrmacht* as it was necessary not to reveal the presence of German soldiers supporting one of the contenders in the Spanish conflict.

The German tank crews, now wearing civilian clothes and carrying false passports, made up a homogeneous group of young German travellers waiting to board a ship to spend their summer holidays under the sun of a country they still knew nothing about. The group was driven to Stettin, a port where they would board a ship in the belief their final destination was Danzig, a former German town that the *Reich* was claiming back from the Polish state.

On 28 September 1936 the members of the Panzer unit boarded the SS *Pasajes* and the SS *Girgenti*, which were also loaded with their impedimenta and all necessary *matériel* for their tasks at the destination.

The 267-man expedition was made up of the *Panzer Gruppe* Staff, two full tank companies, a transport company, a workshop, an armoury and an anti-tank gun training unit, with the following equipment: forty-one *Panzerkampfwagen* I *Ausf* A tanks, ten Büssing-NAG 80 trucks to tow tank carriers, six workshop trucks, eleven light cars, forty-five trucks (including fourteen Vomag tank carriers), nineteen low-loader *Sd. Ah.* 115 tank carriers and eighteen motorcycles, as well as twenty-four 37 mm *Pak* 35/36 anti-tank guns, assorted accessories and spares.

THE SPANISH CIVIL WAR | 53

One of the Pz I Ausf A 'Breda' conversions moves along a Spainish road. Unfortunately its commander has decided to sit on the turret top so his legs cover the details of the new gun mantlet. (Prigent Collection)

Behind the 'Breda' conversion came an unmodified Pz I Ausf A. There appears to be a letter A on its glacis. (Prigent Collection)

The Breda was followed by three more Pz I Ausf A, one with a passenger in a very risky position. (Prigent Collection)

Hptm. Albert Schneider (right) was the commanding officer of the workshop company of Panzergruppe Thoma. In this image he is posing with fellow workshop officer Lt Paul Jaskula (left), who was killed in an air accident shortly afterwards. (Campesino via R. Arias)

The two crewmen of a Panzer I, in brand new uniforms and black berets, posing in front of their war machine, which has been perfectly camouflaged to commence operations with Spanish recruits. (Campesino, via R. Arias)

The German instructors were much appreciated by their Spanish trainees. Their teaching made the Spanish military aware of the superiority of the tactics employed against their Republican enemies, who had better equipment. (Wilhelmi, via L. Molina)

One of the huge Vomag tank transport lorries with an Sd.Ah 115 tank trailer and two Panzerkampfwagen I Ausf. A, all of them belonging to Panzergruppe Thoma. (Campesino, via R. Arias)

On 7 October 1936, the ships reached Spanish waters, and from then on they were escorted by the battleships *Admiral Scheer* and *Deutschland* and the torpedo boat *See Adler*. In the evening they moored in Seville, where the personnel and materiel were landed.

Although the men of the *Panzer Gruppe* were anxious to take to the field, they were not sent to the front immediately since their main mission was to train Spanish soldiers in the handling of the tanks and their combat use interpreting tactical lessons, learnt in their own country, of how modern armoured war should be carried out. Shortly after their arrival in Seville, they were sent to Cáceres by rail in several trips, between 8 and 10 October. A week later, on 18 October, Franco reviewed the troops at their base at the castle of Las Herguijuelas.

By then *Oberstleutnant* von Thoma had already assumed command of the unit, with *Major* Eberhardt von Ostman as his Chief-of-Staff. During November a further thirty-seven men joined them and, along with some of their comrades already in Spain and a further twenty-one tanks – in this case *Panzerkampfwagen* I *Ausf* Bs from *Panzer Regiment* 4 that had arrived in Seville on 25 November on the SS *Urania* – made up the 3rd Tank Company of the *Panzer Gruppe* commanded by *Hauptmann* Karl Ernst Bothe. In addition the *Panzer Gruppe* command post moved to Cubas de la Sagra, Madrid, where the Training School and the workshops were also established.

Accounting for losses and the men who returned to Germany, by late 1936 there were 299 German tank crewmen still serving in Spain. One year later there were only 124, and by late 1938 there were just 108 German tank crew.

From October 1936 to May 1939 von Thoma's men trained Spanish personnel in various operations such as tanks, anti-tank guns, flame-throwers, mine-throwers, gas protection, workshop duties, driving, and in work as armourers.

Panzer Gruppe Thoma, with its officers, NCOs and technical teams, also supported the following operational units on the different battlefronts:
- Four German tank companies, with 16 tanks each.
- Two 'Russian' tank companies, with 22 captured Soviet-built tanks (March 1938)
- Twenty anti-tank gun companies, with 10 guns each (March 1938)

THE SPANISH CIVIL WAR

Two Pz I Ausf As of II Batallón of the Agrupación de Carros de Combate de la Legión. The front tank is the 5th vehicle of the 2nd Section of the 1st Company, numbered 425 on its glacis and with a red-over-yellow tactical marking disc while behind it is the command tank of the 3rd Company with a red/white/red disc. Unfortunately, the number on the command tank's glacis is illegible. (Prigent Collection)

Panzerkampfwagen I

Weight:	5.4 tonnes
Crew:	2
Engine:	Krupp M305 3.5 litre, 60 HP
Speed:	37.5 kp/h
Armament:	2 x MG13k 7.92 mm MGs
Length:	4.02 m
Width:	2.06 m
Height:	1.72 m
Armour:	5 to 15 mm

A Spanish Pz I Ausf A Command Tank

The red/yellow/red disc shows that this Pz I Ausf A is the command tank of the 2nd Company, II Batallón of the Agrupación de Carros de Combate de la Legión It carries the usual Spanish flag marking in the same colours and also the white badge of the Legión. The white marking on the glacis is the letter 'M' with splayed legs, standing for 'Mando' as short for Comando - command. (Prigent Collection)

© COPYRIGHT HILARY LOUIS DOYLE

PANZERWAFFE

This Pz I Ausf A carries on its side the emblem of the Partido Tradicionalista (Traditionalist Party), the cross of Burgundy which was rarely seen on Nationalist tanks. It should be red on a white background, but the colours here appear to differ and may be red on a yellow background at the bottom changing to yellow on a red background at the top. (Prigent Collection)

ABOVE AND LEFT: For driver training the Germans supplied the Spanish with a Panzerkampfwagen I Ausf A 'ohne Aufbau'. As the image shows, as well as the instructor and trainee driver several more trainees could be accommodated sitting in the vehicle. (L. Molina collection)

A very good image of a German Panzerkampfwagen I Ausf. A tank, the regular equipment of the German training unit in Spain and the tank units of the Ejército Nacional. (Negreira, via L. Molina)

THE SPANISH CIVIL WAR | 57

The Republican Army managed to capture a small number of German Panzer I tanks such as this one, which were shown off as war trophies. (B.N., via L. Molina)

ABOVE AND BELOW: A Panzerbefehlswagen I Ausf. B. The German Reich sent a total of four tanks of this model, three for command of the companies established in the Batallón de Carros de Combate,ß and the fourth for command of the battalion itself. The photographs show some of the tanks being tested on Spanish soil. (Marín-Mata, via L. Molina)

A Panzer I Ausf. A transformed into a Flammenpanzer in October 1936 by replacing one of the MGs with the hose of a light flame-thrower. On 27 October 1936 this tank left with the Batallón de Carros de Combate in the direction of Talavera de la Reina, in its advance on Madrid. (L. Molina collection)

Rear view of Panzer I Ausf. A number 223. This was the third tank of the Second Company of the 2º Batallón of the Agrupación de Carros de Combate of the Spanish Legion. This designation was maintained till the end of the Civil War. (Aballe, via L. Molina)

THE *PANZER* I IN THE SPANISH CIVIL WAR

The purpose of the presence of *Panzer Gruppe* Thoma in Spain was none other than the training of Nationalist troops in the battlefield use of the *Panzerkampfwagen* I and the special vehicles of the transport unit and the workshops, as well as assorted *materiél* supplied by the '*negrillos*'[1].

A Spanish tank battalion had been established with personnel from *Regimiento de Infantería* 'Argel' *n° 37* in Cáceres on 1 October 1936. A week later the unit was organised under the command of retired infantry *comandante*[2] José Pujales, who had served in the Renault FT-17 equipped *Compañía de Carros Ligeros de Asalto* (Light Tank Company), and was thus highly experienced in the use and training of armoured equipment.

The Spaniards organised their unit taking as a model the German one that had just arrived in Cáceres: a Staff, two tank companies, a transport unit, workshops and an anti-tank company. On 1 December, when a new company of German tanks joined them, the Spanish *3ª Compañía* was also established at Cubas.

In order to avoid confusion with the various fusilier battalions that the *Regimiento de Carros de Combate n° 2* organised during the campaign, on 1 October 1937 the '*negrillo*' tank battalion became the *Primer Batallón de Carros de Combate* (1st Tank Battalion), which saw a change in its composition on that date, now established with two tank *grupos* with three companies each, two made up of German *Panzer* Is, and one with Russian T-26 tanks captured from the enemy.

Another *Panzer* I company (number 5 and belonging to the so-called *2° Grupo*) was established at Casarrubuelos on the same date, equipped with sixteen new tanks out of the thirty that had arrived from Germany by early September. So as to avoid the administrative problems involved by the diverse origins of the personnel, and in order to give financial and prestige incentives by qualifying the unit as 'storm troops' since 12 February 1938, the *Generalissimo's* HQ decreed the administrative transfer of all the personnel of the *Primer Batallón de Carros de Combate* to the Spanish *Legión*. Two weeks later it was placed entirely under the command of the *2° Tercio de la Legión*[3], designated as the *Bandera de Carros de Combate de la Legión*[4].

On 1 October, because of the ever-growing size of the theatre of operations, the *grupos* making up the *Bandera de Carros de Combate* scaled up their establishments, were supplied with rear repair echelons and saw their personnel figures strengthened. These *grupos* became *batallones,* and the units of the *Bandera de Carros de Combate* not included in the *grupos* remained with the same designations and compositions except for the Workshops Company, which was considerably reinforced and often supported by the Vickers mobile workshops. As a result of these changes, the *Bandera de Carros de Combate de la Legión* became the *Agrupación de Carros de Combate de la Legión*, a designation that was kept to the end of the conflict.

THE '*NEGRILLO*' TANKS

Much has been written on the tanks supplied by Germany to the Nationalist side during the Spanish conflict. Perhaps too many works have been published but certainly few have managed to determine the real extent of the German armoured contribution to the Spanish Civil War.

The total number of tanks supplied to the *Gruppe Thoma* through the *Legión Cóndor*, i.e. the tanks supplied by Germany to the land contingent for organisation and operations at the beginning of the conflict, was seventy-two, which arrived in Spain in three separate shipments of forty-one, twenty-one and ten tanks respectively.

The first shipment of forty-one tanks of the *Panzerkampfwagen* I type arrived on the SS *Pasajes* and

A different mounting of a flame-thrower, on the turret of a Panzerkampfwagen I Ausf. A. The Spanish Civil War saw little use of this vicious weapon. (Aballe, via L. Molina)

THE SPANISH CIVIL WAR

After their arrival in Seville on German ships, the Panzerkampfwagen Ausf. As were sent by rail to Cáceres, where the main armoured unit that took part in the Spanish Civil War was being organised. (Aballe, via L. Molina)

Although twenty-one of the 122 Panzer Is sent by Germany to the Nationalists during the Spanish Civil War were of the Ausf. B model, pictures showing this variant of the German tank do not abound. This image shows the crew of an Ausf. B surrounded by Spanish and German troops. (Aballe, via L. Molina)

An excellent photograph of a Panzer I Ausf. A marked 'F' belonging to the 2º Batallón of the Agrupación de Carros de Combate of the Spanish Legión. This tank was knocked out by enemy fire and was captured by the Republicans in reasonably good condition. (L. Molina collection)

Girgenti in October 1936, along with the German personnel and the rest of the *matériel*, all of which was used to establish the first units of the Nationalist *Batallón de Carros de Combate*. Although surviving documents do not record any specific mention regarding these tanks, it is logical to think that they included at least three command tanks, one for the battalion and another one each for the two companies established. These tanks were used to equip two full companies, of three sections with five tanks each plus one for the company CO, which made a total of thirty-three tanks, i.e. thirty combat tanks and three command tanks. Of the eight remaining, one was for driver training, known as '*Ohne Aufbau*' in German, or without superstructure or turret and intended for use on driving courses. The other seven were kept as reserves to make up the expected combat losses of the unit, later to be assigned to the so-called *Compañía de Depósito* – Storage Company. All the tanks in this batch, excepting the command tanks, belonged to the Ausf. A variant, called 'Krupp' in Spain because of their power plant.

The second batch of German tanks arrived in Spain by late November 1936 – twenty-one *Panzer* Is, probably of the *Ausf. B* variant. Fifteen of them, plus a command tank, were used to establish the third company of the Nationalist *Batallón de Carros de Combate* in December. A further five were kept as reserves to make up losses. Finally, *Legión Cóndor* documents record a third batch of ten *Panzerkampfwagen* I tanks, although both the delivery date and the tank variant supplied remain unknown. It is possible the arrival date may have been early 1937, so to make up the losses so far recorded.

In summary, this accounts for the 72 tanks sent to Spain through the *Legión Cóndor*. However, intense battlefield use and the losses suffered in the Spanish conflict made these 72 tanks insufficient to keep the unit operational, so the Spanish military authorities decided to ask Germany for larger numbers of Panzers.

The corresponding requests were transmitted through the Spanish-German HISMA Ltda. Company, the first on 13 July 1937 and the second on 12 November 1938.

In the main square of a village somewhere in Spain, tanks, improvised armoured trucks, pick-ups, lorries and draft animals assemble with Spanish tank crews and infantry. (via L. Molina)

The first request was transmitted by the *Generalissimo's* HQ, which asked *General* Sander (Sperrle) to try and speed up the delivery of the thirty tanks ordered in Berlin, as well as additional *matériel* including fifty 3.7 cm *Pak* 35/36. The mediation of the head of the *Legión Cóndor* must have been decisive as eighteen *Panzer* I *Ausf. A* tanks arrived by sea at the Arsenal at El Ferrol on 25 August. Five days later, on 30 August, the other twelve tanks making up the thirty requested arrived in Seville. All of them were sent to Cubas de la Sagra, where a 16-tank company was established. The rest were kept as reserves to fulfil the needs of the companies to make up combat losses.

The second request, transmitted through *Major* Wilhelmi, the German liaison officer between the *Gruppe Imker* and the *Generalissimo* HQs, asked for "... *20 German tanks, some of them armed with 20-mm gun or larger calibre.*"

This request was met with a positive response and the twenty tanks ordered were delivered to the *Agrupación de Carros de Combate* on 20 January 1939, all of them of the *Panzer* I *Ausf* A type. This armoured *matériel* completed the total supplies that the Germans sent to Spain during the Civil War, a total of 122 *Panzerkampfwagen* Is of the *A, B* and command (*Panzerbefehlwagen*) variants.

By early 1937, the light weight of these tanks and their lack of firepower with which they were able to confront their Russian adversaries, which were fitted with powerful 45 mm guns, impelled the Nationalist command to study fitting 20 mm guns on Italian (Fiat-Ansaldo CV-33/35) and German (*Panzer* I *Ausf* A) tanks. After fitting Italian Breda 20 mm machine cannons to both tank types it was concluded that the German tank achieved the best performance, and the modification of one tank for each of the existing sections was ordered. Thus it was intended to improve the offensive capacity of the Nationalist armoured units, clearly outclassed in numbers and quality by their Republican opponents.

A total of four *Panzer* I *Ausf As* were thus modified, although the capture and phasing in of a certain number of Soviet T-26Bs made the transformation unnecessary.

The *Gruppe Thoma* supplied the tank unit with an anti-tank gun company for combined operations for support against enemy tanks. That company was made up of eight anti-tank guns known as 3.7 cm *Panzerabwehrkanone (Pak)* 35/36, all of them equipped with Krupp L-2H43 Protze off-road tractor trucks, and a further five guns, which were carried on trucks, for independent operations.

Apart from this company, which formed part of the tank unit, Germany sent nearly 300 guns of the same type and calibre to Spain in several shipments. These were used to establish a powerful *Agrupación de Cañones Antitanque* (Anti-Tank Gun Group) which operated on the different fronts during the Civil War. Apart from the German *matériel*, it used Russian 45/44 mm guns and other types, all of them captured from the Republicans.

[1] Diminutive of *negro*, black in Spanish, a nickname that the Spanish applied to all German personnel and equipment.
[2] Major.
[3] A *tercio* –literally, one third– is about the size of a regiment.
[4] A *bandera* – literally, flag – is about the size of a battalion.

The Polish Campaign

Pz II Ausf b advancing in Poland. Their white crosses are almost completely obscured. (Prigent Collection)

by William Russ

THE invasion of Poland in September 1939 would give the Panzer arm its first test of combat. All of its pre-war training and experience in the Spanish Civil War would confirm whether the doctrine of armoured warfare the Germans had adopted would prove to be an effective battlefield weapon. Of course, General Guderian and the other Panzer advocates in the German Army were not pleased by this sudden thrust into war as the tank force Germany had built up by mid-1939 was mostly made up of light tanks. The *Panzerkampfwagen* I and II models were only intended as training tanks until more suitable models became available. There were a few main battle tanks available: production of the *Panzerkampfwagen* III and IV models had just started but was not scheduled to reach full production until late 1940, and it was not until 1942 that the Panzer divisions were expected to be fully equipped for war. Part of this lack of medium tanks was, however, made up by the acquisition of the Czech Army's inventory of tanks in 1938. The *Panzerkampfwagen* 35(t) and 38(t) tanks were well-armed and robust tanks. Even though these were not quite what the Panzer enthusiasts wanted, the Czech tanks went on to give the Germans good service over the next two years.

For the invasion of Poland the Germans deployed seven Panzer divisions; the 1st, 2nd, 3rd, 4th, 5th, 10th and *Kempf*. The first five were pre-war Panzer divisions consisting of one Panzer brigade with two Panzer regiments, one motorised infantry regiment with two infantry battalions, one motorised artillery regiment with two artillery battalions, one armoured reconnaissance battalion, one motorised anti-tank battalion, one motorised engineer battalion, one motorised signals battalion, and the motorised divisional services which consisted of one motorised supply battalion, two motorised food service companies, one motorised medical company, one Panzer repair workshop, one motorised police unit and one motorised postal unit. In addition, the *1., 2., 4.* and *5. Panzer Divisions* were assigned a *Luftwaffe* motorised anti-aircraft battalion for the duration of the campaign. The *5. Panzer Division* had an additional motorised infantry regiment attached for the campaign and the *1., 2.* and *3. Panzer Divisions* had motorcycle battalions attached as part of their normal organisation. As can thus be realised from the above, the pre-war Panzer divisions had a standard organisation, but were reinforced with additional forces to meet anticipated operational needs.

The *10. Panzer Division* was a recent creation, being formed in April 1939, and was used as an occupation force in the newly acquired Czech territory. The *10. Panzer Division* had only one Panzer regiment with two Panzer battalions, one motorised infantry regiment with three motorised infantry battalions[1], one motorised artillery regiment with two artillery battalions, one armoured reconnaissance battalion, one motorised anti-tank battalion, one motorised engineer company, divisional services (the same as the other Panzer divisions) and one *Luftwaffe* motorised anti-aircraft battalion. The division moved north from Prague in August to reinforce Guderian's corps in Pomerania. The *Panzer Division Kempf* was an even more recent creation, having been formed in East Prussia in July 1939 to suit the OKH's desire for a Panzer unit in East Prussia to support the *3. Armee's* advance into Poland. Since the division was late in assembling, it was the size of a reinforced Panzer brigade. *Panzer Division Kempf* consisted of one Panzer regiment with two tank battalions, one SS motorised infantry regiment with three infantry battalions, one SS motorised

A column of Kfz 13 armoured cars in Poland. Judging by their clean state, the lack of helmets and the happy faces of the crews, these are on the way back to Germany after the fighting was over. Careful examination of the original print shows the boundaries between the grey and brown camouflage paints. The tactical markings are unusual and must show a survival of their unit's original improvised marking before the 1938 regulations laid down an official list of markings. The crew's black uniforms and bulky berets are also unusual, normally being reserved for Panzer crewmen. Possibly this car was still operated by a Panzer unit, though all were supposed to have been removed from Panzer reconnaissance units before the Polish campaign. (Prigent Collection)

artillery regiment with two artillery battalions, one SS motorised anti-aircraft company, one SS armoured reconnaissance battalion, one motorised anti-tank battalion, one motorised engineer battalion, one SS motorised signals battalion and the full complement of divisional services.

There were also other German divisions that contained tanks and these were the Light *(Leichte)* Divisions. The four light divisions were formed in the late 1930s to placate the still strong cavalry element in the army. They were envisioned to function like the horse cavalry division, mainly in reconnaissance and pursuit roles. The standard division was organised as follows: one Panzer battalion, two motorised infantry regiments with two infantry battalions each, one motorised artillery regiment with two motorised artillery battalions, one reconnaissance regiment with one armoured reconnaissance battalion and one motorcycle battalion, one motorised engineer battalion, one motorised signals battalion and the divisional services consisting of one motorised supply battalion, one motorised medical company, two food service companies, one motorised police unit and one motorised postal unit.

By the start of the Polish campaign the light divisions' organisation had been modified to reflect the operational changes in their missions. The *1. Leichte Division* had its tank strength considerably increased from a battalion to a regiment of three tank battalions and a *Luftwaffe* motorised anti-aircraft battalion was added. The *3. Leichte Division* lost a motorised infantry regiment, but had its motorcycle battalion shifted to support the other infantry regiment. The *4. Leichte Division* was also reinforced by a *Luftwaffe* anti-aircraft battalion, leaving the *2. Leichte Division* as the only light division with a standard organisation.

For deployment, the largest numbers of Panzer divisions were concentrated under the command of Army Group South as this was where the major axis of attack into Poland would be made. The army group's *10. Armee* contained the *1.* and *4. Panzer Divisions* along with the *1., 3.* and *4. Leichte Divisions*. The *14. Armee* contained the *2.* and *5. Panzer Divisions* along with the *2. Leichte Division*. Army Group North had the *3. Panzer Division* and *Panzer Division Kempf* with the *10. Panzer Division* in strategic reserve. This deployment reflected the army's reluctance to concentrate any mechanised forces larger than a corps, much to Guderian's and the other armoured enthusiasts' chagrin. Several senior officers in the German high command were still wary of the claims by the Panzer advocates. They felt the infantry and the artillery were going to be the decisive arms in this and any future campaigns and, therefore, tried to relegate the Panzer formations to secondary roles. In numbers, the Germans had a total of 2,481 tanks deployed for front line service[2]. Broken down by type there were 934 Panzer Is, 1,098 Panzer IIs, 87 Panzer IIIs, 195 Panzer IVs, 112 Panzer 35(t)s and 55 Panzer 38(t)s[3]. In comparison, the Polish Army only had 615 tanks and the majority of these were light tankettes distributed amongst the infantry divisions and cavalry brigades. The Poles had only organised two mechanised brigades before the war[4], thus the threat to the Germans having to face masses of enemy tanks was minimal.

These two Pz I Ausf As are seen in Poland in September 1939. Both have the 'Mercedes star' of 4 PzDiv on the drivers' front plates. Note also the white crosses obscured with mud and the black rhomboid plate on the side of the nearer tank with the tactical number 815, denoting tank 5 of 1 Platoon, 8 Company. Each battalion of a regiment had four companies, so this tank belongs to the second battalion though it is impossible to say whether it belongs to PzRegt 35 or 36. (Prigent Collection)

Here Pz I Ausf A 825 follows in exactly the same place and shows that the tanks of this regiment carried large numbers on their turret rears. In front of it is a Pz II Ausf A or B with tactical number 811 on a rhomboid plate at the rear and on the turret sides, with a cross on the turret rear and a white air recognition rectangle on its engine deck. Between them, these two photographs show that the Regiment marked its tanks with the usual rhomboid plates, crosses and air recognition markings but also used large numbers on the rear flanks of their turrets with a cross between them. All the tanks are very dirty, but the original prints do show traces of the boundaries between their grey and brown camouflage areas. (Prigent Collection)

At first the German Army did not meet much resistance from the Polish Army when the invasion started on 1 September. The Poles made the decision prior to the invasion to make their main line of resistance twenty to thirty kilometres beyond the Polish-German border, as the Polish high command knew that they could not man the entire border. This was done in an effort to shorten the line the Polish forces would have to defend. The lone exception was to defend the Polish Corridor, a decision made for purely political reasons. This is where Guderian's XIX Corps was assigned the mission to cross the corridor and isolate the Polish forces holding it. In the early morning hours of 1 September the *3. Panzer*, *2.* and *20. Motorisiert Infanterie* (Motorised) *Divisions* crossed the Polish-German border east and south of Chojnice without much resistance. However, it was not long before the *2. Motorisiert Infanterie Division* had become entangled in a Polish defensive belt south of Chojnice and was not able to move forward until the next day. The *20. Motorisiert Infanterie Division* made better progress by bypassing Chojnice to the north. However the division halted its forward progress, not wanting to have an open flank while the 2nd Motorised was stopped. The *3. Panzer Division* itself ran into a couple of anti-tank positions, but these were quickly dealt with. By the afternoon, the Panzer division had reached the Brda River, which was the halfway point across the corridor. The 3rd Panzer's reconnaissance battalion quickly crossed this obstacle and raced ahead, closely

These two Pz I Ausf Bs in Poland carry no unit identification, but the tactical numbers beginning 'I' show that they belonged to the staff of the first battalion of their regiment. The lack of any crosses on the nearer tank is intriguing, perhaps meaning that it was a replacement drawn from reserves too quickly to be marked with crosses. The cursive 'I' on the front tank is probably a personal marking. Both tanks carry smoke candle ranks mounted on their exhaust silencers, and are too dirty to see any evidence of their two-colour camouflage. (Prigent Collection)

followed by the Panzer regiments. The reconnaissance battalion forged ahead, marching into the night. By late evening the reconnaissance battalion had reached the town of Swiecie on the Vistula River, thus in one day crossing the entire corridor and cutting off the majority of the Polish forces in the corridor. This penetration was a tenuous one and would have to be reinforced over the next couple of days.

The 3. *Panzer Division's* two battlegroups[5] closed in on the Vistula River, both reaching the river by late on 3 September and followed closely by both motorised divisions and the 23rd Infantry Division. Once the XIX corps had established firm contact with the 3. *Armee* forces across the Vistula, the corps turned its attention to the Polish forces left in the corridor. From 3 to 4 September the 2. and 20. *Motorisiert Infanterie Divisions*, plus other infantry divisions of the 4. *Armee*, fought to eliminate the remaining Polish forces in the corridor pocket. The Poles made several desperate attacks to break out of the encirclement, but most of these were beaten back. By the evening of the 5th most of the Polish defenders had either been killed or captured.

With the end of organised resistance in the corridor, the XIX Corps, along with other units of the 4. *Armee*, were transferred by rail over 6 to 9 September to assembly areas in eastern East Prussia. It was planned that the XIX Corps would form the northern pincer as part of a grand flanking manouevre to trap Polish forces east of the Vistula River. Army Group South's XXII Corps was to be the southern pincer moving north out of the Galicia region. Both forces were to manouevre to eventually meet along the Bug River south of Brest Litovsk. By 8 September most of the XIX Corps had assembled around the Masurian Lakes region and kept its original order of battle plus the 10. *Panzer Division*. Von Bock was eager to get the XIX Corps' attack underway as soon as possible because the Poles were evidently disengaging from the German forces east of the Vistula River to form a new defensive line behind the Narew and Bug Rivers. This new defensive line could wreck any possibility of the strategic envelopment envisioned. Only the 10. *Panzer* and 20. *Motorisiert Infanterie Divisions* were ready for combat by the 8th. The 3rd Panzer was still refitting from its losses in the corridor battles and the 2nd Motorised Division had just recently detrained. So, with the support of units of the XXI Corps, the 10. *Panzer* and 20. *Motorisiert Infanterie Divisions* forged ahead and would let the rest of the corps catch up.

The beginning of the offensive on 8 September did not get off to a good start. The 10. *Panzer Division* became entangled in a series of Polish bunkers just south of the Narew River on the first day. With the lead division stalled, General Guderian himself came forward to see what was holding up the advance. After assessing the situation Guderian ordered up the guns of the *Luftwaffe* Flak battalion to soften up the bunkers before the next attack. The next infantry assault, combined with the division's light tanks, successfully broke the Poles' resistance. Thereafter the division resumed its advance south with the 20. *Motorisiert Infanterie Division* following close behind.

From 9 to 13 September there was a rapid advance by the XIX Corps. The 3. *Panzer Division*, taking up the corps' left flank, passed through Bielsk Podolaski and began a larger flanking movement east of Brest Litovsk. The 10. *Panzer Division* was able to cross the Lesna River and drive straight to Brest Litovsk itself by 14 September. A battlegroup of the 10th Panzer was able to take the city, but the Polish troops that were holding the city had retreated into the city's fortress. This would have to be taken by a formal assault. It would

This Pz I Ausf B of 4 PzDiv gives a very clear view of the 1939 division emblem as well as showing what happened to thin armour when struck by even a small armour-piercing shell. It is curious that only the markings on the turret have been smeared with mud to reduce their visibility, leaving the bright white cross on the hull front as a clear mark for enemy gunners. Perhaps this is why it was hit? (Prigent Collection)

A Pz I Ausf A of an unknown unit with a very visible white cross on its turret rear but an obscured cross on the turret side. The latter is hard to see because it has been painted across the open vision port, but its top can be spotted above the port. This tank gives a good view of the extra engine deck armour, protecting the engine air vents, that was found necessary after experience of fighting in Spain. It also carries a smoke candle rack, which is differently-placed to the rack fitted to Ausf B tanks. (Prigent Collection)

take the combined forces of the 10. *Panzer* and 20. *Motorisiert Infanterie Division* plus *Luftwaffe* support before the Brest citadel fell to the Germans on the 20th.

While the 10. *Panzer* and 20. *Motorisiert Infanterie Divisions* were occupied reducing the Brest Litovsk fortress, the 3. *Panzer* and 2. *Motorisiert Infanterie Divisions* continued their advance east and south of Brest from 15 to 18 September to link up with the XXII Corps forces. Following the east bank of the Bug River, the 3. *Panzer Division* had driven some 70 kilometres south of Brest. The Russian invasion of eastern Poland on 18 September, however, brought an abrupt end to this drive and all offensive movement was suspended.

These Pz I Ausf As are seen with captured Polish 7TP tanks at a collection point on 24 September 1939. The nearest Pz I has the white air recognition rectangle on its engine deck armour, and all three show variations of the cross – one white, one white filled in with what appears to be yellow, and one with an apparently yellow cross inside the white one. (Prigent Collection)

A Befehlspanzer I Ausf B command tank in Poland, September 1939. Its grey and brown camouflage pattern is visible, and it carries the tactical markings of a towed artillery unit in white with a yellow figure 4. (Prigent Collection)

All of the Pz II Ausf b in this column have their white crosses obscured with mud and carry white vertical stripes on their turret rears, several painted over the muddied crosses. These seem more likely to be for visibility on night marches than figure 1s. (Prigent Collection)

THE POLISH CAMPAIGN

Panzerkampfwagen III B

Weight: 16 tonnes
Crew: 5
Engine: Maybach HL 108 TR, 250 HP
Speed: 35 km/h
Armament: 1 X 3.7 cm KwK, 2 X 7.92 MG 34
Armour: 5 to 16 mm
Length: 5.665 m
Width: 2.810 m
Height: 2.387 m
Armour: 5 to 16 mm

An Pz III Ausf B is seen in Poland in September 1939.

The yellow tactical number 04 after a Roman II indicates that it belongs to the HQ of the 2nd battalion of its regiment, but since it carries no division sign the actual unit cannot be identified. (Prigent Collection)

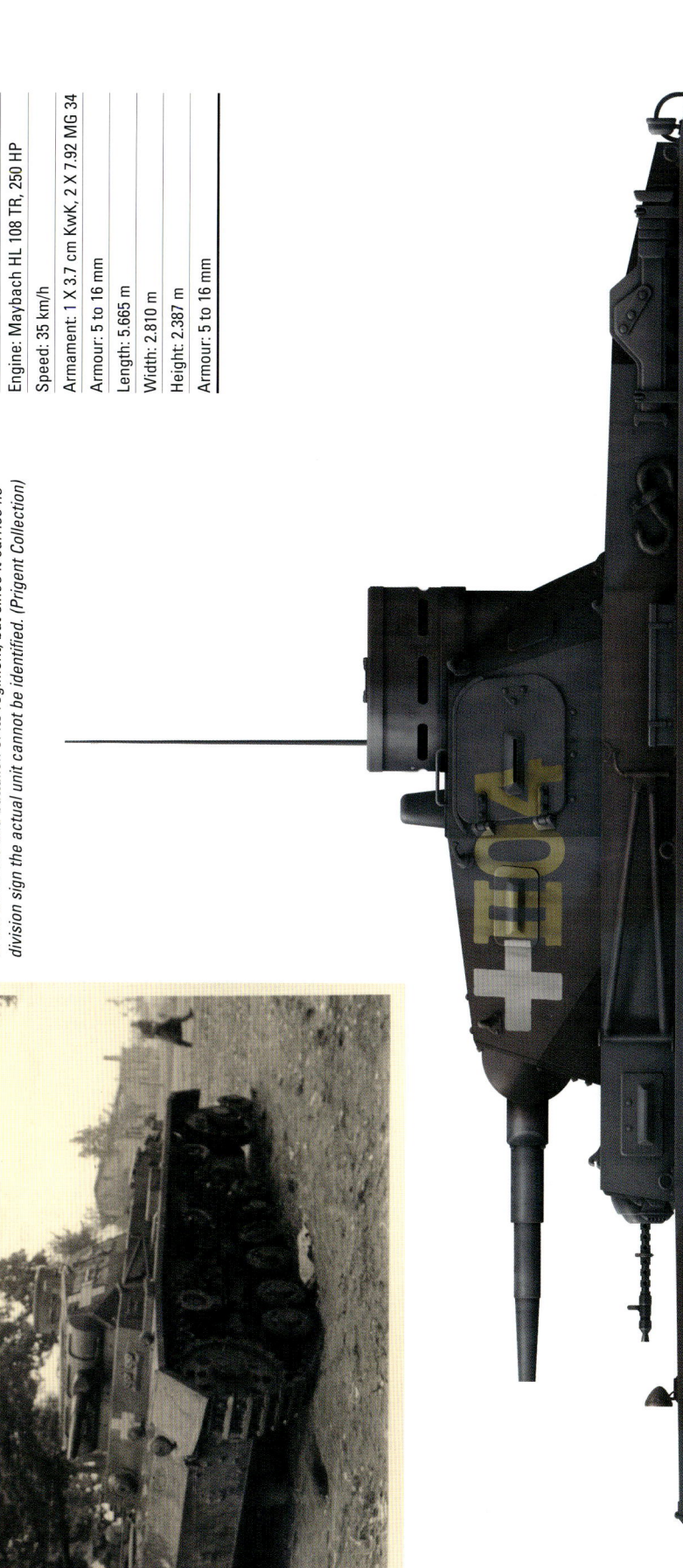

PANZERWAFFE

Two Befehlspanzer I Ausf B advance in Poland between Pz IIs. (Prigent Collection)

THE POLISH CAMPAIGN

It is rare to find two photographs of the same tank, but here are both sides of a Pz II Ausf b in Poland. The dot after its tactical number probably designates the second battalion of its regiment, but no unit sign is visible. The transparent rear rhomboid plate is very unusual and must have been hard to see from az distance. The white air recognition rectangle is clearly seen on its engine deck. (Prigent Collection)

This Pz II Ausf b and the Pz I Ausf As behind it are from Panzer Divison Kempf. Just distinguishable behind them are at least two Pz II Ausf c with five larger roadwheels. The men at the roadside are from SS Infantry Regiment Deutschland. It is possible that the two white dots on the bow of the Ausf b are a division insignia for this temporary division. (Prigent Collection)

This brought an end to the XIX Corps active participation in the campaign and it was soon withdrawn to East Prussia. For its part the *3. Panzer Division* had performed well in the campaign. The division swiftly closed the Polish corridor and aided in the destruction of the Polish troops trapped in the corridor's pocket. In their second phase of the campaign the *3.* and *10. Panzer Divisions* drove deep into the Polish rear sowing confusion and destruction along the way. The 220 kilometre march over an eight-day period by *10. Panzer Division* that cumulated in the capture of Brest Litovsk was a most impressive feat. Guderian's corps showed what well-handled motorised troops could accomplish.

Tasked with driving into the heart of Poland, the *10. Armee's* mission was to be the decisive axis of attack with Warsaw as its ultimate objective. Given this importance the *10. Armee* had the highest concentration of motorised forces with the *1.* and *4. Panzer Divisions, 1., 2.* and *3. Leichte Divisions* and the *13.* and *29. Motorisiert Infanterie Divisions*. The infantry divisions were initially tasked with breaking the Poles' main line of resistance, opening gaps that the following motorised divisions would exploit. Once the actual invasion had commenced on 1 September the Germans realised that the Poles were not making a stand at the border. Instead they had set up a screen of light forces (mostly consisting of cavalry, border guard and national guard units) at the border while their main line of resistance would be some twenty to thirty kilometers beyond the international border. In this case, the Germans rapidly pushed the motorised forces forward to catch the Poles before they had fully manned the main defensive line. The *1.* and *4. Panzer Divisions* did not cross the border until the early morning hours of the 1st, having to wind their way through the already clogged roads that the infantry divisions were using. It was expected that both divisions would gain more manouevring room the next day, but this would not prove to be the case for the 4th Panzer.

After crossing the border, the *4. Panzer Division* set out to reach its most immediate objective of crossing the Warta River by the evening of the 1st. However, the division soon ran into a defensive screen set up by the Polish Wolynska Cavalry Brigade at Opatow. At first tanks of the *Panzer Regiment* 35 were sent forward to disperse the Poles to their front, but this attack was repulsed by the Polish lancers' effective use of their anti-tank guns. Once the Germans had regrouped they moved forward again, only to find the Polish cavalry had fallen back to positions just east of Morka. This time the tanks of the I/36 *Panzer Regiment* attacked the Polish positions with infantry support, but even this assault was repulsed by the enemy's anti-tank and field artillery, forcing the Germans back to Wilkowicko. By noon the bulk of the division had moved up between Opatow and Morka. *General* Reinhardt ordered a general attack on Morka by 13.00 hrs that would include tanks, infantry and artillery. In the division's centre at Rebielice the I/12 Motorised Infantry Regiment with artillery support advanced against light enemy resistance and moved through the forest until it encountered Polish cavalry and an armoured train at the rail line. By 15.00 hrs the main attack on the Morka defenses commenced with the *Panzer Regiment 35* on the right and the *Panzer Regiment 36* on the left. This time the Germans overran the Morka position but were again stopped by a stubborn Polish defense at the rail line west of Morka, taking heavy losses in tanks. After probing for a weakness along the rail line one was found south of Morka. The Germans took immediate advantage of this and funneled the I and II/35. *Panzer*

A column of Pz I and II of several Ausfs in a Polish field, awaiting the order to advance. (Prigent Collection)

This Pz II may be Ausf c, A or B – they cannot be told apart at this angle. It is crossing an engineer bridge in Poland and has the unusual marking of a skull and crossbones on its glacis. (Prigent Collection)

A Pz II at the victory parade in Gdansk (Danzig) in October 1939. (Prigent Collection)

Regiment tanks through this hole, eventually taking them to Miedano well into the enemy's rear. At the same time the 12th Motorised Infantry Regiment launched another attack at the divisions centre at Wilkowiecko, pushing the Polish defenders back to the rail line south of Morka. Both of these attacks finally forced the Poles into a general retreat as this left the rest of their positions outflanked.

The 4. *Panzer Division* had finally forced the Poles back, but at a heavy cost in tanks and men. This first day's action was not a tactical success on the 4th Panzer's part. It showed that the tactical mishandling of attacks on the Germans' part against a battlefield-aware defence by the Poles would mean rough going for the Panzer forces. Meanwhile the *1. Panzer Division* had a much easier time in its initial combat debut. Moving south of the 4. *Panzer Division*, the 1st Panzer crossed the border on 1 September at the Liswarte River against light resistance. With the Division's reconnaissance leading the way, the division reached the outskirts of Klobuck by early evening. The 1st Panzer's infantry deployed south of Klobuck, assaulted the Polish positions and quickly routed the Poles out the town by 20.00 hrs. In comparison to the *4. Panzer Division*, the 1st Panzer's advance from the border to Klobuck was relatively easy with few losses in men and equipment. By the morning of 2 September both divisions prepared to make the turn north to cross the Warta River.

From 3 to 6 September, both Panzer divisions advanced in parallel up the Czestochowa-Warsaw highway, chasing the retreating Polish forces through Radomsko and Piotrkow. Because of their rapid advance both divisions had become strung out along the march route. Supply became spotty for the forward units, and to make matters worse bypassed Polish units were attacking the rear service units. Also Army Group South headquarters was becoming nervous about the Panzers' headlong thrust and wanted *General* Reichenau, the 10. *Armee* commander, to rein in both divisions to allow the infantry to catch up with them. These fears were calmed however, once the army group got a clear picture of the situation on what was

These Pz II Ausf c, A or B of 4 PzDiv have their white crosses very neatly filled in with what appears to be yellow. The division sign is faintly visible beside the driver's vision port of the tank on the right. (Prigent Collection)

THE POLISH CAMPAIGN

This Pz II in Poland has unusually small turret numbers and displays. its white air recognition rectangle across the engine instead of along it. (Prigent Collection)

Pz II Ausf c, A, B or C of PzDiv Kempf advance toward Zelechow, 80 km southeast of Warsaw. The front tank has its turret-front cross obscured but not the side one, while the rear tanks have plain white crosses. (Prigent Collection)

A Pz II Ausf E on a tank transport trailer. The only markings are its white Polish Campaign crosses. (Prigent Collection)

This Pz III Ausf C has lost its central roadwheels, giving a good view of the suspension spring and swingarms. It has no division emblem so its unit cannot be identified. (Prigent Collection)

THE POLISH CAMPAIGN 77

A Pz III Ausf D shares this repair park in a Polish town with several Pz IV Ausf C and trucks. (Prigent Collection)

This Pz III Ausf D in Poland is unusual in having no visible cross on its turret side, though an arm of one is just visible on the turret rear. (Prigent Collection)

A Befehlspanzer III Ausf D1 of an unidentifiable unit in Poland. (Prigent Collection)

These tanks of 4 PzDiv were fully prepared for the invasion of Poland at Neuhammer on 23 August 1939. Lined up behind the Befehlspanzer III Ausf D1 numbered R01 is a Befehlspanzer I Ausf B numbered R02, with a Pz II Ausf c, A or B behind that. (Prigent Collection)

happening at the front on the 6th. Both Panzer division commanders had relayed through the 10. *Armee* headquarters that, even though they had some supply difficulties together with some security issues along the march route, their forces were still in good enough shape to continue their advance on Warsaw. In that case, *General* Reichenau gave both commanders the go ahead to continue their advance. The XVI Corps would remain the 10. *Armee's* spearhead while the VII and IV Corps provided flank protection as best they could.

It was on 7 and 8 September that the 4. *Panzer Division* made its remarkable march on the Polish capital. *General* Reinhardt launched the division forward from its positions just north of Piotrkow on the morning of 7 September with the 5th Panzer Brigade leading the way. The 5th Panzer Brigade rapidly advanced up the main road, bypassing Tomaszow Mazowiecka, shooting up retreating Polish columns along the way. The brigade stopped at Rawa Mazowieka to laager for the night. The next morning the divisions advanced guard set out for Mszconow and once again found little or no Polish forces in its path. By noon the 5th Panzer Brigade had taken Mszconow then halted momentarily to regroup and awaited its final orders to advance on the Polish capital. In the afternoon *Generals* Reichenau and Hoepner came forward to Reinhardt's divisional headquarters for a meeting to discuss whether the 4th Panzer should wait for reinforcements or attempt to take Warsaw by itself. *General* Reinhardt stated that the 4th Panzer was more than capable of taking the capital by itself, especially since intelligence indicated there were few or no major Polish formations between the division and Warsaw. Combining this with the fact that the Poles were putting up little resistance and retreating across the whole front made it more than plain to Reinhardt that the city was theirs for the taking. Both *Generals* Reichenau and Hoepner concurred, as they had already been briefed by the army and army group's intelligence sections who agreed with Reinhardt's assessment. All three worked out the details for the anticipated advance and occupation and the orders were issued.

The 5th Panzer Brigade set out for Warsaw once again at around 14.00 hrs with one battlegroup leading the division up the main highway while a second battlegroup assumed the division's left flank. The first group was composed of the 5th Panzer Brigade headquarters, *Panzer Regiment* 35, 12th Motorised Infantry Regiment, 103rd Motorised Artillery Regiment, 49th Motorised Anti-tank Battalion (minus its 3rd company) and one battalion from the *Panzer Regiment* 36. The second group was composed of the 33rd

THE POLISH CAMPAIGN

A company column of Pz IVs move along a Polish road. The closest tank is an Ausf A, while those in front of it are Ausfs B or C. The legible tactical numbers are all from the 8th Company of their battalion and the bars under the numbers indicate the second battalion of their regiment, but no unit emblems are visible. A car is partially seen on the extreme right carrying the tactical sign for a signals platoon, but its divisional emblem is out of the photograph. (Prigent Collection)

Two Pz IV Ausf B in Hitler's victory parade in Warsaw. (Prigent Collection)

PANZERWAFFE

Pz IV Ausf Bs reentering Paderborn, their garrison town, in triumph on return from Poland, 23 October 1939. (Prigent Collection)

A Pz IV Ausf A crossing a rough bridge in Poland. No unit emblem or tactical numbers are carried. (Prigent Collection)

Infantry Regiment (minus one battalion), *Panzer Regiment* 36 (minus one battalion), 627th Motorised Artillery Regiment with two battalions, the 62nd Engineer Battalion and the 3rd Company of the 49th Anti-tank Battalion. It was not long before the main battlegroup had reached the suburbs of Warsaw. It was at Mokotow and Ochota suburbs that the Germans faced a stiffening of Polish resistance with heavy artillery fire halting progress. At 17.00 hrs the Germans tried one more time to penetrate the Polish positions but they were thrown back. With darkness approaching Reinhardt called off any more attacks for the day, preferring to wait for the next day when proper artillery support could be set up. The General was confident that the 4th Panzer would take the city on the 9th. But he and the fighting troops of the Division were about to find out that tanks are not well suited for urban fighting against a determined foe.

The next morning, 9 September, the German battle groups once again advanced on the Polish positions and almost immediately the attack stalled. The Poles had erected numerous barricades with anti-tank traps and mines in the narrow city streets. This funneled the German attacks into small kill zones that forced the Germans into easily containable areas. By 09.00 hrs *General* Reinhardt had called off all attacks placing the division on the defensive. It was clear to Reinhardt that he would need more infantry and artillery before the city could be taken. High losses of tanks in the past few days fighting in an urban environment had shown that without the other supporting arms, attacking with tanks alone was suicidal. Also the Division's supply route was stretched to the limit and was under constant attack by roaming bands of Polish troops trying to escape the ever-tightening noose the Germans were forming west of Warsaw. When the Division was ordered to make its run on Warsaw, the *31. Infanterie Division* and the SS *Liebstandarte* motorised Infantry Regiment were to close up as fast as possible to protect the 4th Panzer's rear and lines of communication. It would be several days before the *Panzer Division's* positions were secured by the follow-up divisions.

In the meantime, on 7 September, the *1. Panzer Division* had been detailed by the *10. Armee* to pursue Polish forces seeking refuge east of the Vistula River below Warsaw. The division turned east at Tomaszow Mazowiecka following the north bank of the Pilica River, finding very few sizeable Polish units in its path. On the 8th the division turned north to support the 4th Panzer's right flank south of Warsaw. By the time the *1. Panzer Division* had arrived, the *31. Infanterie Division* had taken over the positions previously occupied by the *4. Panzer Division*. For the next ten days both Panzer divisions participated in the Bzura battles, mostly in a supporting role for the infantry. Once the Polish forces in the Bzura pocket had been eliminated both divisions went into the army group's reserve, ending their active participation in the campaign.

In sum, both Panzer divisions had performed well for the task assigned to them even though there were tactical lapses in judgement at times, especially at Morka and in front of Warsaw. Still, the 4th Panzer's remarkable march on Warsaw on 7 and 8 September was an example of what a Panzer division was capable of with the right leadership.

Because of the *14. Armee's* secondary role in the invasion of Poland its Panzer divisions were also assigned secondary roles, which essentially meant they were to play a subservient role to the infantry divisions. This was evident by the deployment of the Panzer and light divisions at the beginning of the campaign. The *5. Panzer Division*, along with the SS *Germania* motorised Infantry Regiment, were deployed under the VIII Corps command to support the infantry divisions advance into Polish Silesia. The 2nd Panzer and 4th Light Divisions were also expected to fill this role advancing out of the Tatra Mountains. But the XXI Corps commander, *General* Ewald von Kleist, had other ideas for the use of his two divisions[6]. Even though *General* Kleist was an old cavalry officer from his days under the *Kaiser*, he saw the potential of the new mechanised divisions and was determined to make the fullest use of their mobility.

In the opening days of the campaign the 2nd Panzer and 4th Light Divisions made their way through the mountain roads facing only border guard and national guard troops. The German advance was initially slow because the Poles made effective use of mines, destroyed bridges and tree barriers along the narrow roads. By late on 3 September both divisions had finally broken through to more open country. To counter the Germans, the Poles had moved the 10th Mechanized Brigade from its reserve position near Krakow to slow their advance. By the morning of the 4th, Colonel Maczek, the 10th Mechanized commander, had positioned the brigade behind the Skawa River between Jordanow and Rabka to block the German advance up the main road. The 2nd Panzer Division assailed these positions without success in the morning hours, reformed, and attacked again in the afternoon. This attack was more successful as the Poles were forced back in the evening hours. Colonel Maczek's force fell back to positions just south of Myslenice, regrouped and awaited the 2nd Panzer's arrival. In due course the 2nd Panzer moved up and assaulted these positions. This time the Poles could not hold their positions as they had suffered many casualties the day before. The 10th Mechanised fell back towards Tarnow throwing up rearguards to slow the Germans down. The 2nd Panzer, however, did not follow up its success since it was ordered, along with the *4. Leichte Division*, to turn east as the *14. Armee* had determined that it was more important to seize bridgeheads over the Dunajec River.

From 4 to 9 September, the *4. Leichte Division* took over as the XXII Corps lead division, crossing the Dunajec River at Tuchow on the 6th. The 4th Light then formed two battlegroups, one on the left that moved north to bypass Tarnow and the other advanced on Debica. The 2nd Panzer itself had been held up when several stray enemy groups set upon the division's rear service elements near Bochnia. Because critical fuel had been destroyed, the tanks had to halt while other fuel columns had to be rerouted through the more

A Pz IV Ausf C of an unknown unit with tactical number 321. (Prigent Collection)

This Pz IV Ausf C is parked in the square of a Polish town. The fighting here is evidently over and the townspeople have come out to have a look at the German vehicle. (Prigent Collection)

A Pz IV Ausf C entering Tomaszow, Poland, in September 1939. Several Panzer and Light Divisions passed through this town so it is impossible to say which one this tank belonged to, though 4 PzDiv seems unlikely because it used its 'Mercedes star' on its tanks and no such emblem can be seen. Although damage to many buildings is evident, those in the background appear untouched. (Prigent Collection)

This Pz IV Ausf C, surrounded by curious infantrymen, has the name Anni on its bow. Although not officially allowed, the naming of tanks was permitted occasionally. (Prigent Collection)

THE POLISH CAMPAIGN

This Pz IV Ausf C of 4 PzDiv was photographed twice on the same day of the Polish campaign, which offers us the rare opportunity to confirm its full markings. The division's 'Mercedes star' is on the glacis together with a white cross. The tactical number 841 is on both turret-side hatches, and also carried on grey rhomboid plates on both superstructure sides. A white cross appears on each forward turret side, just visible in the second photograph behind the radio operator's head, and there would also have been one on the turret rear. In both photographs the gun muzzle and coaxial machine gun have their dust covers in place, the reason being obvious when the photographs are compared because although taken close together, the second one already, shows dust beginning to cover the hull front and its markings, although the sides are still fairly clean. (Prigent Collection)

Panzerkampfwagen IV C

Weight: 18.5 tonnes
Crew: 5
Engine: Maybach HL 120 TRM, 265 HP
Speed: 42 km/h
Armament: 1 x 7.5 cm KwK, 2 x 7.92 mm MG 34
Length: 5.92 m
Width: 2.83 m
Height: 2.68 m
Armour: 8 to 30 mm

© COPYRIGHT HILARY LOUIS DOYLE

A Pz IV Ausf C of 4 PzDiv. Only '44' is visible on the turret number, but it probably belongs to the same unit as the subject of the colour profile on page 85. (Prigent Collection)

secure XVIII Corps rear area. Once the tanks were refueled and on the move again, the 2. *Panzer Division* assumed the corps' left flank using the Bochnia-Tarnow highway as its main axis of attack. It was not long before the 2nd Panzer ran into and destroyed several Polish formations along the highway. The division's lead armoured column, commanded by *Oberst* Ritter von Thoma[7], enjoyed particular success in wiping out various enemy columns along the way before having to stop at the Dunajec River because of the destroyed bridge.

On 8 September the *4. Leichte Division* began a general pursuit of the retreating Polish Army with the objective of reaching the San River. The *4. Leichte Division* moved along the major highway between Tarnow and Rzeszow and arrived at the San River at Radymno on 10 September. The Division probed for any bridges that were capable of supporting the heavy traffic that would have to be carried but found none. The *4. Leichte Division* would have to wait for its bridging columns. The *2. Panzer Division* still lagged behind in its crossing the Dunajec, its progress slowed by Polish rearguards. The Division finally came in line with the 4th Light on the 10th at Lubzczow on the San River. By the 12th both divisions had sufficient bridging equipment to force crossings, and this was accomplished by the evening hours. To help secure their gains the SS *Germania* motorised Infantry Regiment had moved up to the river crossings, as the infantry divisions were still far behind. It would be another two days of hard marching before the 44th and 45th Infantry Divisions could secure the San River bridges.

Once across the San River both divisions were ordered to manouevre their forces to link up with the XIX Corps units moving south along the Bug River from Brest Litovsk. This would trap the majority of the Polish forces still between the Vistula and San Rivers. The 2nd Panzer was given the task of forming the inner wheel of the encirclement by moving up the Jaraslaw-Tomaszow road then marching north to Zamosc. The 4. *Leichte Division* would drive east, then north to arrive at the Bug River, thus linking up with the 3. *Panzer Division* coming from the north. From 10 to 12 September both divisions moved over terrain mostly devoid of Polish forces, encountering only the occasional enemy rear service units. The 4th Light passed through Rawa Ruska on the 14th, cutting the major highway between Lublin and Lvov, covering some 60 kilometres in one day. By the end of the day the 4. *Leichte Division's* forward units had reached the Bug River thus achieving its operational goal in two days. Meanwhile the 2nd Panzer had reached its objectives by the evening of the 14th, taking Zamosc with little trouble.

THE POLISH CAMPAIGN

These Pz 35(t) must belong to 1 Leichte Division because it was the only unit issued with them. The visible tactical number 532 places this sub-unit as II/PzRegt 11 (2nd Battalion, 11 Panzer Regiment), since the other armoured sub-unit was Panzer Abteilung 65, a single battalion. They have seen considerable service at this stage of the Polish campaign, proved by the heavy dust coat that has covered all traces of their camouflage patterns. (Prigent Collection)

This very rare photograph shows one of the Pz 35(t) converted to command tanks for PzRegt 11 and fitted with a frame aerial for its long-range radio. Unfortunately the place name written on the back of the original print is illegible. (Prigent Collection)

This Pz 38(t) with tactical number 312 is crossing a quickly-constructed diversion from a road, probably because the original surface is being repaired by the workmen seen beyond the halt sign. It may belong to 2 Leichte Division, though no unit markings are carried to confirm this. (Prigent Collection)

These Pz 35(t) are seen at Paderborn on 23 October 1939 in the parade that welcomed their return from the Polish campaign. Although they are dirty again after being cleaned before their journey, some traces of the grey and brown camouflage pattern can be seen. (Prigent Collection)

However the operational needs of the army had changed, and the two divisions were now needed for other tasks. The opportunity to destroy the large Polish force (remnants of the Army Lublin) that was moving east between Tarnow and Wieprz could not be passed up. To block the Poles' eastward movement, the 14th Army ordered the 4th Light Division to take over the 2. *Panzer Division's* position around Zamosc. This would make the 4th Light the blocking force while the infantry divisions of VII and VIII Corps would act as the 'hammer' to crush the encircled Polish forces. In due course, the 4. *Leichte Division* abandoned its bridgeheads on the Bug River, taking over the 2nd Panzers positions between Zamosc and Tomaszow by the evening of 12 September. Over the next several days the 4. *Leichte Division* (later reinforced by a battlegroup from the 2. *Panzer Division*) battled the Polish groups desperately trying to escape the ever tightening pocket. Some small Polish groups did manage to infiltrate through the 4th Light's cordon, but for the most part the division held its positions and prevented any larger groups from achieving a breakthrough.

This early production SdKfz 222 is seen in Poland on 6 September 1939. It can be distinguished from later production by its flat, simple vision port covers, the later ones being cast with a bulged shape. The mesh on top of the open turret prevented grenades being thrown inside, and folded up and to the sides to allow the crew to enter the vehicle. (Prigent Collection)

An SdKfz 221 passes through a wrecked Polish town. Like the SdKfz 222 it has a mesh screen on its open-topped turret, but flat instead of raised. (Prigent Collection)

By the 20th the pocket had been eliminated and the 4th Light was placed in the army reserve, thus ending its active participation in the campaign.

Meanwhile, the 2nd Panzer Division was sent south to help the beleaguered 1st Mountain Division that was desperately hanging on at Lvov. Leaving its positions to the 4th Light Division, *General* Veiel sent a battlegroup south that duly arrived at the 1st Mountain's positions on 18 September. But by the time the 2nd Panzer's battlegroup had fully arrived the 1st Mountain Division had been reinforced by the forces of the XVIII Corps and it was therefore not really needed. It was at this time that the 4. *Leichte Division* requested help in holding its positions around Tomaszow. *General* Veiel dutifully turned the division around and headed back to Tomaszow. A battlegroup arrived just in time to reinforce the 4th Light's positions south of Tomaszow where the Poles were making the greatest effort to break out of the pocket. Because of the timely arrival of the 2nd Panzer's reinforcements the Polish attacks failed and the line held. Except for some mopping up operations, this was the 2nd Panzer's last major operation for the campaign. By 24 September the division had been placed in the army reserve.

Overall, von Kleist was pleased with the corps' performance during the campaign. Off to a slow start after struggling through the mountains and foothills, the corps' divisions rapidly outpaced the infantry after crossing the Dunajec River. Both the 4th Light and 2. *Panzer Divisions* sowed confusion and destruction in the Poles' rear areas, greatly aiding the rapid collapse of the Polish armies in southern Poland.

For Guderian and the Panzer advocates the Polish campaign was a vindication for what they said could be accomplished by the *Panzerwaffe*. The Panzer divisions used their mobility and firepower to disrupt the Polish armies' ability to form any kind of coherent defence line, cut major communication lines, and caused general confusion in the Polish rear areas. The prime examples of this were the XIX Corps run on Brest Litovsk, the XVI Corps advance on Warsaw and the XXII Corps race across southern Poland. All of this gave the impetus to expand the Panzer arm to ten divisions after the campaign. Another positive effect was the persuasion of some of the more conservative generals on the effectiveness of the new arm.

The first battles also exposed problems. The Panzer divisions regularly outran the rest of the army's infantry forces leaving a gap that enabled large groups of Polish troops to escape encirclement. These same enemy groups also fell upon the Panzer divisions' rear units and could, as stated previously, disrupt the flow of supplies to the combat units. This is where the motorised infantry divisions could have made a difference, but they were not grouped with the Panzer divisions. They were used more to plug holes in the line with

THE POLISH CAMPAIGN

PzSdKfz 263 (8 rad)

Weight: 8.10 tonnes
Crew: 5
Engine: Buessing NAG L8V/GS 7.91 litre, 155 HP
Speed: 85 km/h
Armament: 1 x 7.92 mm MG34
Length: 5.85 m
Width: 2.20 m
Height: 2.90 m
Armour: 8mm

A SdKfz 263 radio car being serviced during a pause in the Polish campaign.

It bears only the white crosses used for identification and the very low registration number WH 755. There would have been a white cross and the registration number on its hull front as well as the cross on its rear that is greatly obscured by dust. (Prigent Collection)

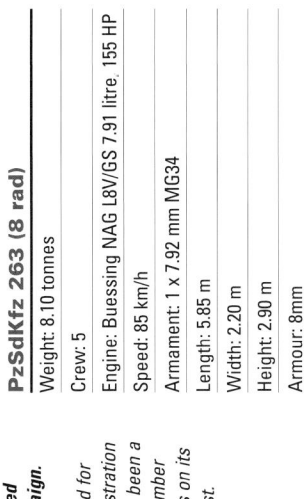

© COPYRIGHT HILARY LOUIS DOYLE

A six-wheeled SdKfz 232 that has been hit in the engine compartment by enemy fire, with paint burnt off as a result but still showing the different tones of its grey and brown. Its cross is a rare type, neatly overpainted in grey to leave a white border. (Prigent Collection)

the marching infantry[8]. Also, not all the Panzer divisions were used to their fullest potential. The 5. *Panzer Division* and *Panzer Division Kempf* were used to support the infantry divisions they were paired with, thereby wasting their mobility. The four light divisions performed well enough themselves, but actual battlefield conditions had shown them to be too 'light' for the constant combat they were subjected to. A cross between a motorised and a Panzer division, the light divisions did not have enough tanks nor enough infantry to be a well-balanced unit. All four of the light divisions were converted to Panzer divisions after the campaign. On the tactical level there were problems with infantry and armour cooperation, but improvements were made during the winter of 1939-40. All of these lessons would have to be quickly absorbed as the Panzer arm was about to face a sterner enemy in the form of the French and British armies.

[1]. The motorised infantry regiment was detached from the 29th Motorised Division.

[2]. There were also 388 Panzers held in reserve. Broken down by type they were: 260 Panzer Is, 67 Panzer IIs, 11 Panzer IIIs, 11 Panzer IVs, 34 Panzer 35(t)s and 5 Panzer 38(t)s. These numbers include the independent Panzer battalions.

[3]. These numbers do not include the unarmed command tanks. There were a total of 134 available.

[4]. These were the 10th Mechanised and Warsaw Mechanised Brigades. The Warsaw Brigade fielded 43 tanks (26 TKSs, 17 Vickers). The 10th Mechanised had 231 tanks (13 TKs, 13 TKSs, 98 7TPs, 45 R-35s, 17 Vickers and 45 FT-17s).

[5]. *Kampfgruppen* Kleeman and Angern. Both were formed around the two Panzer regiments.

[6]. Initially the 2nd Panzer and 4th Light Divisions were under the command of the XVIII Corps from 1-2 September. This was a ploy to disguise the intended use of both corps from Polish intelligence.

[7]. Von Thoma became famous later in the war for his various commands in the North Africa.

[8]. The lone exception was the XIX Corps use of its motorised divisions throughout the campaign. This was likely due to Guderian's insistance.

A rest break in Poland gives the commander of this eight-wheeled SdKfz 263 the chance for a cigarette. The tools stowed on its front have first been painted grey and then the white cross painted over them. (Prigent Collection)

This 8-wheeled SdKfz 231 is very dirty but its grey and brown camouflage can still just be seen on the original print. Facing the viewer on the front mudguard is a version of the tactical sign for an armoured car unit, unfortunately covered in dust so impossible to read clearly. (Prigent Collection)

Captured vehicles were put into use. These TKS tankettes were captured by 6 Company of Infantry Regiment 76 on the morning of 12 September 1939 in Zareby-Boledy, 107 kilometres northeast of Warsaw, and photographed for a celebratory postcard. It still carries the Polish camouflage of horizontal bands in sand-grey, green and brown but the Regiment has chalked on its own markings. (Prigent Collection)

Not all Polish tanks were the famous 7TP series. This is a Vickers Mk E, still carrying its pre-1936 camouflage in fairly bright tones of sand, green and brown, captured in Schepetowka. (Prigent Collection)